MW01536469

HARDPRESS

ISBN: 9781313161114

Published by:
HardPress Publishing
8345 NW 66TH ST #2561
MIAMI FL 33166-2626

Email: info@hardpress.net
Web: http://www.hardpress.net

F
3708
E59

F 3708E59

Cornell University Library

Ecuador :its ancient and modern history,

3 1924 021 200 047

Cornell University Library

BOUGHT WITH THE INCOME OF THE

SAGE ENDOWMENT FUND

THE GIFT OF

Henry W. Sage

1891

A 359534.

23 VI 16

9306

DEC 13 1942

MAY 4 1948

OCT 22 1962 M P

APR 8 1960 M P

NOV 12 1963 M P

JUL 15 1964 M P

MAR 25 2004

S

ECUADOR

"The output of the books upon Latin America has in recent years been very large, a proof doubtless of the increasing interest that is felt in the subject. Of these the South American Series edited by Mr. Martin Hume is the most noteworthy."—TIMES.

"Mr. Unwin is doing good service to commercial men and investors by the production of his 'South American Series.'"—SATURDAY REVIEW.

"Those who wish to gain some idea of the march of progress in these countries cannot do better than study the admirable 'South American Series.'"—CHAMBER OF COMMERCE JOURNAL.

DRYING COCOA IN A GUAYAQUIL STREET.

ECUADOR

ITS ANCIENT AND MODERN HISTORY
TOPOGRAPHY AND NATURAL RESOURCES
INDUSTRIES AND SOCIAL DEVELOPMENT

BY

C. REGINALD ENOCK, F.R.G.S.

AUTHOR OF "THE ANDES AND THE AMAZON," "PERU," "MEXICO,"
"THE SECRET OF THE PACIFIC," ETC.

WITH 37 ILLUSTRATIONS AND 2 MAPS

T. FISHER UNWIN

LONDON: ADELPHI TERRACE
LEIPSIC: INSELSTRASSE 20

F 19.

A 359534

(*All* rights reserved)

PREFACE

THERE has been hitherto no comprehensive book in English dealing with the republic of Ecuador, a void which the present volume is intended to fill. The country, as will be shown, is one of peculiar interest from various points of view, whether to the trader, the traveller, or the general reader. The book is offered as a study in " human geography " in the field covered, a theme such as has been the underlying one in the author's various works upon other lands, both in this series and elsewhere.

C. R. E.

LONDON, 1914.

CONTENTS

8 CONTENTS

ILLUSTRATIONS

ILLUSTRATIONS

MAPS

cribed as the most remarkable assemblage of cyclopean peaks in the world, culminating above the perpetual snowline. Nothing can exceed the stupendous grandeur of the great avenue of snow-covered volcanoes, extinct or active, which forms the approach to Quito and terminates near the Equator. Whether it was the ancient inhabitant of the land, developing his early civilization before the advent of the Spanish voyager or horseman, whether it be the laborious peasant of the Andine uplands, or the chance traveller, all have been startled or impressed by the presence of these great mountains, as indeed at times they have been menaced or desolated by their eruptive activity.

Topographically, and as a result climatologically, Ecuador presents very marked contrasts. Beneath perpetual snowfields lie fruitful valleys ; perennial winter reigns above perpetual spring ; the fruits of the tropics hang less than a day's march distant from Arctic plant forms ; and the warm seas of the torrid zone bathe shores which slope upwards to the icy *páramos*. In the same territory, within a range of forty leagues, those " dragons of the prime," the loathly alligator in the hot slime of the tropic river, and the boa-constrictor of the forests, give place to the perfect forms of upland deer or *vicuña*, and to the great condor, circling above the edge of the snow-clad volcano ; and from the beautiful coco-palms of the Guayas to the humble lichens of snow-bound Chimborazo is, geographically, but a step.

Ecuador occupies that portion of the South American continent which protrudes farthest west into the Pacific Ocean. It was upon the Ecuadorian coast that Francisco Pizarro, the renowned conqueror of Peru, and his companions first learned of the existence of a great empire—that of the Incas—lying beyond the Andes, whose grey and distant escarpments rose like a mighty curtain between them and the mystery of the unknown civilization beyond : an empire where gold was used for household utensils, where beautiful stone-built temples and palaces abounded, and where flourished an ordered social system, superior in certain respects to anything that the world had produced. Even before the time of the Incas a strange, semi-civilized people dwelt in Ecuador : a people who had first landed on its coast in great rafts, whom tradition or fable has recorded were giants, who left evidences of their arts in the curious sculptured stone chairs on hill platforms, now covered by the jungle ; and who ascended to Quito to found the stable and cultured Shiri nation, which preceded the Incas and the Spaniards.

Through those rugged regions pressed the fanatic Spaniard, with the sword and the cross, to make new history in that old world, somewhat erroneously termed " new." It was from Quito that intrepid voyagers, having descended the eastern slopes of the Andes, found and embarked upon a great river, the Napo, and, always seeking El Dorado, emerged upon the mighty Amazon, navigating for the first time its three-thousand-mile course to the Atlantic—a voyage which has few equals in the history of inland explorations, by reason of its risks and hardships. Yet, as if in a measure of compensation for the stupendous uplands and the still savage Amazonian region, Nature has endowed Ecuador with the most beautiful and fruitful fluvial system in the whole of tropic America—that of the Guayas and its affluents, traversing a district producing a large proportion of the world's supply of cocoa and chocolate, and falling into the Pacific at Guayaquil.

The fluvial system of the Guayas is the only considerable group of navigable waterways, and the Gulf of Guayaquil the only great indentation, in the whole of the vast Pacific littoral of South, Central, and part of North America, for a distance of several thousand miles ; features which give to Ecuador a marked geographical individuality. The world owes to the early people of Ecuador a debt of gratitude for one of its most valued food products, the potato, which, evolved by the Indians of the Andes from the bitter wild variety, was first brought to the notice of the Spaniards near Quito. Among the gifts of Latin America—Mexico, Brazil, Peru, Bolivia, Chile, Ecuador, and others—to the world, gifts which include the peculiar and valuable products of rubber, chocolate, quinine, cocaine, etc., the potato can scarcely take a secondary place.

The surface of Ecuador presents in a very marked manner the peculiar structure and attributes which characterize the topography of the western slope of South America, such as are shared to a large extent by its neighbour, Peru. There are three very distinct regions, and for a clear comprehension of the general condition of the country these must be grasped. The first of these is the cis-Andine, the littoral or coast zone, lying between the Pacific Ocean and the foot of the Andes ; the second the inter-Andine, embracing the slopes, tablelands, and peaks of the Cordilleras of the Andes ; the third the trans-Andine, forming the upper part of the Amazon basin. These three divisions present absolute differences in respect of climate, vegetation, general aspect, animal life, and even of human life. Had Nature designed to construct a model, whereby the varying characteristics of her handiwork might conveniently be displayed within a measurable compass, such a purpose could scarcely have been better exemplified than in that part of the earth's surface embodied in a section taken across the republic of Ecuador. Above the hot lowlands of the coast, covered with dense vegetation in places and sterile in others, lie bleak tablelands, crowned by perpetual snows, notwithstanding their proximity to the equator. All grades of climate are encountered, all conditions of aridity or humidity. On the upper edge of this topographical and climatic model are encountered the creatures and vegetation of cold climates ; lower down are those corresponding to temperate climates ; whilst at the base swarms that profuse and fantastic life, whether of plant, animal, or reptile, whose home is in the dense jungle or the sluggish mud of the tropical streams. Similarly is it with the vegetable world, the products useful to man, whose cultivation developed as civilization spread. The orange, the banana, and other well-known fruits, cocoa, coffee, and other products, give place to wheat and potatoes as higher elevations are gained. As to man, the highest condition of his indigenous civilization came into being on the uplands. The coastal lowlands in places menaced him with fevers and other disorders, whilst the forests of the Amazon basin only sheltered the naked savages who depend upon primitive nature for their subsistence.

The Ecuadorian coast zone mainly consists of low-lying plains, formed in great part by Tertiary and Quaternary deposits, alluvial sands, earth, and detritus brought down by the action of mountain streams from the Cordillera. It differs considerably from the corresponding region in Peru and northern Chile, stretching for 2,000 miles or more to the south, in that it is much broader, the Andes lying farther from the coast in this part of the continent ; that it possesses numerous navigable rivers, which in Peru do not exist on the littoral ; and that it is in part covered with dense vegetation, as contrasted with the Sahara-like character of large portions of the Peruvian and northern Chilean coast. The littoral of Ecuador stretches from 1° 20′ north of the equator to latitude 3° 14′ south.

The structure of the high division of Ecuador is a very marked and peculiar mountain system.

2

Broadly, it comprises the two great parallel ranges of the Andes, known respectively as the eastern and western Cordillera, from twenty to fifty miles apart, joined by counterforts or " knots "—*nudos,* as they are locally known. This system extends through the length of the republic, from north to south, for somewhat less than 500 miles. In the northern half the great valley or series of plateaux between the two ranges, in which the principal centres of upland population are found, is overlooked on either side by the high peaks, some of which are active volcanoes. The average height of the Cordilleras from which these culminating points arise may be taken as 11,500 feet, the peaks rising to 19,000 feet in some instances ; and that of the plateau, a great longitudinal valley between, is 8,250 feet above sea-level. In this great, high valley numerous rivers have their rise, from the snows and rains of the Cordillera, and, breaking a passage through deep canyons in the enclosing ranges, make their way either to the Atlantic or to the Pacific. The position of the water-parting of South America formed by the Andes, lying near the Pacific coast throughout the whole length of the continent, renders the physical structure of Ecuador of considerable interest. From both Cordilleras spurs or lateral ranges descend east and west, in the one case dying out on the Amazon plain, in the other on the edge of the Pacific coast. In this elevated region surprising changes and contrasts are encountered, as happens in all Andine and Alpine countries. There are pleasing sub-valleys and fertile plains, watered by clear rivulets and bearing the orange and the myrtle, cereals, cattle, and all else necessary for the life of its human occupants, bounded by rugged, inclement uplands and sterile slopes, overlooked by the volcanoes ; the result of whose activity has, over wide districts, rendered life impossible. The uplands

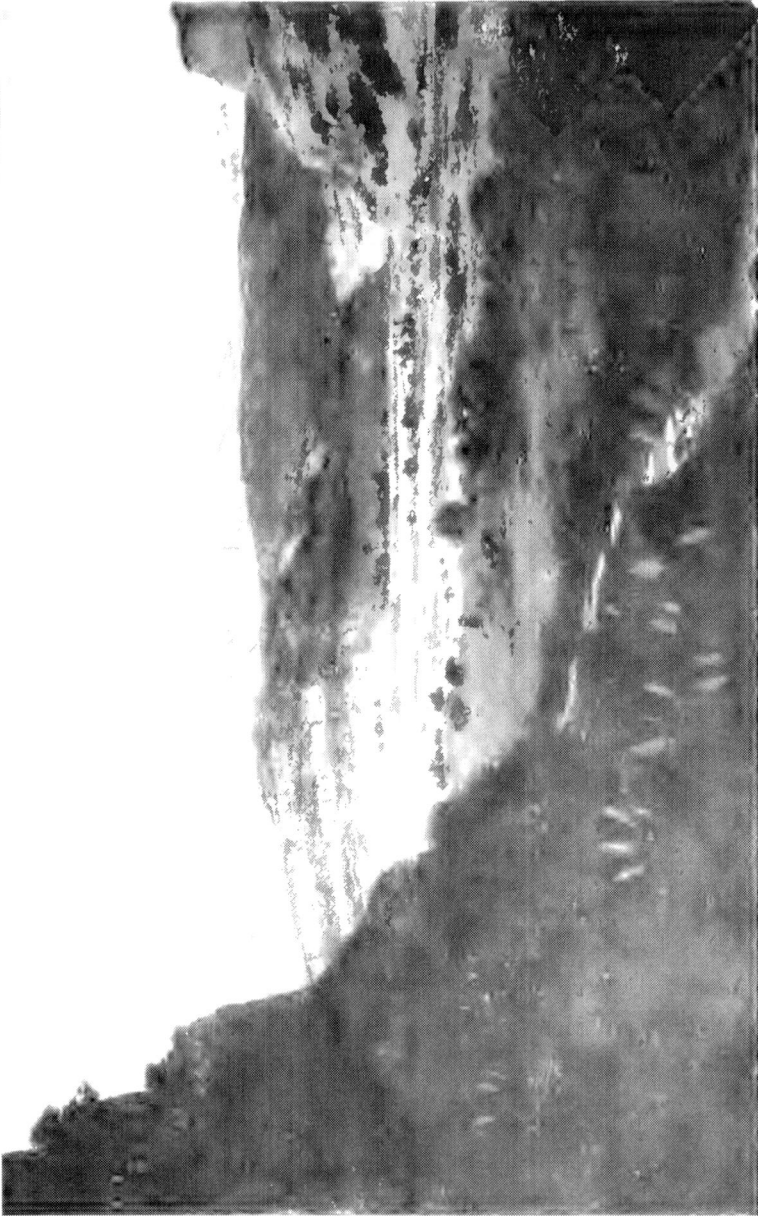

COTOPAXI: THE WORLD'S HIGHEST VOLCANO.

[To face p. 24

of Ecuador and the snowy volcanoes have of late
years been rendered more easily accessible by reason
of the Guayaquil to Quito railway, one of the most
noteworthy lines in the world, constructed under great
difficulties.

KR.

Upon the eastern slope of the Andes, from the high
tableland and ridges, there are, however, no such
means of travel, and in Ecuador and Peru, in this
zone, there is revealed what might be described as
an unfinished world. The descent is rapid. From
the cold uplands, treeless and without vegetation,
except for the long *ichu* grass and the twisted,
stunted shrub-life in the *quebradas* or ravines, the
traveller plunges into a region of arboreal wealth
run riot, in a warm, humid climate, often shrouded
in mists, which lie in banks of curious form along
the valleys. Here and there, as the descent is made,
great precipices are disclosed, old and grey, or sometimes recent, where landslips, brought about by heavy
rains acting upon the steeply-hung strata, have fallen
crashing among the trees beneath, where their debris
remains, rapidly to be covered by flowering shrubs
and plants. The living rock itself, disclosed by the
fall, does not long remain unclothed. Gleaming
cascades leap sheer over dizzy verges, their spray
floating among the treetops as they fall into the
water-worn rock basins, fashioned smooth and symmetrical. Great caves and chasms open to the view,
and at times the route of the seemingly impossible
trail winds and zig-zags up this or that flank of the
ravines to gain some high headland, whereon the
panting mule and his rider—if the way be practicable
for more than the foot passenger, which commonly
it is not—stand to rest and contemplate the difficulties
of the passage. It is a landscape veritably displaced
and contorted that greets the view in these remarkable zones ; above rise peaks and ridges absolutely
inaccessible, below great leafy labyrinths, and the

mystery and wild beauty, of the whole are a measure
of recompense for hardship undergone.

There is much of interest in the hydrography of the
Andes. The great streams, which rising among the
snows of the Andes thread their way along vast
plateaux several miles above sea-level, gathering innumerable tributaries, flowing past obscure and
desolate upland Indian villages, whose simple and
ignorant yet hardy and patient people wrest a living
from these inclement uplands, pouring thence over the
lips of the plains, issuing, it might be said, from the
very mouth of the Andes, descend in torrential courses
down the rugged breastplates of the Cordilleras, to
where their waters give life and fertility to gentle
plains and verdant woods, yielding all the fruits of the
tropics. The hydrographic system of the Cordilleras,
regarded as a vast hydraulic machine, raising first,
and then distributing by gravitation the waters necessary for organic life, is curiously instructive.

The eastern region of Ecuador is similar, to some
extent, to the northern part of the coastal region, as
before remarked, but it is less mountainous. Below
the foot of the Andes, where the rivers which foam
down the Cordilleras become navigable for canoes or
steamboats, the face of the country presents enormous
tree-covered plains, only broken by relatively small
undulations. This vast wilderness of vegetation,
which extends throughout the Ecuadorian *Oriente*,
and embraces the *montañas* of Peru and Bolivia, and
passes into the *selvas* of Brazil, traversed only by the
rivers, has a peculiar character, which impresses itself
on the mind of the traveller. It is majestic in certain
aspects, but becomes at times melancholy, sombre, and
oppressive. There is no horizon. The view is everywhere barred by trees, whose green walls enclose the
channels of the rivers to the very verge. There are
in eastern Ecuador no open, grass-covered plains,
permitting distant views of the hills, such as the

uplands afford, or such as in Colombia and Venezuela distinguish the Amazon lowlands of those countries. Yet, to the naturalist, the wealth of animal life is alluring, even in the sombre forests.

The people of Ecuador, as fully described in a subsequent chapter, are composed of the Spanish race, originally conquerors and colonists, and in a small degree conserving European purity of blood, and the various shades of intermixture with the aboriginal race, thus forming the *mestizo* race, such as predominates throughout the mountain republics of South America (as also in Mexico). This race forms the typical Ecuadorian, as it does the Peruvian or other Latin American race (except in Argentina and the River Plate region generally, where the Indian forms but a small element). In many respects this race must be considered as an intelligent and hardy people, although suffering from various drawbacks due to environment and customs. The purely savage tribes of Ecuador, the *infieles* or *salvajes*, inhabit the Amazon region, the upland people being all Christianized.

The official language of Ecuador is Spanish, or *Castellano*. The bulk of the people, however, who constitute the classes more approaching the Indian, still speak the Quechua language, which was that of the pre-Hispanic Inca regimen. Both the Spanish and the Quechua languages are rich and pleasing, and this quality is strongly borne out in topographical nomenclature and terms. Spanish terms of this nature have been preserved throughout this book with the purpose of familiarizing the reader or the traveller with what is an inseparable part of the atmosphere of the country.

For the adventurous traveller the portion of South America covered by the republic of Ecuador offers considerable attraction ; some of the eastern districts are almost unexplored, lying in that part of the continent which is most remote and inaccessible. From these uplands there is no easy means of communication to the east ; the primitive mule trails, over which pack animals and horsemen have stumbled ever since the conquest, afford the only available means of transit. From Quito the traveller may follow the trail of Gonzalo Pizarro and of Orellana, making his way down the eastern slope of the Andes to the headwaters of the Napo River, embarking thence in canoe and steam-launch to reach the Amazon, and so to the Atlantic coast in Brazil.

There are many undeveloped resources in the republic of Ecuador awaiting a better political and economic regimen and the growth of a more enlightened social system ; but before considering these it is necessary to the purpose of this work to enter, in broad outline, upon the history of the country.

CHAPTER II

THE PREHISTORIC KINGDOM OF QUITO

THE history of Ecuador, in its earlier period, is the history in large part of the conquest of that mysterious territory first known to Europeans as "Peru," the land lying south of Panama. But the history of the region, albeit to a certain extent vague and indefinite, goes back far beyond the time of the landing of Pizarro on the inhospitable Tumbez coast, and is lost in the semi-fabulous traditions of the Incas, a thousand years ago. From the history to the archæology of Peru and Ecuador the student is, indeed, conducted still farther back in time, perhaps to periods which were contemporaneous with early Egypt and Babylon, when even upon this remote and inaccessible American shore intelligent man was evolving his temples and his laws.

It is only of very recent years that any detailed knowledge about the ancient people of the Ecuadorian coast in pre-Hispanic times, and of the objects left thereby, has been obtained. The western coast of South America, in that portion lying north of Peru, from the Gulf of Guayaquil to Panama, forming the littoral of Ecuador and Colombia, was but little studied archæologically until recent years,[1] and the same condition prevailed to some extent with regard to the interior inter-Andine tablelands of Ecuador and Colombia.

[1] See the chapter on Antiquities.

In the last-named republic, the culture-area of the Chibchas, is found an important people, whose description belongs to Colombia rather than Ecuador, and that of the Quimbayas, with evidences of other independent cultures. Bogotá was the centre of the Chibcha area, and Cali and Popayan of others. The dense and humid forests of Darien and Panama would seem to have acted as a barrier between South America and the famous Chiriqui culture-area of Costa Rica and Panama, but it is known that the Mayas of Mexico sent out colonies from time to time which reached the west coast of Central America, and remains of their settlements were found as far down as the Chiriqui lagoon. All these regions lay between the vast culture-area of the Mayas and Aztecs of Yucatan and Mexico on the north and of the Incas of Peru to the south. The connection between these two old civilizations of North and South America is scarcely apparent, although further archæological study may determine a more considerable contact. The myths and stories of migrations in ancient times seem to point to such contact, as do various archæological details. That wanderers from Mexico to Peru should have found their way down the Isthmus of Panama, the narrow neck of land joining the twin continents, it is only reasonable to suppose. Such migration would, of course, have crossed where the line of the great Panama Canal now severs the Isthmus. It would be beyond the scope of this book to describe in detail the various theories of origin of the pre-Colombian cultures of America. Whether these cultures were autochthonous, the result of the natural evolution of man in his surroundings and of reaction to environment, or whether they were of imported origin cannot be dogmatically affirmed or denied. There is no reason why early contact with Asia should not have been made, through the drifting or sailing over of junks from China, or by emigration across Behring Strait, where the coast of one continent is visible from the other. There appear to be various points of evidence supporting the view of imported culture in pre-Hispanic times, although arguments against such seem to be equally strong. The whole subject is one of great interest.[1] Under any circumstance it is practically established that North and South America were originally peopled by the Mongol race, and the likeness between the American brown race and the Mongolians is often very marked.

At the time of its prehistoric obscurity Ecuador was peopled by a number of tribes of different grades of culture, speaking different languages. Velasco, the principal historian and geographer of the kingdom of Quito, has left an enumeration of these primitive natives, upon which subsequent writers have drawn. They embodied a number of " independent States " and " tribes " or " principal provinces." These " States," as rearranged by Wolf,[2] beginning at the north with the province of Carachi and extending to Loja, on the borders of Peru, were as follows :—

Huaca, Dehuaca, and Tusa, 3 small undivided States ; Pimapiro, a medium-sized State with 4 tribes ; Imbaya, a large State with 8 tribes ; Otavalo, large, 7 tribes ; Cayambi, large, 3 tribes ; Poritaco, Collahuaso, and Lingachi, 3 small States near Quito, with few tribes ; Quito, large, with 34 tribes ; Latacunga, large, 15 tribes ; Angamarca, medium (Colorados and Yungas) ; Hambato, small, 4 tribes ; Mocha, medium, 5 tribes ; Puruhá, large, 30 tribes ; Chimbo, medium, 5 tribes ; Tiquizambi (or Tixan) small, 3 tribes ; Lausi (or Alausi), medium, 8 tribes ; Cañar, large, 25 tribes ; Paltas, small, 3 tribes ; Zara, large, 13 tribes.

[1] The subject is fully discussed in the Author's book, *The Secret of the Pacific*. T. Fisher Unwin : London, 1913 (2nd edition).

[2] Wolf, *Ecuador*. Leipsic, 1892 (Spanish and German).

The foregoing were those of higher Ecuador, and the following were of lower or maritime Ecuador :—

Tumbez and Mayavilca, 2 small confederations ; Poceos and Machala, 2 small States ; Lapuna, on the island of that name ; Guancavilcas, large, 17 tribes ; Manta, large, 10 tribes ; Cara, large, 8 tribes ; Tacames or Atacames, 13 tribes.

To the east of the Cordilleras were : Jaenes, with 10 tribes ; Pacamores, with 12 tribes ; Yaguarzongos, with 12 tribes ; Jibaros, 13 tribes ; Huamboyas, 2 tribes ; Macas, 8 tribes ; Quijos (or Canelos), 5 tribes ; Cofanes, 5 tribes ; Sucumbios, 5 tribes ; Mocoas, 5 tribes. Furthermore, Velasco in his list of Indian nations of the Missions of the Marañon, enumerates 43 nations with 130 tribes and 20 " doubtful " nations. The total of all the " nations " enumerated by Velasco reaches 100, and, according to this authority, each had its separate language, with a total of more than 430 tribes, all having different dialects. Thus, within the area of ancient Ecuador, it may well be said that there existed a veritable Babel, a linguistic and ethnic chaos possibly without equal. But probably many of these distinctions would have disappeared on closer examination, and they depended partially upon un-trustworthy Indian information ; and Velasco's enumeration was doubtless that, to a large extent, of mere *pueblos* or villages, which he dignified by the name of " nations." Confusion has also occurred by reason of the mixture of spelling of Cara and Quichua names. The various districts are, however, marked out to a certain extent by the geographical names given by the Indians themselves, which are very significant. It is noted that the terminant *bi* or *pi* means " water " or " river," the equivalent of the Quechua *yacu*, and the first-named term was that used by the Cayapas Indians of Esmeraldas.

Quechua, the great language of the Andes, was not spoken by the Caras, but was introduced by the Incas.

It is stated that the nation of the Quitus was not at that period greatly distinguished from those nations which surrounded it, either by its spirit of enterprise or by a more advanced civilization. It belonged, it is true, to the most populous of the nations, but probably others, and especially the Cañaris, were more advanced in various branches of culture, as disclosed by their archæological remains.[1] Quito required some outside impulse to bring about the grandeur it subsequently attained, and this impulse came from the conquest of Quito by the Caras.

There is no knowledge obtainable of the earliest settlement of the Ecuadorian coast. The first people of whom definite facts are known were the Caras, who were a people marked out from the other natives. It is maintained that the Caras, as distinct from the indigenous tribes, were an immigrating or invading people, who came by sea on large rafts in a not very remote epoch, possibly during the sixth or seventh century of the Christian era. They were superior in intelligence and culture to the natives, bellicose and conquering, and they rapidly covered the territory of the barbarians of the district. Their first theatre of operations was Manabi, from Caraquez Bay to Manta, and it is said that they founded a city at that latter point. Thence they gradually extended their activities elsewhere. The history of the Caras is, however, wrapped in speculation and obscurity, and their migration uncertain. It is only known that they deserted the coast of Manabi by degrees for that of Atacames and Esmeraldas in the north, and for the interior by following the rivers to the vicinity of Quito. According to Velasco, this migration was made to escape the unhealthy climate,

[1] Gonzalez Suarez, *Estudio historico sobre los Cañaris.* Quito, 1878.

but this was probably not correct, because their first environment of the coast region is healthy, and the second, that of the woods, unhealthy ; and the real reason for the migration was probably that of their nomadic and adventurous character. Probably a portion of the Caras people remained in Manabi. The path of the Caras to Quito was stated by Velasco and others to have been by the valley of the Esmeraldas River, and the ascent of the river in *balsas*, or rafts. The geographical names remaining give some clue to their dwelling-places. Until about the year 1000 the Caras remained in possession of the district of Quito, and from that time dates the rise of Quito to some native splendour. It is true that there are no exact chronological data relating to the first three centuries of this regimen until 1300.

Velasco, the native historian of Ecuador, who wrote in 1789, and who defended the Ecuadorians against the literary attacks of European writers, states that the Caras had been settled on the coast before their ascent of the Esmeraldas River for two hundred years, during which time eight successive chiefs reigned over them. Their conquest of the Quitus was in 980 A.D. The religion of the Caran-Scyris was that of sun and moon worshippers ; and a temple to the sun was built near Quito, on the hill now known as the Panecillo. The eastern door of this temple is described as having had " two tall columns before it, for the purpose of determining the solstices, and twelve pillars on one side of the temple, as gnomons, to point out, by their order, the first day of each month." Thus these people followed the rude astronomical system such as was so considerably employed by the Incas. On an adjacent height was a temple to the moon. They built vaults over their dead, piled up with earth and stones, forming mounds known as *tolas*. The Scyris had, however, little knowledge of architecture, such as so

remarkably distinguished the Incas ; but they ex-
celled as lapidaries. In the headdress of the Scyri
king a great emerald was worn as a royal mark.
Their conquests were made principally in the north,
where they built forts with villages around them,
inhabited by troops. The writings of Velasco have
been regarded as somewhat marked by credulity.[1]
Velasco was a Jesuit, and on the expulsion of his
order from South America he retired to Italy, where
he wrote his book, whose material was largely drawn
from unpublished manuscripts. The early history of
Ecuador, however, is supported by other writers, and
is sufficiently established. The objects of antiquity
found on the coast, especially the remarkably
sculptured stone seats and other matters, attest the
advanced skill of some unknown people long prior
to the Inca advent.

The kings of Quito bore the general title of Caran-
Shiri, the distinguishing names of the first ten or
eleven chiefs having been lost. Little by little these
rulers extended their sway over a very considerable
territory, covering the inter-Andine districts as far
as the region which now forms Colombia, the province
of Pastos, to as far south as the province of Puruhá,
near Mocha (Ecuador). The tradition of the last and
best period of the Shiris, which lasted about 150
years, began with the pacific conquest of the great
province of Puruhá, and, in fact, it may be said that
the political history and geography of Ecuador begins
with that time.

The desert-like coast region, at the beginning of
the Christian era, was, according to a doubtful con-
jecture or statement by Velasco, " invaded by giants."
Bandelier, however, places the invasion in the
fifteenth century, quoting from an unpublished work
of Gutierrez, but the statement is not generally borne
out by other authorities. The various references by

[1] According to Prescott.

the old Spanish writers to these alleged giants are interesting. According to tradition, the giants landed on the Ecuadorian coast at Santa Elena Point, which juts far out into the Pacific, forming the westernmost extremity of the continent in Ecuador, disembarking from large boats or *balsas*. This advent was during the time of the Caras on the coast. The tradition, which was universal among the Indians at the time of the Spanish conquest, is recorded by all writers. The boats or rafts of the native people of Ecuador were formed of canes bound together, and sometimes of *balsa* wood. In the account by Diego de Almagro, in the *Relacion de los Primeros Descubrimientos de Francisco Pizarro y Diego de Almagro*, Ruiz, the pilot of Pizarro, describes these craft, one of which was captured by the expedition. These are described later on.

Speaking of the giants, Zarate says : " Near Santa Elena there are certain veins extending into the sea which contain bitumen, which looks like alquitran,[1] and the Indians say that giants of great stature inhabited the land at this point, four times as large as a man. They do not say whence these came, but say they ate fish and were great fishermen, and went in *balsas*, each one in his own, because the rafts could not carry more than one. They devoured Indians, thirty-two each, and went naked, and were very cruel in killing the Indians." It is further affirmed by Zarate that the Spaniards "saw two massive sculptured figures of these giants, a male and female, and that the Indians preserved from father to son many particulars of the giants, especially as concerned their end, which was brought about by the advent from heaven of a young man, shining like the sun, who drove the giants into a valley and killed them with flames of fire, marks of which remain upon the rocks still." The Spaniards gave little credence

[1] Now a centre of petroleum production.

to these stories "until the time when Captain Juan de Olmos of Trujillo, Governor of Puerto Viejo, in 1543, hearing about them, caused excavations to be made in the valley, which laid bare enormous ribs and bones, which if they did not appear with heads, nevertheless could not be believed to be of human beings." These traditions of the giants had been recorded by the *quipos*, or knotted cord mnemonic system of the Peruvians. Another writer, Bollaert, records the traditions concerning the abandonment of the coast regions by the Caras, that it was by reason of the advent of the giants, who came on floats of rushes. Tradition further states that the giants took possession of the Cara women and killed the men, and it is added that Pizarro was supposed to have seen stone statues eight feet high, with mitres and other insignia, representing the giants who had been annihilated by Divine wrath, and that there were great ruins attributed to the giants and wells made thereby. The statement of Zarate that the Spaniards saw the sculptured figures of these giants, it has been conjectured by Bandelier, may have arisen from the existence of the large stone seats or benches of Manabi, which are the most remarkable antiquities of Ecuador. These stone seats are carved in some cases with supports of human and animal figures, and are found only in that particular part of Ecuador.[1] It is noteworthy that the early Spaniards made no mention of these curious stone seats, which are not found among the antiquities of any other part of the Americas. As regards the great bones, which the Indians supposed to be those of the giants, these were parts of the skeletons of mastodons, which have been found in various districts in Ecuador and Peru, including Santa Elena. Doubtless the stories about the landing of giants at Santa Elena may have had their origin in the remote past, from the advent of

[1] See the chapter on Antiquities.

some warlike people who arrived in craft of some
nature.   Traditions of landings on the Pacific coast,
both in Mexico and Peru, show that there may have
been contact with the outside world long before the
discovery of America by Columbus, as before remarked.   Fable and archæology are strangely inter-
mixed in .Western American lore.   The remarkable
stone colossi, or figures of enormous men, some of
them seventy-five feet high, which exist on Easter
Island (belonging to Chile) were fabulously ascribed
to " wicked giants before the Flood." [1]
.With the death of the eleventh Shiri the male line
of the Caras came to an end.   The Shiri law prohibited the reigning of a daughter, who was the only
issue of the Shiri.   But the law was abrogated and
replaced by a new one, under which, in default of
an heir, the daughter might reign in company with
such a prince as she might choose for her consort.
This law was well received by the people, and the
Princess Toa married the son of the provincial head
of Puruhá, by name Duchisela.   By this method both
an heir and an alliance were secured to the Shiri of
Quito, the kingdom being enlarged by the acquisition of Puruhá, a rich territory which had always
resisted assimilation.   The Shiri died in the year
1300, and his successor, Shiri XII, reigned pacifically
for seventy years, dying at the age of one hundred.
After him came the son, Shiri XIII, with an equally
peaceful term of sixty years ; and during this period
the kingdom became greatly enlarged towards the
south, taking in Huancabamba, Piura, and Payta
(part of modern Peru) under treaties and alliances.
The Cañaris, the Paltas, the Zargas, and some maritime States were incorporated in the kingdom.   Some
of the smaller States doubtless sought the alliance
with the larger from defensive reasons, due to the
menace of the great Inca Empire to the south, whose

[1] Described in *The Secret of the Pacific, op. cit.*

growing power had extended far, and had alarmed a large part of the South American continent. The system of conquest by the Shiris of Quito was very different from that of the Incas. The latter followed a system of centralization, consolidating their conquests by introducing their own religion, laws, customs, and language, and establishing in the subdued provinces civil and military authorities ; but the Quitos contented themselves with a simple treaty of alliance, with a small tribute, a species of confederation, leaving to the associated provinces their own native governors, languages, and customs. This system, whilst it accorded well with the naturally non-social character of the American tribes, was not conducive to strength in times of war. Such a war befell Shiri XIV. He came to power in 1430, and reigned thirty-three years, only twenty of which were peaceful. The name of this chief was Hualcopo Duchisela. At that time the kingdom of Quito, which had enjoyed uninterrupted peace for 150 years, covered practically the same territory as the modern republic of Ecuador, with the exception, perhaps, of the ultra-Andine region, or Amazon forest belt. The nations on the Pacific slope were subject or allied, and the monarchy was the only one in South America that rivalled the Inca Empire in respect of its extent and the number of its inhabitants and grade of civilization at that period.

The methods by which the Shiris attained their relatively high grade of culture, whether they were the result mainly of outside influence, or whether of a natural development, are matters not easy of investigation. It was a similar process to that which underlay the life of the Incas. The question as to whether the latter owed the impulse towards higher government, civic life, and the development of arts and crafts, such as they had reached in so remarkable a manner, to outside impulse and early contact with the Old World, or whether it was a natural and autochthonous process born of their own soil, has not been determined. In similar case were the people of Quito. Yet it is known that the Caras, who appear to have caused this impulse, were superior to the native tribes at the time of their advent, more advanced in the arts of government, war, and peace, that they were of an intelligent and even noble character, and of an open, enterprising spirit. Where they came from is a mystery. But they entered like a ferment into the small kingdom of Quito and the inert mass of surrounding nations and tribes of the uplands, and seemed to be possessed of a mission to civilize and develop the backward human element with which they were thrown into contact. Always alert, they sought ordered means of improvement, and were, furthermore, favoured by an uninterrupted series of successes and events, added to the favourable environment, the powerful influence of the healthy and invigorating upland climate of the Andine tablelands, and a soil that responded to agriculture and the establishment of permanent dwellings ; and thus their development may well seem to have been a natural one. The physical and moral conditions which surrounded the Shiris for over 400 years were thus very similar to those enjoyed by the famous Incas.[1]

But the termination of the flourishing state of Quito approached, and the Incas were to be the agent of its downfall. Vast as the continent was, the law of conflict denied room for both monarchies upon it, and during the latter half of the reign of Hualcopo Duchisela, the Shiri Empire, the old kingdom of Quito, began to decline.

Native historians of Ecuador have given considerable attention to their ancient history, and their works (in Spanish) may be consulted. The advent of the Inca invaders has now to be considered.

[1] See the Author's *Peru* (2nd edition).

CHAPTER III

THE COMING OF THE INCAS

THE history of the Incas, and the very fragmentary knowledge which exists concerning their predecessors, the " Andine people " as they have been termed, belongs properly to the history of Peru rather than to that of Ecuador. The beginning of the history of these remarkable people, the Incas, lies in the grey dawn of myth and fable ; whilst the doings of their predecessors, from whom they doubtless inherited the principles of their civilization, are only recorded in the ruined walls of the stone structures they left on the Andine uplands, and in pottery and textile fabrics, often of very beautiful manufacture, discovered in their burial-places. Otherwise their history is a closed book. The principal monument of the " Andine people " is the sculptured monolithic doorway of the ruins at Tiahuanako, in Bolivia, near Lake Titicaca, but there are other vestiges scattered throughout Peru. The work of the Incas is generally separable therefrom. Into an account of the remarkable civilization of the Incas, their laws, temples, and industries, it is not the purpose of this book to enter.

The Incas of Peru, whose power and influence had reached a very high state, began to regard with jealousy the flourishing Shiri nation. It was always the policy of the Inca Empire to extend its borders, and in 1450, under the great Inca emperor Tupac Yupanqui, the Eleventh Inca, the idea of northern conquest or "rectification" of the frontier first crystallized into action. The first operations following upon this impulse were easy. The weakness in the federal as opposed to a central system of Shiri government contributed to this. The southern provinces of the Quito Empire, those south of Azuay, were conquered by the forces of the Incas under Tupac Yupanqui without any bloodshed, a treaty of peace and friendship being entered into by these States, easily led by the seductive promises of the Incas, such as were customarily made in their conquests. The first notice of the Inca invasion arrived at Quito simultaneously with the news of the defection of the frontier and some of the maritime States. At the same time these States had sent their ambassadors to Huancabamba, offering the Incas friendship and alliance, and the latter, in the act, replied by sending governors, captains, and priests to instruct these new provinces of the empire in the required form of government. The Incas followed up this easy success by immediate action, marched triumphantly through the great provinces of Zara, Paltas, and Cañar, and only paused at the southern base of the Azuay mountain knot, the very portal of the ancient kingdom of the Shiris.

It is to be recollected, in considering this rapid advance and resolute purpose, that the Incas were dominated, not only by the lust of conquest but by religious fanaticism. The Incas were "sons of the Sun," in their own belief. They were the chosen, sent by Heaven to civilize the earth, to spread abroad the cult of their father, the Sun. In their own estimation they were men-gods, this reigning family of fabulous origin, and to disobey them was to sweep aside the benevolent attributes they ordinarily acted upon and to incur their semi-Divine wrath. The King of Quito was in no condition to defend his possessions from this attack. Arms and armies under his regimen were unorganized, and far from pretending to recover what had been taken, his chief concern was to defend what remained. Tupac Yupanqui, however, halted for two years in Cañar, building palaces, fortresses, and temples, after the Inca custom, establishing a firm base of operations and recruiting his army from the new allies, guessing that, on the other side of Azuay, his task would be far less easy, for there would be encountered the faithful vassals of the real kingdom of the Shiris.

The conquest of the province of Cañari was one of the greatest exploits of Tupac Yupanqui, whose activity in reducing other neighbouring nations and incorporating them in the Inca empire had marked him out from his predecessors. The conquest of Cañar was undertaken after the reduction of Huánuco, where the Incas built extensive stone structures.[1] These included a palace, a temple of the Sun with beautifully formed stone doorways, and a town of round and square houses, covering an extensive plain. The whole forms a very typical but little known group of Inca structures, which lies at an elevation of over 11,000 ft. above sea-level.

On the road to Cañari, Tupac conquered the province of Paltas, and according to Cieza de Leon,[2] later took from that place the delicious *palta* fruits (alligator pears) and implanted them in a warm valley near Cuzco, the Inca capital. The Incas gave great attention to such subjects. South of Huánuco they had conquered a place called Papamarca, meaning " the village of potatoes," so called from the fact that these tubers grew very large at that point. Such matters were valuable to the life of the empire, and

[1] Visited by the Author, and described before the Royal Geographical Society ; see the Author's *The Andes and the Amazon* and *The Secret of the Pacific.*

[2] *Royal Commentaries of the Incas.*

in all the conquered regions the Incas caused irrigation canals to be made, established terrace cultivation,
and greatly improved agriculture and the means of
life for the inhabitants, so redeeming them from their
former more primitive conditions. It was small matter
for surprise, therefore, that these tribes readily
accepted the Inca dominion. The Palta Indians followed the curious custom of flattening their heads,
by the method of binding small boards on the back
and front of the craniums of young children, and
tightening them daily, until the child was three years
old. This ugly custom gave rise to a term of oppro-
brium afterwards of " Palta-head " or " flat-head "
to any Indian whose head happened to be flatter than
usual. The Cañaris were at first divided in their
reception of the invading Incas, but submitted. They
were moon-worshippers, and tree and stone (jasper)
worshippers, but they accepted the Inca cult of the
Sun. The Inca greatly favoured this province of
Cañari, building palaces adorned with gold and silver,
the doors of which " were inlaid with plates of gold,
in which emeralds were set," and Tupac specially implanted here the beneficent Inca laws. Rich clothing
and gold cups—according to Cieza de Leon—were
brought in, and the stones of the palaces were carried
from Cuzco, the Inca capital of Peru, a vast distance
away. Such stones were looked upon as sacred, and
it was regarded as a special privilege to have them
brought from Cuzco. The Indians " in order to
enjoy such honours would think nothing of bringing
the stones over so long and wearisome a road, which
must be over four hundred leagues in length, and so
rugged that it would not be credible to any one who
had not travelled it." ¹ Whatever may be the truth
of these statements, the character of the Andine Indian
is such as would readily have lent itself to such

¹ The Author, well acquainted with portions of this "road" of
the Andes, can bear witness to its inaccessibility.

operations. Tupac Yupanqui, having arranged the affairs of government in Cañari, returned to Cuzco to attend to affairs of his rule at the empire's centre. But the spirit of conquest being strong within him, he returned, and pushed on farther, overcoming small tribes and establishing the Inca rule. The maritime provinces under the Quito sway, that of Huancavillcas especially, sent ambassadors to Tupac, as before mentioned, asking for the benevolent Inca rule and institutions, and captains were sent to implant these, with presents and kindly instructions. According to Spanish writers, Tupac himself went to the Huancavillcas country, where he first saw the sea on the shores of Guayaquil ; and collecting a large fleet of *balsas* or rafts, he embarked there. It is said that the Inca discovered two islands in the South Seas. It is possible but not probable that these were the Galapagos Islands.[1] But the natives of Huancavillcas turned traitor, and killed the Inca captains and instructors. Tupac heard of this, but dissimulated, as at the time he was unable to chastise the offenders.

Tupac Yupanqui again returned to Cuzco, but after a period once more set out to conquer Quito, assembling an army of 40,000 men at Tumipampa. Hualcopo, the Shiri king, had profited by the delay, and had fortified part of the province of Puruhá and the small States of Tiquizambi and Alausi, which extended to the northern base of Azuay. As soon as Tupac Yupanqui with his army passed this mountain the Inca chief made the usual proposals of peace and friendship under Inca domination, such as customarily preceded the Inca conquest, but these were indignantly spurned by Hualcopo.

But the personal valour of the Shiri and his subjects was without avail. Nor did the high and broken territory of this frontier impede the march of the Incas, nor the crossing of the profound gorges and

[1] This is a debated point.

rivers, which have their rise in this the water-parting of the South American continent. Some of these rivers flow eastwardly to join the Marañon and Amazon on their way to the Atlantic, others westwardly to the Pacific Ocean. The Incas were well accustomed to operate in territory of this broken character, which indeed was similar to that which formed their own native environment ; and the snows of Chimborazo and Sangay, which lay before them, were but a replica of their own perpetually white-clad and ice-bound summits. The tenacious resistance of the Shiri troops, under their general, Epiclachima, brother of the king, did not prevail against the more experienced and, veteran Inca soldiers, and after various bloody encounters the States of Alausi and Tiquizambi were lost, and the forces of Quito retired to their *páramos*, or high plains of the Trocajas knot, between Tixan and Guamote, to prepare for a decisive battle.

Tupac Yupanqui, seeing that the conquest of Quito would be long and arduous, sent for his son and heir, Huayna Capac, in order that he might acquire experience in the war. This prince had given indications in his childhood of great talents, and of royal magnanimity, and the name given to him meant " one from childhood rich in magnanimous deeds " ; the word " Capac," synonymous with greatness of mind and the peculiar Inca qualities, having generally been applied to the chiefs of this remarkable dynasty from its founder, Manco Capac, onward. A quality in especial possessed by Huayna, which he observed both as a prince and a monarch, and for which the Indians venerated him, was that he never refused a request . made to him by a woman, whatever her age, rank, or condition, and this characteristic influenced some of his later acts.

Ill-fortune followed the people of Quito at Trocajas. After three months' skirmishing around the fortress, the Incas inflicted a severe defeat upon them, in which the valiant Epiclachima was killed, and 16,000 soldiers. Hualcopo retired upon Liribamba, capital of Puruhá, but finding little support there, fell back upon Mocha, leaving the whole province to the Inca forces. The Mocha fortress was an advantageous strategic point surrounded by woods, with lakes connected by canals. Reinforcements from Quito joined Hualcopo there, and he reorganized his army, and placed in command Calicuchima, son of the dead general, an expert young man. New hopes arose in the army. The repeated offers of the Incas for honourable subjection were haughtily refused, and attack followed attack by the Peruvians. But a serious reverse attended the Inca forces, and they lost heavily. In view of this unfavourable turn of affairs, Tupac Yupanqui, seeing his troops being thinned, and recognizing the difficulties of the campaign, raised the siege, and contented himself with firmly establishing the Inca rule in the subjugated provinces, building fortresses and establishing governors. This done, he again retired to Cuzco, in 1460, in triumph, leaving Huayna Capac in command. Hualcopo, the Quito monarch, did not long survive the grief of his defeats and lost provinces, and he died in 1463.

At Hualcopo's death his son Cacha Duchisela became king, the fifteenth and last Shiri of Quito. Cacha at once set to work to recover the lost provinces, and, fortune favouring, he became master of Puruhá, with Tiquizambi and Alausi, destroying the fortress of the Inca and putting the Inca soldiers to the sword. Thus he again extended the realm of Quito to the northern foot of Azuay, but despite all his efforts he could not compass the southern side, due to the obstinate resistance of the Cañaris, who preferred to remain faithful to the Incas. Cacha fell ill at Liribamba, and his nephew Calicuchima remained in command of the army. The Inca Tupac Yupanqui, greatly, angered by the reverses, news of which reached him in Peru, would have set out once more for Quito. But, feeling that his end was near, he summoned his son Huayna Capac, and charged him with the punishment of the traitorous Huancavillcas and the conquest of Quito. Then Tupac bade his son and people farewell, saying that his father the Sun had called him to his rest. So perished this great ruler, leaving an immortal memory throughout his empire by reason of his clemency and benevolence. His body was embalmed after the Inca custom, and, says Garcilaso de la Vega, his chronicler and descendant, " I saw it afterwards, in the year 1559, when it looked as if it were alive." [1]

Huayna Capac, his mission the reduction of Quito, set forth from Cuzco in 1475, having passed a year in the ceremonies attending the obsequies of his father. He was accompanied by 40,000 warriors.[2] He travelled the road along the Cordillera to Huancabamba, and descending to Tumbez, entered upon a pacific conquest of the littoral provinces of the kingdom of Quito. Force was rarely necessary, except with the island nation of Puná. These people, by means of a treacherous act, inflicted severe loss upon the Incas. The chief of the island, Tumballa, described as proud and vicious, the possessor of " many women and boys," and a sacrificer of human hearts and blood to his idols, called the people together and charged them to resist the customary pacific Inca advances. But it was obvious to the tribe that they could not oppose the necessary force of arms to the Peruvians. A message of peace was therefore treacherously returned, and the Inca, satisfied, visited the island and strove to establish the Inca laws. Certain officers of the blood royal were then sent, and the natives were to carry these over in rafts. When

---

[1] *Royal Commentaries of the Incas.*   [2] *Ibid.*

the Inca had departed, the curacas of Puná con-
spired, embarked the officers in two rafts, and
in ferrying them across cut the ropes which bound
the *balsas* together, casting the lncas into the water,
where they were drowned. Others they killed with
great barbarity, putting their heads on the doors
of their idolatrous temples. Upon receiving news
of this treachery Huayna Capac entered into deep
mourning, and, setting out, took terrible revenge upon
the chiefs of Puná, causing them to be killed in the
same manner in which they had murdered the Inca
officers, whether by drowning, decapitation, or
quartering. It is recorded that various of the tribes
in the regions of Ecuador (and probably it was
true of parts of Peru) practised sodomy, which was
a vice of the Puná chieftain, and Huayna Capac
undertook the punishment of a tribe in Manabi on account of this criminal condition, wiping it out entirely.

During this time Cacha Duchisela, the Shiri king,
was rapidly declining in health. But his mind did not
share the ills of his body, and he formulated careful
plans for the organization of his forces, which, under
Calicuchima, were carried out. Amid the snowy
heights of Azuay the vanguard of the Puruhaes de-
tained for long the onward march of the Inca forces.
But, aided by the Cañaris, the Peruvians opened a
way, and upon the bleak and melancholy *páramos* of
Tiocajas, where years before their fathers had fought,
battle was again waged, and with the same fatal result
for the forces of the Shiri. Completely defeated,
Cacha retired upon the fortress of Mocha, as his
father Hualcopo had done ; but, still more unfortunate, Cacha could not prevent the advance of the
Incas. Having lost almost all his army, not so much
by death as by desertion and disaffection, Cacha was
forced to abandon the provinces of Mocha, Ambato,
Latacunga, and Quito, which seemed insecure, and to
pass to the northern provinces. Followed by the

Inca, he first fortified himself at Cochasqui and then at Otalvo.[1] Here the valiant Caranquis, who had always been the faithful vassals of the Shiris, fought with such bravery that from the defensive the army passed to the offensive, and the Inca, escaping from an attack, was obliged to raise the siege of the Caranqui fortress and to suspend operations. He ordered strongholds to be made at Pesillo, and turned back to Tomebamba, with the purpose of calling up from Cuzco and the other provinces fresh forces of the imperial troops. In the meantime the Caranquis attacked and took the Pesillo fortress, and killed its garrison, an exploit which was at once answered by Huayna Capac with a strong detachment of soldiers, under the command of his brother Auqui Toma. Encountering no resistance, this general advanced to Otalvo, but he fell in the first attack. Discouraged by his death, the Peruvians halted. Huayna Capac then advanced, bent on vengeance, and the attack was renewed, but without result. At length by means of a subterfuge, in which the Incas pretended to flee and then made a flank attack, the castle was taken and burnt. The cheated Caranquis fell confused before the enemy, and only a captain and a thousand men escaped, taking refuge in the forests. Cacha fled to the famed Hatuntaqui fortress, the last hope of his remaining vassals, and around this stronghold his troops were concentrated. The Shiri king, notwithstanding his wasting infirmity, caused his servants to carry him in his chair to the place of greatest danger in the combat. The Inca sent him the last invitation to an honourable surrender, with the hope of avoiding further bloodshed. Cacha made reply that the war was not of his seeking, that he was defending the integrity of his people, and that he would die before submitting. The attacks continued, and at first it seemed that the tide of battle might

[1] Velasco and Cevallos.

turn in favour of the Shiri. But these hopes were vain, for, suddenly struck by a lance, which penetrated his body, the brave Shiri fell dead in his chair. Disaster followed : the vanquished army gave up its weapons and surrendered, proclaiming however, at the last moment, upon the stricken field, the right of accession to kingship of Paccha, the son of the dead king. But with the battle of Hatuntaqui fell the dynasty of the Shiris, and on the plain which had formed the fatal battleground the traveller may observe to-day the numerous tumuli beneath which repose the remains of those who once formed the army of the kingdom of Quito. Thus was played out in those high regions, overlooked by the Andine snows and volcanoes, one of those fateful dramas of early America, analogous in many ways with the historic struggles of Old World dynasties.

Immediately after the battle of Hatuntaqui, Huayna Capac took as one of his wives the daughter of the dead Shiri, hoping by this alliance to placate the vanquished Quiteños. Huayna had, as was customary with the Inca princes, a multitude of concubines. The real heir to the throne of Peru was Huascar. The meaning of this name was " cable " or " rope," and it arose from the circumstance that Huayna Capac celebrated the birth of his son in Cuzco by causing an enormous chain or cable of gold to be made for the nobles to hold in their hands as they performed their national dance at the festival. According to Zarate and Garcilaso, this chain was " 700 ft. long and as thick as a man's wrist." The Spanish chroniclers, however, did not as a rule minimize the wonders of the incidents with which they dealt. But the favourite son of Huayna Capac was Atahualpa, whom he had had by his Scyri queen, and who afterwards perished at the hands of the Spanish conqueror of Peru, Francisco Pizarro, as described in its place.

Huayna Capac, after the defeat of the Quiteños, penetrated to the north of Quito and the provinces lying beyond, but he founded the royal centre at Quito. The Caciques came from the coast valleys with presents, among which were "a very fierce lion and a tiger," two animals which afterwards figured in the history of the Spanish advent. The Inca king returned to Cuzco and visited or sent emissaries at this period to the remotest confines of the empire, including what is now Chile, and Tucuman in Argentina, beyond the Andes. He erected some of the famous buildings of Cuzco ; and the walls of the palace of Huayna Capac, built with massive polygonal-shaped and accurately fitted stones, are among the noteworthy archæological features of Cuzco to-day.[1]

During the Inca's absence the Chachapoyas people rebelled, and killed the Inca governors. Chachapoyas is a large province in northern Peru, lying on the east side of the Marañon, north of Huanuco. Huayna advanced with an army to the Marañon, where numerous *balsas* or rafts of maguey, a very light wood, were collected, and a floating bridge of these was made. The rebels, fearful of the impending punishment, fled, only the aged, infirm, and women remaining. Then it was that the attribute of Huayna, formerly mentioned, of never refusing the petition of a woman, came into prominence. The Chachapoyas people knew of this quality. They sent to meet the Inca a woman who had been a mistress of Tupac Yupanqui, his father, and this brave woman, urged by the supplication of her kinsfolk and the defenceless condition of her people, set out, accompanied by a large deputation of other women and matrons, resolved to throw herself at the feet of the terrible monarch. No man accompanied them. They met Huayna and his army about two leagues from Cajamarquilla, and

[1] See the Author's *The Andes and the Amazon*.

prostrated themselves to the ground. " O sole lord," exclaimed the matron, " remember that thou hast the name of Huac-Chacuyac,[1] lover of the poor and defenceless. I implore pardon for these poor people ; or, if vengeance must be done, let it fall only upon this poor body. Consider that thou art a child of the Sun. To-morrow thou wilt regret having given way to anger. Stay thy hand ! " Then she was silent, whilst her companions took up the supplication.

The Inca chief, it is recorded, remained long in suspense. At length he raised the woman from the ground, informed her that her action had saved the people, that he pardoned them, that she was indeed a worthy woman and *mama-cuna*.[2] With that Huayna Capac reversed the order of his march and, having appointed fresh governors for the province, departed whence he came. The people of Chacha-poyas, repenting of their ways and overcome by the magnanimity of the Inca, built upon the spot where the meeting had taken place a sacred well, surrounded by three walls, the interior of which was " of fine cut stone with a cornice above." [3]

Following upon these events, Huayna Capac set out on a long-planned expedition to the Ecuadorian littoral, for the purpose of establishing the Inca civilization among the savage tribes inhabiting it. He reached Manta, the harbour afterwards called by the Spaniards Puerto Viejo. The people were gross idolaters, worshipping the sea, fishes, tigers, lions, serpents, and so forth, and—chief object of their veneration—a great emerald, " said to have been as large as an ostrich's egg." This precious stone was displayed at festivals, and the Indians

[1] The name is taken by the first Inca Manco Capac, and adopted by his descendants.

[2] Curiously the word *mama*, in the Inca language, has the same significance as in English and Spanish.

[3] *Royal Commentaries of the Inca.*

came from great distances to worship it. It was called Umiña, and presents of smaller emeralds were brought to it, for the chiefs and priests of Manta gave out the—to them—comfortable doctrine that the large emerald "regarded the smaller ones as its daughters," a covetous creed which greatly enriched the place with these precious stones. Many of these emeralds were found at the time of the conquest by Pedro de Alvarado and his companions, and it is recorded that they "tested" them by "breaking the stones on an anvil," saying that real stones ought to resist the hardest blow. The great emerald, however, was especially hidden, and the Spaniards never found it. The people were described as sodomists, and as extremely cruel and barbarous with their captives of war, flaying them alive and filling their hides with cinders, placing them thus stuffed at the doors of their temples. They also had the repulsive custom of head-flattening in childhood, by means of boards strapped on the cranium. Some writers have endeavoured to mitigate these accounts of the early Ecuadorians as to the native vices.

The Inca sent these people the customary summons to submit, which they did, seeing that resistance was useless. Huayna then advanced to the Caranqui province and subdued the inhabitants in like manner. These people also indulged the singular head-flattening custom, with others equally repulsive. The Inca then went on to the Indians of Passau (Cape Pasados, on the Equator), who were, as regards their bestial customs, of similar character, with no knowledge of agriculture, living in hollow trees, painting their bodies and faces and subsisting largely on fish, which they speared with great dexterity from the shore or in their *balsas*. It is recorded that the Inca, thinking it would be a waste of time to endeavour to civilize such savages, took himself and his army, away, and left the natives of Pasado to their savagery. He then returned to Cuzco.

The next incident of Huayna's reign, as concerns Ecuador, was the rebellion of the Caranquis, who had accepted the Inca rulers. It was a long and obstinate conflict to overcome them, but terrible punishment was meted out. The Inca caused 20,000 [1] of the rebels to be drowned in a lake, that of Yahuar-Cocha, whose name means " the lake of blood," which it bears to the present time. The number given, other writers remark, was probably that of the combatants who fell on both sides. When the punitive expedition was accomplished Huayna returned to Quito, greatly troubled by the constant insurrections of the various provinces of the northern empire. There was a shadow upon the mind of the great Inca ruler, a portent of some disaster to befall his nation. These forebodings were later to be realized, for the caravels of the white man, although at that moment the Inca did not know it, were about to traverse the waters of the Pacific upon the coasts of the empire.

[1] According to Cieza de Leon.

CHAPTER IV

THE SPANISH ADVENT

THE story of the discovery and conquest of the lands lying upon the west coast of South America, the vast territory known to the Spaniards as " Peru," after the crossing, in 1513, by Balboa of the Isthmus of Panama, is one of the most stirring and romantic in the annals of exploration. It would be beyond the scope of this book to enter into detail of the famous conquest of Peru by Pizarro and his companions except in broad outline and as concerns the territory which now forms the republic of Ecuador.

Vasco Nuñez de Balboa was the first to dream of the conquest of Peru, and to him doubtless the glory of it would have belonged had he not been foully executed by reason of the machinations of the ruthless Pedrarias Davila. Francisco Pizarro was one of the explorers who accompanied Balboa in the expedition across Panama, and stood with Balboa upon that famous " peak in Darien " (its identity has not been precisely determined), and with him first beheld the great South Sea, or Pacific Ocean. When in 1522 Andagoya returned with glowing accounts of his expedition along the coast south of Panama, accounts which fired the imagination of the Spaniards, already aroused by the exploits of Cortés in Mexico, two of the colonists of Panama, Francisco Pizarro and Diego de Almagro, with a third associate, Fernando de Lluque, an ecclesiastic, entered into partnership for the purpose of further exploration,

and pooled their capital and obtained two small ships.
A body of men was engaged, consisting largely of
low-class Spaniards, who were recruited with some
difficulty, and Pizarro set sail from Panama in
November, 1554.   Almagro was to follow.   Ignorant
of the season, the voyage was begun during the
period of adverse winds, but the vessel reached and
entered the small River Birú, which had marked the
limit of Andagoya's exploration.   The name of this
stream, according to Zarate, was that which, under
a mispronunciation, gave origin to the name of Peru.
The territory entered was not promising.   It consisted of swampy, forested land—dismal, uninhabited
solitudes ; and Pizarro's men, expecting to have
encountered some Dorado, where riches might lie
easy to their hands, rebelled, and were for returning
to Panama.   But Pizarro was of sterner stuff.   He
knew, moreover, that this expedition, which had cost
him and his partners vast effort and expense, was
the one chance of his lifetime for glory and wealth.
But as the whole party was in danger of starvation, he sent the vessel back to the Island of Pearls,
in Panama Bay, for supplies, a voyage of no great
distance.   Waiting for the return of the caravel,
some of the company died of starvation, as no food
was obtainable from the tropic jungle.   In their
extremities an Indian village was discovered.   The
Spaniards entered among the astonished natives and
devoured the maize and coconuts which formed the
Indian larders, heedless of the owners' protests.   But
there were other matters of interest for the Spaniards.
They saw the glint of gold.   Here was that alluring
metal for which they had come, in the form of rude
ornaments upon the bodies of the natives.   This
gold was only the prelude to more sensational
matters.   For Pizarro learned, by such signs and
language with the natives as was possible, that,
beyond the forests and the high mountains behind

them lay a great empire and potentate, whose terrible name had descended even to that primitive tribe by the sea. This was the first news of the Inca empire which the Spaniards received, and the potentate referred to was doubtless Huayna Capac, who some thirty years before the period had overcome the kingdom of Quito.

Their bodily sufferings alleviated to some extent, and their minds animated by this piece of news, Pizarro and his companions awaited day by day the return of their vessel. It came some six weeks afterwards, laden with provisions. Their sufferings were forgotten ; they embarked and left the shores of Port Famine—as they appropriately termed the place—and struck out southwards along the coast. But many hardships befell them. In a fight with Indians Pizarro nearly lost his life, and several Spaniards were killed. Disillusion came upon the expedition, and a return was made to Chicama, near Panama. Meantime Almagro had followed in his caravel with some sixty men. Sailing on the same track, he touched at the points reached by Pizarro, encountered the same fierce savages, and went as far south as the San Juan River. This river lies a few miles north of the port of Buenaventura, in Colombia, in latitude 4° north, and is a waterway which in modern times has been considered as a possible route for a trans-isthmian canal. Thus the total southern distance accomplished so far was small. Pizarro sent back his ship to Panama, and Almagro also returned there. Great difficulty was encountered in overcoming the opposition of Pedrarias Davela, Governor of Panama, to a further voyage of exploration to the south, and but for the aid and influence of the third associate of Pizarro and Amalgro, the sagacious Churchman Fernando de Lluque, the discovery of Peru would not then have been prosecuted. Considered almost mad by the

colonists of Panama, the three confederates entered
into a further compact, and Pizarro and Almagro,
piloted by Bartolomé Ruiz, the most experienced
navigator in those waters, again set sail for the
San Juan River.   From the Indians of the region
considerable booty of gold was obtained, and,.flushed
with this small success, the hopes of the Spaniards
rose still higher.   But from the numbers of the
Indians the Conquistadores knew that their forces
were insufficient to enter upon any great conquest.
Almagro therefore returned with the gold to Panama
for reinforcements, while Pizarro encamped upon the
territory, and Ruiz sailed southwards to explore the
unknown coast below them.

The pilot reached the bay now known as San
Mateo, the Island of Gallo, and the headland on the
Ecuadorian coast called Cape Pasado.   This cape
lies slightly south of the Equator, and thus the valiant
Ruiz was the first European to cross the Line in
the western Pacific.   Suddenly there appeared on
the horizon a strange sail.   No vessel of the white
men could be in those waters ; what, then, could it
mean ?   As the caravel approached the strange
craft it was seen to be a native raft, with a
number of Indians on board.   The Indian raft (in
somewhat similar form such craft are still used in
the Guayas River, as described in a subsequent
chapter) was made of great logs of the very light
balsa wood, lashed together and covered with a platform, carrying a mast with a large square sail of
cotton, and having a rude rudder and a movable keel.
Aboard this strange craft were Indians, dressed
in woollen clothes of fine and curious texture,
embroidered with figures of birds and flowers,
brilliantly dyed, and in the possession of its voyagers
were curious articles, such as an obsidian mirror and a
pair of scales for weighing gold, with other matters.
Ruiz was astonished to contemplate these evidences of

a considerable native culture. He learned from the occupants of the raft, two of whom had come from the northern coast of Peru (Tumbez), wonders relating to the monarch and people of those regions, of their vast flocks and herds, their stone palaces, the gold and silver, so common that the metals were used as household utensils. Here, indeed, was a stimulant after the kind that the Spaniards loved..

Tacking northwards again from Point Pasado, Ruiz hastened to rejoin Pizarro. It was time, for the Spaniards with him were exhausted from want and hardship. They had penetrated into the interior of the tropic forests, where monkeys chattered and great boas and alligators haunted the jungle and the swamps, and many had fallen from fever and the attacks of the savages. Except for the wild potato, the coconut, and the bitter mangrove fruit, the explorers had had little to sustain them, whilst the attacks of the mosquitoes rendered it necessary to bury their faces in the sand if any sleep was to be obtained at night.

But again these hardships were forgotten, under the stimulus of Ruiz's news, and to add to their satisfaction Almagro and his vessel sailed in, laden with fresh supplies and bringing reinforcements, including a band of eager Spaniards who had arrived at Panama from Spain. Pizarro embarked ; Gallo and San Mateo were reached and passed, the villages along the coast became more numerous, healthy patches of open land cultivated with fields of maize and green meadows opened out, and Atacames, near the great Esmeraldas River (in Northern Ecuador), was reached, and anchor cast before its port. The Spaniards " saw a town of two thousand houses, whose inhabitants they found possessed of gold and precious emeralds." But the natives proved no easy subject for conquest. Armed canoes shot out from the shore, supported by ten thousand warriors on the beach. In a fight after landing Pizarro fell from his horse, and the natives, astonished and terrified at the apparent separation into two parts of the horseman, which they had imagined to be one formidable animal, fell back, and the Spaniards were enabled to regain the ship.

Again Pizarro and his companions realized the inadequacy of their forces, and the apparent impossibility of conquering what seemed to be so well populated and organized a land without far greater resources than those they commanded. A council of war was called. Some were for going home and giving up the enterprise ; Almagro was for returning to Panama for reinforcements, suggesting that Pizarro should await their return. But the latter objected to this proposal. At Panama all had left creditors, and possibly imprisonment would await them there ; and as to remaining, Pizarro upbraided Almagro with desiring the easier life of shipboard, whilst he himself should endure the hardships of the deserts again. Almagro replied that if necessary he would remain, but from words the two partners came to blows, and had not Ruiz interposed an end might have been made of one or both. However, the plan of Almagro was adopted. But their followers had also to be reckoned with. These little relished a continuance of their sufferings. Where was the treasure they had been promised? What credit or profit was there in fighting a pack of miserable savages? As far as they were concerned, the whole expedition seemed to be a cheat and a failure, and some of the men wrote letters to send in the ship with Almagro, begging the Governor of Panama to recall this disastrous expedition. The astute Ruiz, however, seized these letters on board, intending to destroy them. But his purpose was frustrated by the ingenuity of a soldier, who concealed a letter in a ball of cotton, sent as a present to the Governor's wife. This epistle duly reached its destination when Almagro arrived at Panama. The Governor, Pedro de Los Rios, incensed at the poor result of the expedition, and deriding the representation of Almagro and Lluque that success awaited a further voyage, immediately dispatched two vessels with orders to bring back Pizarro and his companions.

But Almagro and Lluque sent their confederate a letter, telling him not to return, but to remain firm, and promising sooner or later to rejoin him. This was sufficient for Pizarro. Calling together the half-mutinous and discontented followers, he stood before them and traced a line on the sand with his sword— the famous line which has gone down to history. " Comrades," he said, " on the south of this line lie hardship, hunger, and possibly death : on the north side ease and salvation. On the south is Peru, with its riches ; on the north Panama, with its poverty. Choose which you will ; for my own part I go to the south. Who follows? " With these words Pizarro stepped across the line in the sand, upon its southern side. He was immediately followed by Ruiz and by Pedro de Candia, a valiant Greek of great stature who was seeking fortune with the band, and by eleven others of the company. The names of these thirteen faithful spirits are preserved in the Convention made afterwards with the Crown of Spain, in which they were commemorated for their constancy.

It was one of those moments in the life of a man where the tide of defeat or of success was to be taken. Constant to their quest, these heroes of ocean chivalry, a mere handful, deliberately chose the desert and its future rather than an inglorious return. Tafur, the officer sent to bring them back, was, however, animated by no such spirit, and, grudgingly leaving a few stores behind, he set sail with the two ships for Panama, Ruiz accompanying him, but with the determination of co-operating later with Almagro and Lluque. Pizarro pitched his camp on the small island of Gorgona, off the Colombian coast, having constructed a raft for the purpose of reaching it. There was water and game for their sustenance and the mosquitoes were less formidable. Morning prayers were regularly said, and here the Spaniards, with little occupation except that of watching the monotonous waves, awaited the somewhat forlorn event of reinforcements from Almagro.

But Almagro was true to his promise, and at length the Panama Governor, under a sense of responsibility, permitted the dispatch of a vessel to Gorgona, with orders that the expedition should positively return within six months. Pizarro and his followers were embarked, sail was set again for the south, Cape Pasado was passed, and after twenty days' journeying from Gallo the caravel entered the smooth waters of the Gulf of Guayaquil, a region never before traversed by the white man's keel. The shores were fringed with green, and far to the east the gleaming crests of Chimborazo and Cotopaxi shone, surmounting the mighty chain of the grey and rocky Andes. The vessel passed the Island of Puná and came to an anchor off the entrance to the bay of Tumbez.[1]

The apparition of the floating castle on their shores quickly attracted hordes of Indians, and large *balsas* came forth full of warriors. The two natives of that place, who had been earlier captured by Ruiz and were on board the ship, mixed with their countrymen and recounted the wonders, qualities, and doings of their captors, who, fortunately, had treated them well. Other *balsas* then came out, loaded with fruit and provisions—bananas, coconuts, maize, and other products of the fruitful Tumbez valley.

[1] Santa Clara Island.

The llamas greatly excited the Spaniards' curiosity, although they had seen Balboa's rude drawings of these animals before. An Inca noble, who by chance was at Tumbez, his person decorated with gold ornaments, visited Pizarro on board the vessel, and was presented with an iron hatchet, that metal being then unknown to the natives. It was here that Pedro Candia went ashore as an emissary, bearing a sword and cross, together with his carbine, which latter he fired for the delectation of the natives, perforating a board with the ball. The valiant Candia had gone alone, like some knight-errant, but he entered the Indian town, and returned safely on board with marvellous accounts of what he had seen. Among the wonders were " gardens filled with artificial flowers wrought in gold." It is to be recollected that Tumbez was a favoured place of Tupac Yupanqui and the Incas, with a fortress, and was the terminus of the road to Quito. However exaggerated may have been the glowing accounts of the enthusiastic Greek, there was sufficient of truth in them to turn the Spaniards half mad with joy.

Passing on from Tumbez, Pizarro and his companions reached Payta, on the coast of Peru. In every place the Spaniards received the same accounts of the mighty kingdom of the Incas, whose stronghold lay beyond the Andes, looming upon the eastern horizon. Sailing on, after buffeting with storms, the town now called Trujillo was reached, and, having penetrated nine degrees farther south than any other navigators, the Spaniards decided to return.

The further adventures of Francisco Pizarro and his companions belong mainly to the history of Peru. He returned to Panama with the news of a rich Indian empire. But " a few gold and silver toys and some Indian sheep " (the llamas) did not arouse any enthusiasm in the Governor's breast, and, raising a sum of money, Pizarro left for Spain to present his case before the King of Castile. His earnest story and bearing, and the curious and valuable objects he brought, ensured Pizarro a favourable reception at the Spanish Court, with royal favour and promise of support in a further expedition. But the arrangements for his return journey followed very tardily, and were only expedited by the Queen's efforts. Her Majesty, in the *Capitulacion* which she caused to be drawn up, secured to Pizarro the right of conquest of Peru or New Castile, as the region was to be termed.

Almagro and Lluque were also fully rewarded, and nominated to important posts. Pizarro was specially exhorted to preserve the good native state of government of the Indians. It is to be recollected that the Spanish sovereigns generally strove to protect the Indians, whose subsequent cruel treatment was the work of the greedy colonists. It must further be recorded to the credit of the Spanish sovereigns that they strove to secure the teaching of Christianity to the Indians, and the ships sent out were required to carry a certain number of priests as a complement to the rude soldiery. Pizarro visited his native town in Estremadura before embarking again for America, and took with him his brothers, one of whom, Gonzalo Pizarro, was to figure largely in the early history of Ecuador. Overcoming many difficulties, Pizarro at length left with his expedition for America. At Panama there was a quarrel with Almagro, but in January, 1531, the conqueror of Peru set forth on his third and last expedition.

The first landing upon the southern coast was made at Coaque, where a cruel attack on the Indians was made, and the ships were sent back to Panama for more men and horses. They carried a value of 20,000 *castellanos* [1] in gold taken from the natives. The Spaniards marched on along the coast, suffering considerable hardships and some disease, and, subduing various places, reached the island of Puná by means of rafts across the separating gulf. At the same time a vessel arrived from Panama with supplies and various royal officers. The island of Puná was inhabited by a warlike race of Indians, the same who had resisted the Incas, and a stubborn fight was necessary to ensure occupation thereof, in which several Spaniards were killed, Pizarro himself being wounded. The arrival of two vessels from Panama, under Hernando de Soto, relieved the situation however, and the Spaniards made their way to Tumbez, thus entering upon the real conquest of Peru. How they struggled along the sunbeat deserts of the coast, ascended the rocky wall of the Andes, hitherto untrodden by the horseman, and what befell them there are matters which do not belong to the history of Ecuador, but are part of the conquest of Peru, to the affairs of which kingdom it is now necessary to give a final glance.

Under Huayna Capac the Inca empire had reached its greatest development and power, and after his death and at the time of its invasion by the Spaniards the State was already beginning to decline. It included what are now the republics of Ecuador, Peru, Bolivia, and Chile. But Huayna Capac, who had done more than all the preceding Inca emperors to enlarge the empire, was also the instrument in the division which preceded its downfall. Huayna Capac, as customary among the Inca monarchs, had a large number of wives. He had numerous male children, two of whom, Huascar and Atahualpa— the last the son of the Scyri princess—inherited the kingdom. Feeling his end approaching, Huayna divided the possession, Huascar taking the southern

[1] A *castellano* was worth about eight shillings.

portion, with Cuzco as its capital, and Atahualpa the northern, whose centre was Quito. The last years of Huayna were passed in that city, and his death took place near the close of 1525, about seven years before Pizarro's arrival at Puná, as far as the date has been truly ascertained. His body was embalmed and transported to Cuzco, to rest in sacred state with those of his ancestors. One of Huayna's works was the making of the famous Inca roads between Cuzco and Quito, works of great utility, but whose importance has been much exaggerated by the early Spanish writers. Some of the finest edifices in Cuzco were also attributed to Huayna ; he established a system of posts upon the roads and did much to increase the material welfare of the people, whilst the Quechua language was brought into general use. Had the empire continued to flourish and develop, it might possibly have reached a degree of civilization approaching that of the great historical despotisms of Asia or Africa.

Huayna Capac doubtless received news of the earlier arrival of the white men on the Panama coast of South America, and the matter impressed him strongly. Tradition states that supernatural occurrences heralded the fall of the Inca empire—flaming comets, earthquakes, and so forth. On his deathbed, according to tradition, Huayna recalled a prognostication that had been earlier made, that after twelve Incas had reigned—Huayna himself was the twelfth —a valorous race would appear, a white, bearded people, who would overcome the empire. " I go to rest with our father the Sun," he added. But it would appear that the great Inca had not always regarded the sun as an infallible power. Some years before, at the great feast of Raymi, the festival of the Sun, at Cuzco, the chief priest had observed that the monarch looked up from time to time at the orb with considerable freedom, an action prohibited and considered almost sacrilegious ; and he inquired why the Inca did this. Huayna replied : " I tell you that our Father the Sun must have another lord more powerful than himself ; a thing so inquiet and so bound in his course could not be a god." Before he died Huayna Capac admonished his successor ever to carry on the noble traditions of their dynasty, in fulfilling their title as " lovers of the poor." Indeed, a civilization and rulers who had so organized the material resources of the realm and the life of the community that none were in want, and where no class oppressed another, as was indisputably the case under the Inca empire, well merited such a title, and that the system should have been destroyed by the ruthless individualism of the Europeans is one of the most melancholy incidents in history.[1]

For five years after the death of Huayna Capac, Atahualpa and Huascar governed their respective realms, the boundary between which was practically that of the republics of Ecuador and Peru at the present time. Encroachment upon this boundary brought about a quarrel between Huayna's two sons, and thus even at that early period warfare was induced over questions of frontier in South America. Atahualpa invaded Peru, raided the Cañaris, and advanced to Cajamarca and dispatched an army towards Cuzco. Huascar was defeated, and at that moment — it was early in the year 1532 — the Spaniards were landing. The cruelties practised by Atahualpa later culminated in the murder of Huascar. Atahualpa had already proclaimed himself emperor of both kingdoms when Pizarro and his Spaniards entered the town of Cajamarca on their invasion from the coast. Whatever Atahualpa's faults, his cruel

[1] The Author, at the request of the Economic Circle of the National Liberal Club in London, lectured before that body on " The Land Laws and Social System of the Incas" (1912).

murder by the Spaniards in the plaza of Cajamarca is an indelible stain upon the name of Pizarro and his companions. This treacherous act took place on May 3, 1533. Cuzco, the Inca capital, fell in November, and Pizarro firmly established the Spanish dominion throughout the whole vast Inca empire with comparatively little resistance. Had the empire not been divided by the dissension between the two Incas, the history of the conquest of Peru might have been very differently written, but Fate had so disposed events that the European advent took place when comparatively little resistance could be offered thereto.

CHAPTER V

SPANISH RULE

THE real conquerors of Ecuador were Diego de Almagro and Sebastian de Benalcazar. These, by the order of Francisco Pizarro, in 1534 penetrated from San Miguel de Piura, near Payta, into the provinces of Loja, Cuenca, and other mountainous regions of Ecuador, to Quito. They fought several battles against Atahualpa's chiefs, who disputed their passage, and entered Quito on December 6, 1534. But very little treasure was encountered in the city, to Benalcazar's disappointment. From Riobamba, Almagro returned to Peru, and Benalcazar, having consolidated Spanish rule in Quito, overcame the Pasto and Cauca districts, whilst his captains founded settlements on the coast, from Guayaquil to Esmeraldas, and strove to overcome the districts of Canelos and Napo.

It was at this period that the attempted conquest of Quito by another Spanish *conquistador*, independent of Pizarro, took place. Pedro de Alvarado, an officer who had fought with great renown in Mexico under Cortes, and who had been appointed by Spain as Governor of Guatemala, the ancient kingdom of the Quiches, which he had conquered, conceived the plan of invading Quito. He affected to regard that kingdom as beyond Pizarro's sphere of influence in Peru, and with a strong force of 500 followers, including 230 cavalry, forming the best equipped expedition that so far had invaded

IN THE WESTERN CORDILLERA

[To face p. 72

the southern seas, Alvarado landed in the Bay of Caraques, on the Ecuadorian coast, in March, 1534. Striking out direct for the mountains, the expedition soon found itself in a maze of inclement wilds amid the snows of the Cordillera, and the Spaniards, accustomed to the warm climate of Guatemala, suffered severely, whilst the Indians who formed part of the force perished by hundreds. Their track across the cold uplands and snowy passes was strewn with discarded articles and the bodies of men and horses, which latter, indeed, the starving soldiers were obliged to devour in default of other food. Even the gold plundered from the natives was regarded as an incubus in a situation where food was the great necessity. Adding to the terrors of the expedition was an eruption of a great snowy volcano near their line of march, which filled the air with ashes, whilst the noise of the outbreaks resounded over the face of the land like the reports of artillery. It was Cotopaxi, in activity at that moment. Traversing the snowy pass, the adventurers entered upon the plain of Riobamba, a quarter of the force having perished in the ascent from the coast. Here disillusion awaited them. There were marks of horses' hoofs in the dust of the trail, upon what Alvarado and his followers had supposed was a region unknown to the white man—evidences that horsemen had been before them. In effect, the expedition of Benalcazar had already passed that way, and Quito had fallen. Alvarado's march was one of the most noteworthy and disastrous in the history of the conquest.

During the absence of Benalcazar in his search for the dreamed of Dorado of Cundinamarca, in 1538, Pizarro named his brother Gonzalo Governor and Captain-General of Quito, Popayan, and all the region that he might discover, unjustly ousting Benalcazar. Following upon these events, Gonzalo

5

Pizarro and his lieutenant Orellana made their famous but terrible journey to the land of the Quijos, an unfortunate expedition, which, however, resulted in the discovery of the Napo River, a great stream flowing to the east, and in the memorable first navigation of the great Amazon.

It was the beginning of the year 1540 when Gonzalo Pizarro, with 350 Spaniards, 150 of whom were mounted, 4,000 Indians, and a herd of swine for food, set out upon this expedition. They ascended the Andes, the great Cordillera to the east, suffering severely from the cold, and whilst crossing it experienced a terrific earthquake. On the eastern slope the climate changed, and the open uplands gave place to deep ravines and matted vegetation, with great heat and torrential rains. After months of toilsome travel the expedition reached Canelas, the land of cinnamon. The beautiful bark-bearing trees spread out on either hand, but it was the tales of gold from wandering Indians, who spoke of a rich land beyond, that lured the explorers on. The impenetrable jungle closed in upon them, and a way could only be opened by cutting through the thickets with *machetes*. Their clothes were torn to pieces, their provisions gave out, and the herd of swine became dispersed, and the men were obliged to kill and eat of the thousand dogs of ferocious breed which they had taken with them to hunt down Indians. At length the weary Spaniards emerged upon the broad stream of the Napo, which, although only a tributary of the Amazon, appeared, in comparison with their own rivers of Spain, one of the largest they had ever seen. After struggling painfully along its banks, still lured on by the tales of occasional Indians as to a fruitful country beyond, Gonzalo and his companions decided to construct a vessel. This they did, from the timber of the forest, with nails made from their horses' shoes.

This " brigantine " cost the expedition two months' work, and could carry only half the company. Its command was given to Francisco de Orellana, a cavalier of Trujillo, on whose constancy Gonzalo thought he could rely, and, marching and floating, the explorers pressed on down the river, traversing the dreary forests of the Napo. Their last pound of food exhausted, they devoured the remaining horses, and these gone, the saddles, for there is but little of food to be found in the montaña of the upper Amazon.[1] The explorers again learned of a rich country, always " a few days' journey " in front of them, which was said to be situated at the point where the river fell into a vaster stream. But Gonzalo Pizarro called a halt. It was agreed that Orellana, with part of the company, should journey on ahead in the vessel, and return with provisions for the remainder of the starving explorers. Accordingly the brigantine set forth, and was soon lost to view on the swift current of the Napo.

This was the last that Pizarro and his companions ever saw of the vessel and its company. They waited, whilst weeks went past, without any return of Orellana, and at length, faint and weary, they set out again towards the supposed fruitful land. Two months of difficult travelling were accomplished before the confluence of the Napo and the Amazon was reached, and the Spaniards gazed despairingly upon the mighty flood which poured away to the east into that unknown continent. All hope of a meeting with Orellana was given up. There was no fruitful land, no El Dorado, no resting-place or consolation of any description. Realizing this, the return journey to Quito was resolved upon. Suddenly a half-naked white man was discovered wandering

[1] The Author personally found this to be the case in an expedition in Eastern Peru, and was obliged to make forced marches through lack of provisions.

in the forest whose features seemed familiar. He
proved to be Vargas, one of Orellana's companions,
and it was a melancholy tale he told. Borne down
by the swift current, the brigantine had reached the
Amazon in three days, but no fruitful country had
been seen, no supplies were obtainable, and to return
against the current seemed impossible. In the face
of these difficulties Orellana had decided to abandon
Gonzalo and his companions to their fate, to descend
the Amazon to its mouth, and thence proceed to
Spain and claim the glory of the discovery. But
Vargas had opposed this dishonourable course, and
as a result was himself abandoned in the forest.
Orellana and his companions accomplished their
design. Time after time the vessel escaped being
dashed to pieces in the rapids, and the ship's company from the attacks of savages in canoes, and after
incredible hardships the mouth of the Amazon was
reached on August 26, 1541. The explorers coasted
along the shores of British Guiana and Trinidad,
and thence Orellana made his way to Spain. The
difficulties of such a voyage, of nearly 3,000 miles
down an unknown river, were necessarily vast, and it
was little short of a miracle that it was accomplished.

There was no alternative for Gonzalo and his
followers but to return to Quito. The journey was
one of the most terrible in the history of America.
Many of the company fell by the way, and perforce
were left to die in the forest ; and of that great
body of men which had set out with high hopes
of conquest, only eighty Spaniards reached Quito,
with half the original number of Indians, a year
having been consumed in the march. The sur-
viving members of the expedition arrived worn to a
shadow with fever, hunger, and privation. As they
approached Quito, the few white inhabitants of the
place went forth to meet them, and the first act of
the return, be it recorded to the explorers' credit,

was to repair to the church and offer up thanks for the arrival of such as had survived.

The fortunes of Gonzalo Pizarro had changed in other respects during his absence from Quito. Civil war between the conquerors of Peru had thrown the governance of New Castile into great disorder. The shameful execution of Almagro, at Cuzco, after a mock trial, following soon after the battle at that place between the adherents of Almagro and Pizarro, with other disorders, brought from Spain a Crown judge, to inquire into the affairs of Peru. This judge was Vaca de Castro, but his arrival was greatly delayed by storms at sea, in which it was at first reported that the emissary had perished. A still more terrible event than the death of Almagro was to shock the country—the murder of the famous *conquistador* to whose enterprise Peru owed its discovery. Francisco Pizarro was foully assassinated by the enraged followers of Almagro, who were exasperated by the delay of justice for them due to the tardy arrival of the royal judge. The *conquistador* was stabbed by the assassins whilst at dinner on Sunday, June 16, 1541.

The character and person of the Marquess Francisco Pizarro have often been described. It is stated that he was a tall, well-proportioned man, and although not of much education, had a soldier-like bearing, with a certain dignity which had stood him in good stead at the punctilious Court of Castile upon his presentation there. He was temperate, and had great powers of endurance, and to his indomitable purpose the difficulties of the conquest sufficiently attest. Probably his main defect was that of not keeping to his promised word, and in this respect he has been described as perfidious. Yet his constancy was great in other matters. To the foregoing defect his fatal quarrel with Almagro was doubtless due.

As a result of an urgent message from Alonzo

de Alvardo, who had been one of Pizarro's powerful
captains, the licentiate Vaca de Castro then took
up an active part in the affairs of the country. The
Spanish emissary, after a tempestuous voyage, had
remained at Buenaventura to recruit his health. The
perplexities of the situation weighed upon him, but
in loyalty to Spain he continued his march to Quito,
where he was joined by Benalcazar. Here Castro
displayed the royal commission which authorized him
to assume the governing, of Peru. The, son of
Almagro, who had succeeded to the leadership in
Peru, disputed his authority, and Castro advanced
towards Cuzco. A battle was fought, in which the
royalists triumphed, and young Almagro was
executed. From Quito Gonzalo Pizarro, who had
returned from his expedition to the Napo, offered
his services to Castro, and after the victory was
summoned to Cuzco. He was, however, admonished
to retire into private life. Vaca de Castro was a
man who commanded respect, and, although no
soldier, he assured his position, and had Charles V of
Spain maintained him as Governor of Peru it would
have been better for the country.

It was at this period, 1542, that Las Casas completed his celebrated treatise on the *Destruction of the
Indies*. Las Casas was the pious ecclesiastic whose
work for the protection of the Indians of the Spanish
possessions has earned him as great a glory as that of
the *conquistadores* who oppressed them. He inveighed
before the Spanish Court against forced labour and
the ruin of the aborigines in South America, en-
trenching himself strongly on the ground of natural
rights. As a result, a code of ordinances was ordered
to be drawn up, Casas having appeared before a Royal
Commission at Valladolid, and a system of laws for
the regulation of the American colonies was devised.
It was also decided to send a Viceroy to govern Peru
as representative of the Spanish sovereign. This

functionary was to be accompanied by a Royal
Audience of four judges, with extensive powers both
civil and criminal, constituting a species of Council,
and Los Reyes, or Lima, as it began to be called, was
named as the metropolis of the Spanish empire on the
Pacific. These ordinances received the royal sanction
in November, 1543, and thus was the celebrated
Ley de Indias first promulgated. Instead, however,
of naming Vaca de Castro, the most suitable person,
as Viceroy, a Spanish knight, Blasco Nuñez Vela, was
selected by the King. The new laws aroused a commotion among the Spanish colonists, who saw that
the benefit, to them, of slave labour might disappear,
and that the other imposed rules of conduct and
general ordinances would act against the freedom of
action hitherto enjoyed. Had Vela suspended the
ordinances until the Crown could be consulted upon
the advisability of rescinding them, peace might have
been secured, but he announced that he would fulfil
his mandate to the letter. He was installed as first
Viceroy at Lima (1544), but a revolution against his
authority soon forced him to prepare for war. Gonzalo Pizarro, whose ambition for power had been
kindled, was called to the leadership by the opponents
of the royal policy, who themselves were careful to
carry the colours of Spain, and did not take the field
as mere revolutionaries. It was at this juncture that
Manco Inca, the last of the Inca line, having been
raised to a position of puppet kingship by Pizarro, was
massacred by some of Almagro's adherents.

Vela's position rapidly became critical. He performed various arbitrary acts, among them placing
the well-meaning Vaca de Castro and other cavaliers
under arrest. Meantime the judges of the Royal
Audience arrived at Lima. They showed disapproval
of the Viceroy's actions, and after further excesses of
Vela's, declared against him, and amid a popular
tumult outside the palace the Viceroy was arrested.

The Audience then called upon Gonzalo Pizarro to lay down his arms, but he refused, and marching at the head of his adherents, entered Lima, and was proclaimed Governor of Peru, pending his Majesty's pleasure, the oaths of office being administered by the judges of the Royal Audience.

This body, however, soon fell to pieces. Blasco Nuñez Vela had been deported to Panama for his return to Spain, but, in company with Castro, who had escaped from arrest, he returned, determined to establish himself at Quito. A number of volunteers joined him, and he received promises of support from Benalcazar, the loyal commander established at Popayan. Gonzalo Pizarro followed hard upon Vela's trail, and one of the most terrible marches in the history of the country was made. At times the Viceroy's soldiers were starving ; there was no food, except occasionally a few handfuls of parched maize from the Indians, and wayside herbs, which the Spaniards were obliged to boil in their helmets in default of other cooking utensils. Horses were left to die, or were hamstrung. The sufferings of Gonzalo's party were of a similar nature, almost duplicating the horrors of his Amazon march. Blasco at length entered Quito, but was ill-received in that city, and he held on towards Pasto, which lay in the jurisdiction of Benalcazar. Pizarro followed, both bands struggling on painfully over the inclement uplands, losing large numbers of their followers by reason of the hardships of the road. The retreat of Vela was one of the most severe journeys ever undertaken at that period, covering more than two hundred leagues of mountain territory, but the Viceroy reached Popayan, and was kindly received. Gonzalo Pizarro established himself at Quito, but by a stratagem decoyed the Viceroy into returning, in order that battle might be given. Benalcazar and the Viceroy marched upon Quito, and the great battle of Añaquito followed on January 18,

1546, on the plains near Quito. The Viceroy's forces numbered about 400 men, those of Pizarro twice as many, each having some 140 cavalry. But the result was disastrous for Vela, who was slain with a third of his troops. Falling wounded on the field, his head was cut off by a black slave of Pizarro's and stuck upon a pike, and thus perished the first Viceroy of Peru. The name of Gonzalo Pizarro resounded from Quito to Lima and Cuzco as that of the country's deliverer. He returned to Lima, and was acclaimed Protector, the soldiery and the Bishops of Cuzco, Quito, and Bogata accompanying him, and he became undisputed master of the entire country.

The advent of a new Viceroy, Pedro de Gasca, and the ultimate fall and execution of Gonzalo Pizarro are matters which belong to the history of Peru. From the time of the first Governor, Francisco Pizarro, to the establishing of independence in Peru, that country and Quito were governed successively by forty-four viceroys. The Jesuits arrived in 1567, and introduced the first printing machine into the New World, established churches and colleges, and acquired great wealth. In 1573 the first *auto-de-fé* under the Inquisition took place at Lima, and that desolating institution remained until the fall of Spanish rule. The Spanish colonies suffered from the strict monopolistic system of Spain as regarded their commerce, and the Indian *curacas* sorrowfully watched the gradual extinction of their people under the iniquitous working of the *mita*, or system of forced labour in mines and plantations. The institutions of Spanish rule were firmly established; beautiful churches appeared in every town, the centres of religious fanaticism, and the Spanish character was indelibly stamped upon that vast region of America for good or ill.

All the Spanish colonies, denominated *tierra firme—*

Nuevo reino de Granada, Nuevo reino de Castilla, Nuevo reino de Toledo, Tucuman, Paraguay, and Buenos Ayres—were governed until the year 1717 under a single Viceroy, who resided in Lima, the capital of the *Nuevo reino de Castilla*. This vast viceregency was composed of the *Audiencias* of Panama, Caracas, Sante Fe, Quito, Lima, Cuzco, Charcas, Santiago, and Buenos Ayres. That which now forms the republic of Ecuador was constituted in 1564, with the name *Presidencia de Quito*, also called *Reino de Quito*, but its jurisdiction extended over a much greater space than at present. Its first president was Don Fernando de Santillan, the *Oidor* of the *Real Audiencia* of Lima. Together with the presidency was established the *Real Audiencia*, which nevertheless was eliminated, as was that of Panama, by reason of the establishment of the viceregency of the *Nuevo reino de Granada*, which took place on March 27, 1717. Whether to moderate the power of the viceroys, or whether to facilitate the administration of such large viceregencies, the King of Spain determined to establish a second viceregency, that of *Nuevo Granada*, with its capital at Santa Fé, now called Bogatá. To this belonged afterwards the Presidencia of Quito. For reasons not quite clear the new viceregency was abolished in 1723, and the government centralized again at Lima, re-establishing also the *Real Audiencia* of Quito. But in 1739 the Nuevo Granada viceregency was again established, preserving at the same time the *Real Audiencia* of Quito.

At that time the *Presidencia* of Quito, according to the *Recopilacion de Indias*, extended on the north to Pasto, Popayan, Cali, Buza, Chapandica, and Guarchicona, reaching on the northern coast as far as the port of Buenaventura inclusively ; on the south to Payta, including that port, and in the interior to Jaen ; on the east to the *pueblos* of Canelas and Quijos, with " all that might be discovered on that side." The discoveries made specially by the missionaries of Quito passed beyond the confluence of the rivers Yavari and Amazon. The presidency had seven lesser *gobiernos* under its sway—Popayan, Guayaquil, Cuenca, Macas, Quijos, Jaen de Bracamoros, and Maynas ; five *corregimientos*—Ibarra, Otavalo, Latacunga, Riobamba, Chimbo, and Loja ; and the *tenencias* of Ambato and Barbacoas. To the *gobierno* of Cuenca belonged the *tenencia* of Alausi, and to that of Guayaquil those of Babahoyo, Baba, Daule, Portoviejo, Santa Elena, Puná, Naranjal, and Yaguachi.

The ecclesiastical government in South America was shared by three " metropolitan churches," which were those of Nuevo Granada, Peru, and Chacas. Quito, which politically and as to military control was under the Viceroy of Santa Fé, depended ecclesiastically upon Lima. Of the other churches within the presidency some were under the control of the Lima archbishopric and others under that of Santo Fé.

The machinery of government of the Spanish Crown in Ecuador, the virtues and defects of its governance, were to follow the same course as those of its ancient predecessors, the Shiris and the Incas, and the old city of Quito was to look forward to another phase of its life. The time of Spanish decadence arrived, and one by one the rich colonies of the New World were to pass under the control of the mixed race which had sprung up in Latin America. The growth of liberal and revolutionary ideas in the civilized world at the period made itself felt, even in those remote regions. The advantages and the defects established by Spanish rule in South America are strongly visible to-day. There was much of beauty and utility in it, much of oppression and fanaticism. A mixed race, formed of Spaniard and Indian, grew up in Peru, Ecuador, and elsewhere, during the time of the viceroys, forming the various nations of the continent, whose social development at the present time offers so many problems.

CHAPTER VI

THE REPUBLIC

UNDER the political divisions before described, the *Reino de Quito* remained until the beginning of the nineteenth century. For 250 years there had been no change in its political geography. But when the time of independence arrived geographical and social changes of a notable character took place. Quito was not altogether indifferent to the cry of independence in South America. Dr. Eugene Espejo and Pio Montufar, both of Quito, entered into cooperation with Nariño and Zea, the revolutionary leaders at Santa Fé, and a political association was instituted at Quito. After the failure of the first revolution in Quito, which took place in 1809, many other efforts were made to throw off Spanish rule, but without result, until, on the 9th October, 1820, Guayaquil definitely obtained its liberty, after various defeats. The following year the Venezuelan general, Antonio José de Sucre, sent by Bolivar and assisted by a contingent from Peru, under Andrés de Santa Cruz, began his campaign against the royal troops in the Sierra, or mountain districts, and on May 22, 1822, obtained a decisive victory. This was at the famous battle of Pichincha, so called from the field of battle, which lay upon the slopes of the snowy volcano of that name, overlooking the city of Quito.

Two days after the battle a capitulation was signed by Aimerich, the last President of Spanish government in Quito, and with this the independence of

APPROACH TO QUITO.

the whole of the ancient kingdom of Quito was sealed, 288 years after the time when the vast dominion had been conquered for Spain by Benalcazar. The presidency of Quito accepted the Constitution of Colombia, and was incorporated into that great republic. The famous liberator, Simon Bolivar, arrived in the same year at Quito, and descended to Guayaquil ; and his whole influence was necessary to cause that department to adhere to the republic of Colombia rather than to that of Peru, which latter proceeding many of the inhabitants desired. A political union was effected with New Granada and Venezuela, having as its basis the republican Constitution instituted at Cucuta in July, 1821. The triple federation took the name of Colombia, and thus the flag of that nation flew over the vast territory from the mouth of the Orinoco, on the Atlantic, southwards to the mouth of the Tumbez River (between Ecuador and Peru to-day), on the Pacific, including almost the same area as that controlled under the old vice-regency of Santa Fé.

But the great republic of Colombia was not destined to endure long. It lasted only eight years, without in that period having been able to attain either political solidarity or civic tranquillity. The inevitable fate befell it which has followed all the Latin American republics : that, once the struggle for independence was over, civil war and fratricidal strife began among liberators and liberated. A disagreement with Peru in 1828 resulted in the invasion by a Peruvian army of Ecuador, and the occupation of Cuenca and Guayaquil ; and although peace was restored in the following year, after a victory by the Ecuadorians at Tarqui, it was an earnest of the jealousies to be aroused among these neighbours of the Andes. Separation from the Colombian federation took place in 1830. By an Act signed in Caracas on November 24, 1829, Venezuela had declared itself as a separate republic, and set up a Congress on 6th May, 1830. Almost at the same time, by the Act of May 13, 1830—the year of Bolivar's death—it was resolved in Quito to separate Ecuador from the federation, and to this Act Guayaquil, Cuenca, and other towns adhered. A Congress was convened on August 14, 1830, in the city of Riobamba, and José Flores, a Venezuelan by birth, was elected as its first President. Flores, although he had to contend against many home and foreign difficulties, maintained a strong position for fifteen years.

The towns of Pasto, Buenaventura, and Popayan, which had always depended from the presidency of Quito, under Spain, incorporated themselves voluntarily, at that period, with the State of Ecuador, and all the provinces of Cauca were represented by their *diputados*, or members, in the first constitutional Congress of the republic in 1831. But Colombia did not look with favour on this incorporation, and claimed all the provinces of the old *Gobierno* of Popayan, without—according to Ecuadorian historians—taking into consideration the wishes of the people of those districts, nor the reasoned protest of the Quito Government. A war between the two countries followed, but Ecuador was to lose. Ecuadorian historians record that the result, fatal to their demands, was brought about by the treasonable actions of General Lopez at Popayan and of Colonel Saenz at Pasto. As a consequence of this defeat a treaty of peace was entered into between Ecuador and Colombia, and signed in Pasto on the 8th of December, 1831. Under this treaty the boundary between the two republics was fixed on the River Carchi, a tributary of the Upper Mira, flowing into the Pacific, in accordance with Article 22 of the Colombian law of June 25, 1824. This definite boundary has been preserved up to the present time.

General Flores was succeeded in 1835 by Vicente Rocafuerte ; but four years afterwards he again became President. In 1843, for a third term, his election was brought about, but shortly afterwards Rocafuerte accepted the title of *generalissimo*, together with a sum of money amounting to 20,000 *pesos*, and consented to leave the country. and its government to his rival politicians. During Rocafuerte's second term of office an important measure was brought about—that of the establishment of peace with Spain. Rocafuerte was followed by Ramon Roca, who was elected President in 1845, holding the post until 1849. A temporary settlement in the question pending with Colombia was effected during his term, and a convention with England against the slave trade was concluded, together with a commercial treaty with Belgium. But a rupture with New Granada took place under his successor, Diego Noboa, the President of only a few months' term. Noboa had been elected after a period of great political confusion. The cause of the trouble with New Granada, or Colombia, was the receiving as refugees by Noboa of Conservative politicians who had been forced to flee that country, and the fall and exile of Noboa followed. From 1852 to 1856 J. M. Urvina was President, a democrat at first and a Dictator afterwards. An attempt to reinstate Noboa under Flores failed, and Francisco Robles in 1856 became President. It was at this period that the French decimal and metric systems of coinage and measures were adopted, and various progressive measures lie to the credit of those years. Robles abdicated in 1859 and left the country. He had refused to ratify the treaty with Peru, under which the siege of Guayaquil had been raised.

Dr. Garcia-Moreno, who was elected to the presidency in 1861, was a man in some respects of progressive ideas and measures. He was a professor of chemistry, a poet, and a journalist, and perhaps the most noteworthy spirit of his times in Ecuador. He became the recognized leader of the Conservative Party, and was elected by the National Convention in Quito. Among Moreno's conceptions was the railway from Guayaquil to the capital ; and he endeavoured to develop the material resources of the country, as opposed to the mere political ambitions of most of his predecessors. It was a steadfast doctrine of his that progress could not be attained whilst widespread poverty existed. During Moreno's term the President and forces of Colombia —the latter under Mosquera—attempted to encroach upon Ecuadorian territory, and Moreno sent an army against the Colombians. This was completely defeated, and Moreno resigned, his resignation, however, not being accepted. But the publication of some of the President's private letters, in which it was shown that he had spoken favourably of a French protectorate over Ecuador, excited distrust of his policy. This view of Moreno's was doubtless induced by the state of political anarchy of his country. Further, certain despotic acts and his purpose of introducing a dictatorship embittered his political rivals. He was also accused of a too fervent papistry and retrograde methods as regarded religion and education, and in 1865 Moreno retired from office. The character of Moreno is worthy of closer study than can be given to it here.[1]

During the years 1865-7 Geronimo Carrion held the presidency. This term of office was marked by an alliance by Ecuador with Chile and Peru against Spain. An expedition had been sent by Spain to the Pacific coast of South America, under Admiral

[1] Such may be found in *Latin America : its Rise and Progress*, by F. Garcia Calderon. London : Unwin, 1913.

Pinzon, with two frigates, ostensibly to carry out scientific work. But by the acts which were committed it became evident that Spain was seeking to recover her lost foothold in those regions. The then President of Peru, Pezet, temporized with Spain, but Bolivia and Chile set aside the quarrel upon which they had entered over the matter of Atacama and combined, and the Chileans captured a Spanish gunboat. Peru also entered into an alliance with Chile to confront the Spaniards, but Callao and Valparaiso were bombarded, with heavy losses on both sides. The Spanish navy withdrew and returned to Spain, and, due to the friendly interposition of the United States, the way was found for a treaty of peace. Spanish subjects had been banished from Ecuador and Peru as a result of Spain's action.

Following on Carrion's resignation some important changes were made by the Congress of Ecuador. The power of the President to imprison persons whose political opinions might seem adverse to public order was regarded as full of danger, and this was annulled. A further measure authorized was the naturalization of Bolivians, Chileans, Peruvians, and Colombians in Ecuador. In 1868 Javier Espinosa was elected President, but he had scarcely assumed office when, in August of that year, a terrific earthquake devastated the country, in which estimates of a loss of 30,000 lives were made. The shock laid in ruins the public buildings of Quito, and several other large upland towns were completely destroyed. This perturbation of Nature was followed by one in human politics, and a revolution which broke out in Quito in the following year brought the presidency of Espinosa to its end.

The National Convention appointed Carvajal to the presidential chair, but, in defiance of this measure, the former President, Garcia Moreno, secured his own election, and became President in 1869. But

6

Moreno had not changed the policy which had antagonized him to many of his countrymen. He showed the same persistent intention to establish a religious despotism, in which the clergy should be supreme and the President only second thereto. A terrible political murder followed upon these matters, such as so frequently has stained the modern history of Spanish America, and President Moreno was assassinated in August, 1875, at Quito.

The successor to Moreno, Dr. Antonio Borrero, had but a short term of office, for in 1876 a revolution, headed by General Ignacio Veintemilla, broke out in Guayaquil. The Government forces which were sent against him, under General Aparicio, were defeated at Galto in December. Veintemilla was declared President, and was so elected by Congress in the following year. Veintemilla was a Radical, and it was in accordance with the desire for a more liberal policy that the revolutionists had embarked upon their campaign. The old forces of clericalism and conservatism had become oppressive. The revolutionary President caused the Constitution to be altered to a more liberal character, and aimed blows at the Clerical Party, abolishing, among other matters, the concordat with Rome. But Veintemilla over-reached himself, and entered upon that fatal dictatorship which has so often led to the overthrow of its authors in Latin America. In 1878 he caused himself to be declared the elected President for a further term of four years, and at the end of the period, instead of making way, as required by the law, for a successor, he assumed dictatorial powers and retained his office as Chief of the Executive. Exasperated by this action, the Clerical Party and the Moderate Liberals joined forces, and brought about a popular uprising throughout the republic against Veintemilla. Driven from Quito, his rule was restricted to the littoral provinces of Guayaquil and Esmeraldas ; but he failed to retain even these, and his antagonists, under General Rinaldo Flores, drove him from Guayaquil and forced him to flee to Peru in June, 1883.

It was at this period that Peru was emerging from her terrible struggle with Chile, during which she lost her valuable nitrate provinces. The Chileans had defeated Peru by land and sea, not, however, without heroic resistance on the part of the Peruvian army and the people of Lima. The famous sea fight of the *Huascar*, the deaths of those sea-heroes Grau and Prat, of the Peruvian and Chilean navies respectively, the fateful struggle on the Morro of Arica and the death of the heroic Bolognesi, as also the bloody struggles among the burning deserts of Tarapacá and the siege and fall of Lima, were incidents of this great war, whose issue in the main was the possession of the nitrate provinces. The Treaty of Ancon was signed in 1883, but the rankling question of Tacna and Arica remains still unsettled. These matters, however, belong to the history of Peru, and Ecuador took no part therein, except as a spectator.

The next President of Ecuador was Dr. Placedo Caamaño, who, at first called upon to take temporary direction of affairs, was, in 1883, formally elected President for the period terminating in 1888. The term of Caamaño's presidency was marked by several revolutionary outbreaks ; but these were suppressed, and in 1888 Dr. Antonio Flores followed, with a term of four years' rule, free from political disturbance. This condition, however, did not endure, for upon the election of his successor, Dr. Luis Cordero, in 1892, the country was once more plunged into political strife and bloodshed.

The cause of these troubles was somewhat peculiar, in having been due to foreign affairs rather than to domestic matters. It was the period of the war between China and Japan, and in 1894 the Govern-

ment of Chile, having arranged for the sale of the
cruiser *Esmeralda* to Japan, and desirous of avoiding international complications, caused the transfer
of the vessel to Japan through Ecuador. The
method proposed for the transference was that in
the Ecuadorian waters of the Galapagos Islands,
600 miles off the mainland, the flag of Ecuador
should be replaced by the flag of Japan, and the
vessel delivered to the representative of that country,
who had come over to receive it. This arrangement was, in fact, carried out, and the *Esmeralda*
was transferred to the Japanese colours in the lonely
waters of the Galapagos. But the transaction did
not meet with popular approval in Ecuador, and
when the part taken therein by President Cordero
became known popular indignation was aroused
and caused, or was made the excuse to cause, a
revolution, which was headed by General Eloy Alfaro.
A year's desultory fighting between the rival forces
disturbed the troubled republic, and as a result of
the final battle the Government forces were overcome, and President Cordero abandoned his office
and escaped from the country.

Alfaro was a born Radical and anti-clerical, and
had entered the political arena at an early age.
Exiled and penniless at one time, he had to endure
considerable privations. His career was typical of
that of the peculiar class of Latin American adminis-
trator, whose meteoric or bloodstained periods of
power succeed each other with such frequency in
Central and South America. Alfaro appears to have
been animated by a hatred of the somewhat corrupt
and retrograde priestcraft which controlled the
country. Upon his victory he assumed dictatorial
powers as supreme head of the republic, and continued in that administrative capacity until, in
February, 1897, it was declared that he was elected
President. But the election was by no means

BUILDING THE GUAYAQUIL—QUITO RAILWAY.

[To face p. 85.

accepted unquestioned by the country, and a series of revolutions against Alfaro's administration plunged the unhappy community into strife and bloodshed for several years. These risings were due in large part to the intrigues of the clericals, whose powers had been greatly curtailed by Alfaro, the influence of the clergy being thwarted whenever possible, an influence, unfortunately, too often exercised in evil practices. During this period the contract for the completion of the Guayaquil-Quito railway was signed, a progressive step of great value to the country. In August, 1901, General Alfaro handed over his office to General Leonidas Plaza, who had been " elected " to succeed him and who was the President's chosen candidate.

The anti-clerical policy inaugurated by Alfaro was continued by President Plaza. The law permitting civil marriage, also divorce, was a victory for the progressive element ; and what amounted in a priest-ridden country to a social revolution was effected in 1904, when the Church was put under State control, the establishment of new religious orders prohibited, and all religions were placed in a position of legal equality. Towards the close of Plaza's term of office even stronger anti-clerical measures were brought about. The great possessions of the Church were declared national or State property, and were let to the highest bidders. Thus did the inevitable reaction from the dogmas and oppression of papistry in this part of South America take place.

In 1905 the Opposition felt itself strong enough to endeavour to change this progressive policy, which had run into too marked extremes. The Church was not necessarily an evil institution throughout, nor was its influence inevitably retrograde. The Latin American people cannot rush into materialism without serious injury to their social state, and in any case the bulk of the people support their Church. The election to the presidency of a candidate, Lizardo Garcia, a wealthy merchant and director of the *Banco Comercial y Agricola* of Ecuador, was carried out. But the anti-clerical forces were too strong, and General Alfaro, with a *pronunciamiento* and appeal to arms, overthrew Garcia, ejected his colleagues from office, and again assumed the presidency with dictatorial powers. He was declared by the army Supreme Dictator.

In January, 1911, Emilio Estrada was elected President. Estrada had been Alfaro's candidate, but later Alfaro repented of his choice, and popular rumour had it that on Independence Day the army would proclaim him Dictator. But surprise and disappointment awaited Alfaro, when a popular outbreak took place, his own soldiers joining against his unconstitutional methods. The populace was invited to arm itself at the barracks ; suddenly the cry " *Viva la Constitucion!* " was heard, mingled with the noise of firearms, below the window of the room in which the astonished General-Dictator was dining. Alfaro and his sons were only saved from the fury of the mob by the intervention of the Chilean and Bolivian Ministers, and they took shelter in the Chilean Legation. There was little real fighting, although the streets were rendered unsafe by reason of the firing of their weapons by bands of drunken soldiery. The object of the disturbance in part was to establish another politician, Dr. Emilio Teran, as President. Teran had been sent earlier as Ecuador's representative to Great Britain. He was a person of some attainments and worthy of a better fate than that which befell him, for he was assassinated by a personal enemy, Colonel Quirola, who took the opportunity of political tumult to wreak private vengeance, a not infrequent occurrence in Latin America. Teran's adherents, however, terribly revenged his death, for, on the following day, the murderer was dragged from his cell and assassinated, his corpse then being mutilated after the barbarous fashion of such happenings in times of political struggle in Spanish America.

Alfaro's written abdication was demanded and complied with, and Emilio Estrada, the constitutionally elected President, took office at Quito. Alfaro was allowed to leave the country, after pledging himself to remain abroad for at least one year, although the popular desire was for his execution. Estrada was not a popular candidate with any party, but he was welcomed as a change from Alfaro's dictatorship. He died on December 22, 1911, at Guayaquil, and the country was once more plunged into revolution, accompanied by bloodthirsty excesses. Support was offered to the Government by General Leonidas Plaza, as well as by General Montero, the military commander at Guayaquil. But Plaza's offer was regarded in that city as a sign that the Government espoused his pretensions to the presidency, and under that pretext, Montero, in a *pronunciamiento* on December 27th, announced himself as Supreme Chief of the nation, and a revolution followed. It was stated that, previous to Estrada's death, there had been a conspiracy in Guayaquil, a result partly of a dispute between the Government and the Duran Wharf Company, in which Estrada was a shareholder. The wharf had been leased by the Government for a period of ten years to the company, to whom, at the expiration of the term, £600,000 was owing, and in default of payment possession was retained by the company with Estrada's support.

The incidents that followed upon this dispute and revolution may be narrated, both as bringing the history of the country up to the present time and as showing the unstable foundation upon which constitutional government in Ecuador appears to rest, and the sanguinary character such dissensions may assume.

The Government forces, after considerable fighting, entered Duran, the terminus of the Guayaquil-Quito railway, across the river from Guayaquil. By a ruse the revolutionary forces were enticed across the Guayas and were mowed down by rifle-fire and machine-guns, hundreds falling easy victims to General Plaza's strategy, the total of killed reaching 1,000, with many wounded and but a few casualties on the Government side. At this juncture Eloy Alfaro arrived and joined Montero, and the two leaders, with a body of troops, remained in possession of Guayaquil, protected by the river. Montero swore that if the Government troops should attempt to cross the town should be reduced to ashes. Under these circumstances the British and United States Consuls at Guayaquil offered their mediation, which was accepted by both sides, and an agreement was signed by Plaza for the Government and Montero and Alfaro for the revolutionists. Under this agreement the revolutionists were to capitulate with the honours of war and the guarantee of amnesty. But whilst the details of the capitulation were still under arrangement by the Consuls, a body of the Guayaquil inhabitants, opponents of the revolutionists, attacked the disarmed soldiers, who fled, Montero and Alfaro being made prisoners. This act, being in contravention of the agreement, was protested against by the Consuls, who sent strong representations to the Government at Quito, but without effect. A portion of the Government army returned to Quito, and were welcomed with showers of roses from the balconies and windows. Following upon a popular demand, Montero was tried by court-martial at Guayaquil, found guilty of high treason, and sentenced to dismissal from the army, with disgrace, and to sixteen years' imprisonment. This sentence was considered inadequate by the populace, enraged at the wanton revolution in their midst, and Montero was shot, either by his guards or by the crowd. The mob cut his throat after the shot was fired, "to make sure of his death." Alfaro and his brother and some of his companions were sent by train to Quito to await trial. An epidemic of yellow fever broke out at Guayaquil, and hundreds of soldiers were attacked, among the many dead being the captain of the United States gunboat which was stationed at Guayaquil. It was stated that 2,000 died of the fever. Alfaro and five other leaders of the revolution were lodged in jail at Quito, protected by a guard against the mob. But the final vengeance was to fall. A few minutes afterwards the mob forced the iron door of the jail without resistance being offered by the armed police, and proceeded to the prisoners' cells, notwithstanding that only the warders were supposed to know where these were situated.[1] There they murdered Alfaro and his companions in cold blood, with "hideous atrocities."

These acts were condemned by Plaza and some others of the Government leaders. But the situation was critical : there was not a dollar in the treasury, and the fall of the Government followed. The railway had been paralysed for weeks, and the mail of six steamers was lying in Guayaquil. The provisional Government, which had been established after the death of Estrada, controlled the affairs of the country until March, 1912, when General Plaza was elected President of the republic by a large majority and without further disturbance. Plaza took steps to re-establish the credit of the country by sending overdue remittances to the foreign bond-

[1] The *Times*, March 26, 1912.

holders in London. A period of tranquillity followed, with improved trade and other prospects for Ecuador, which have continued up to the close of the year 1913, although there were some minor revolutionary disturbances.

CHAPTER VII

BOUNDARIES AND AREA

THE republic of Ecuador, officially known as *La Republica del Ecuador*, occupies a triangular-shaped area of territory fronting upon the Pacific coast, and extending eastwardly across the Andes into the Amazon valley. On the north-east it is bounded by the republic of Colombia and on the south by the republic of Peru. Ecuador takes its modern name from the fact that it lies directly under the equator, which traverses the northern part of the country.

Ecuador is, in point of size, the smallest of the South American republics with the exception of Uruguay. Its area cannot be regarded as fully determined, for the boundary with its southern neighbour is still in dispute. The maps of the country are very defective. Those issued by Peru claim a large part of the territory which Ecuador regards as her own, whilst the Ecuadorian maps extend their limits into the region which Peru claims, and in which the latter country has established certain outposts and occupation. According to Wolf,[1] in his comprehensive work : " If Ecuador were in possession of all the territory claimed thereby, and which it believes it should enjoy, the total area of the republic would be approximately 714,860 square kilometres (or 275,936 square miles, of which 2,888 square miles represent the Galapagos Islands). But of this area Peru occupies the follow-

[1] *Op. cit.*

ing : (1) In Tumbez, the region between the River Tumbez and the River Zarumilla, 513 square miles ; (2) in Jaen, the region between the right bank of the Chinchipe River and the left bank of the Marañon, 3,242 square miles ; (3) in Mainas, all the region at the right side of the River Amazon, 41,380 square miles. Further, Peru has set up a claim to the Oriente region at the left side of the Amazon, between the River Chinchipe and the Brazilian frontier—that is, to the foot of the eastern Cordillera—calculated approximately as 149,190 square miles, a total of 194,325 square miles. Under such conditions Ecuador would be left with only 74,050 square miles of territory. As to the claims of Colombia, any calculation including the area claimed by that republic is impossible. The calculation made by Villavicencio, giving Ecuador 16,000 square leagues (and the Galapagos Islands 800 square leagues), which has been passed on to all the modern geographies and the school books of the country, is entirely wrong."

It will be necessary here to glance at these rival claims, which have formed a subject of bitter contention between the three republics interested. The areas of territory in dispute are, although remote from civilization, of considerable size, and are likely to be of much value in the future development of that at present backward region of the upper Amazon and its affluents.

Some of this disputed territory intervenes between Ecuador and Brazil, and the Ecuadorian maps show Ecuador extending to the Brazilian frontier. The Peruvian maps in some cases show Peru covering almost all the territory of the Amazon watershed in Ecuador, with a north and south line running but a short distance to the east of Quito and Riobamba, which on the map appears a fantastic claim. The commonest map is that which gives Ecuador a boundary with Colombia upon the River Napo, and it is of extreme importance to Ecuador to have access to this large, navigable river, giving communication with the main Amazon system, the Marañon. If this territory were disallowed to Ecuador, the republic would be confined to a comparatively small area, covering only the Andean strip and the Pacific littoral. The possession of the Napo, whilst of vital importance to Ecuador, is not of such importance to Peru, which possesses several large affluents navigable to the Amazon, especially those which flow from the south into the Marañon. Peru possesses, in fact, what is almost equivalent to an Atlantic seaboard, for ocean steamers traverse the Peruvian Amazon, or Marañon, for several hundred miles, giving outlet through Brazil to the Atlantic Ocean. Iquitos, the eastern capital of Peru, lying 2,500 miles from the mouth of the Amazon, is, in fact, in direct communication by steamer with the Atlantic and so to Liverpool or New York without transhipment.

The line taken as the provisional south-eastern boundary of Ecuador runs from Huiririma-Chico on the Napo River, about latitude 2° 50′ south and longitude 73° 20′ west, running west-south-west to the Santiago River.[1]

The portion of the Ecuador-Peru boundary which crosses the Andes leaves the Santiago River (a stream which enters the Marañon near the head of navigation of that stream, at the *Pongo de Manseriche*, or Manseriche rapids) at a point north of the confluence, in latitude approximately 14° 12′ south and longitude 78° west. Thence it runs west across the Andes to the head waters of the Macara River, on the Pacific watershed, follows that to the Chira, or Achira, of which it is a tributary, to a point where a small stream, the Alamo, enters from the north, at about 80° 17′ west longitude. Thence it turns nearly

[1] This provisional boundary is that shown on the map of Ecuador in the *Encyclopædia Britannica*.

at right angles and runs slightly west of north to the southern shore of the Gulf of Guayaquil upon the Pacific. A small area in the Chira valley is claimed by Peru.[1]

The north-eastern boundary of Ecuador would, if the desire of that republic were fulfilled, extend to the Putumayo River—that territory rendered infamous of late by reason of the ill-treatment of the native Indians, and which is claimed by Colombia, Peru, and Ecuador. The Putumayo flows parallel, roughly, with the Napo at a distance of sixty to eighty miles north of that stream, and empties into the Amazon in Brazil. From Huiririma-Chico, on the Napo River, the Ecuador-Colombia line, provisionally, runs up the Napo to the north-west, along the Coca and San Francisco Rivers, tributaries of the Napo, to the Andean water-parting. This water-parting from near where the Equator cuts it forms the dividing line northwards for about eighty miles, whence the boundary turns to the west and cuts the Pacific coast at the head of Panguapi Bay, latitude about 1° 34′ north. The Mira River flows into this bay, and a small section of the territory is disputed by Colombia, Ecuador claiming the main channel of the Mira as the boundary, and Colombia a small district south of that channel, bounded by a line running due west from the mouth of the southernmost of the various outlets of the Mira to a point of intersection with that river.

The boundary disputes between Ecuador and Peru and Peru and Colombia have on more than one occasion almost brought the various republics into war. Soldiers or settlers of one or the other disputants in remote outposts of those little travelled solitudes of contention have from time to time trespassed or committed some outrage or sought to establish authority. From such incidents to a patriotic

[1] *Encyc. Brit.*

commotion in Quito, Bogatá, or Lima was a rapid step. Nothing is more easily inflamed than the Latin American spirit, whenever the " sovereign rights " of its claimed territory are alleged to be " outraged." In reality there is little fundamental difference between the people of these republics, whether in appearance, speech, accent, or any other characteristics. Peruvians, Ecuadorians, or Colombians, to the foreigner, are much alike, yet nowhere is the boundary line of a *patria* more sharply and artificially set up. The disputed territories in some cases are almost uninhabited except by scattered tribes of Indians, and are partly composed of almost impenetrable forests and malarious swamps, separated by hundreds of miles from any civilized centre. Under such conditions the bitterness of contention and difficulty of settlement seem a matter for surprise, viewed dispassionately.

The boundary troubles began in the first instance when the rule of Spain and Portugal over South America was thrown off. The limits were not always well defined, and the resulting boundaries of the independent nations which grew to being suffered accordingly. Nevertheless, the old Spanish limits are those to which the boundaries are generally referred, and evidence, often slender enough, is advanced by one or the other party, based on ancient decrees or documents which emanated from the Crown of Spain, and in some cases on papal decrees made during the colonial period.

The question of boundary between Ecuador and Peru was made the subject of a treaty by the two countries towards the end of last century, in which it was agreed to submit the matter to the arbitration of the King of Spain. Extensive preparation of documents, limits, and claims was made by both parties. But the King's decision was very greatly delayed, and a number of years passed with growing friction between the two arbitrating nations, and when at length it was announced that the, royal arbiter was about to render his decision, information leaked out that this was very favourable to one of the parties and adverse to the other, and in 1908 outrages on Ecuadorian officials in Peru occurred, followed by an attack on the Peruvian Legation and Consulate in Ecuador. Popular feeling was greatly excited, and the armies of both republics were rapidly mobilized. In view of the danger of war, the Governments of Brazil and Argentina, as well as the United States, offered to mediate in the matter, but this was accepted by Peru and declined by Ecuador, as was also a proposal for a Hague tribunal arbitration. Actual fighting, however, was happily averted. The intervening Powers were informed by the Government of Ecuador that the rumoured terms of the King's decision would not be acceptable ; that in their view the matter had not been impartially demonstrated, and they proposed that the jurisdiction of the arbitrator should remain in abeyance, and that direct negotiations should be entered into between the two disputants. Peru, however, professing feelings of delicacy as to thus putting on one side the royal services, even though (according to Peruvian authorities) " they knew it would be adverse to their legitimate hopes," refused to accede to that course. As a result of these dissensions and proceedings the King of Spain renounced the office of arbitrator, and the status of the dispute obtaining before the 1887 treaty was reverted to. For a period following this Ecuador was plunged into fierce political trouble and revolution, and questions of boundaries became secondary. Peru maintained possession of nearly the whole of the disputed territory, and strove to develop various undertakings for increasing Peruvian claims and standing.

The boundary contentions between Peru and

Colombia affect Ecuador to some extent, and somewhat similar conditions obtain as regards the fluvial system involved. The Peruvian claim, which would cut off from Ecuador its Oriental or trans-Andine provinces and the enjoyment by that republic of access to the River Napo, with its facilities of navigation to the Amazon, extends northward back of Ecuador beyond the River Putumayo to the River Caquetá or Yapura. These rivers, the Napo, Putumayo, and Caquetá, are the large tributaries which, as described later, form part of that series of roughly parallel waterways which descend from the Ecuadorian and Colombian Andes, flowing south-east into the Marañon and Amazon. Just as the Napo is of value to Ecuador as an Amazon-Atlantic outlet, so is the Putumayo of value to Colombia. The Caquetá alone is insufficient for Colombia as a navigable stream, for, although its tributaries and upper reaches are valuable as waterways for internal navigation, steamers cannot reach the Amazon therefrom by reason of the great Araracuara falls and rapids. As regards economic necessities it would seem essential for Colombia to retain her rights on the Putumayo, which stream affords means of steam navigation up to the foot of the Andes near the seventy-sixth meridian, or only about 200 miles from the Pacific coast, the Andes intervening. Peru claims the region traversed by this important river. The Putumayo has, as elsewhere described, become almost a byword of infamy, due to the unspeakable atrocities practised upon the Indians of the region by the Peruvian and other rubber-gatherers, yet it is noteworthy that Peru seemed to evince comparatively little repugnance for the acts committed, and easily shouldered the responsibility, and doubtless the reason of their attitude was the implied recognition of their ownership of the territory involved in the charges against their governance of it. " The Peruvians are

7

diplomatists by tradition, and they would consider these annoyances but a small price to pay for their implied recognition of rights which, as a matter of fact, are doubtful, and have long been the subject of bitter disputes." [1]

Certain of the maps of Ecuador depict that country as extending to the Marañon, with the southern frontier formed by that river, instead of the provisional line as defined by actual occupation, that from the Napo to the Santiago, as described before. The map known as the great map of Fray Enrique Vacas Galindo, of the Order of Friars Preachers, depicts Ecuador as extending to the Marañon. Similarly with the map of the Pan-American Union, Washington, 1894. This map, however, includes Iquitos as in Ecuador, a manifestly impossible condition. Into the Marañon, across this region, flow the Rivers Morona, Pastasa, Tigre, and others, having facilities of steam navigation, as described in treating of the river system. The ownership of this territory by Ecuador bases its claim upon what is known as the Pedemonte-Mosquera Protocol of 1830. The Peruvian authorities, on the other hand, assert that neither of these frontier lines is correct, and characterize as untenable any Ecuadorian pretensions 'to extend to the Marañon. They state that Peru has occupied the territory on the Santiago and Morona Rivers since the beginning of the nineteenth century. As regards the Pedemonte-Mosquera Protocol of 1830, it is asserted by Peru that " the document is apocryphal, and that any statement based upon it is invalid ; and that the Peruvian Government maintained before the Arbitration Court of Madrid that the said Protocol never had any existence, and that on the date when Ecuador claims that it was signed in Lima by the Peruvian Minister for Foreign Affairs, Señor Pedemonte, and the Colombian Minister, Señor

[1] The *Times*, South American Supplement, April, 1913.

Mosquera, the latter was several days' sail on his way to Guayaquil." [1] Further, it is maintained by Peruvian authorities that Peru has been in effectual possession, *de jure* and *de facto*, of all this territory, since 1803, the year in which the administrative dispositions made by the King of Spain in the Royal Cedula of July 15, 1802, came into force, constituting the governorship and commandancy-general of Maynas with all the territories watered by the northern and southern tributaries of the Marañon and Amazon " to where by their falls and rapids they cease to be navigable " and annexing to the Viceroyalty of Lima the new political and administrative area, in which were comprised all the countries watered by the Santiago and Morona, northern affluents of the Marañon. [2] To these Peruvian statements impartial annotators have replied that the territory was regarded as still in dispute between Peru and Ecuador, and that the accuracy of such a claim is not affected by proving that one of the disputants is *de facto* and *de jure* in a stronger position than the other. [3]

As remarked in the historical section of this book, Nueva Granada, which included the presidency of Quito, became a Viceroyalty in 1739. The Colombian Government lays claim to all the territory of that Viceroyalty for Colombia and Ecuador in conformity with the *uti possidetis* [4] of 1810, under whose principle the boundaries of many South American republics were settled. When the Quito Government was formed, in the middle of the sixteenth century, it embraced Macas, lying between the Santiago and Morona Rivers, Canelas, between

[1] Peruvian Chargé d'Affaires in London ; letter to the *Times*, June, 1913.
[2] *Ibid.*
[3] Editorial note of the *Times* to the above letter, June, 1913
[4] *Uti possidetis*, " As you hold in possession."

the Morona and Pastaza, Quijos, between the Pastaza
and Napo, and the *Misiones* of Mocena and Sucumbios, between the Napo, Putumayo, and Caquetá,
which missions were dependent upon Pasto, the head-
quarters of the Jesuits and Franciscans.   Under the
name of Maynas the region was formed into a
province early in the seventeenth century.   The *real
cedula*, or royal decree, upon which Peru bases her
claim to the Putumayo, Napo, Pastaza, and other
rivers north of the Marañon, was issued in 1802, but
Colombia denies its validity.   This decree came about
as a consequence of the expulsion in 1767 of the
Jesuits, who had established a number of villages
on the rivers, dating in some cases from 1616, and
when they left the Indians relapsed into savagery
again.   The decree ordained the formation of a
diocese of Maynas, which included the region on
both sides of the Marañon, extending up the great
streams both from the north and from the south
" as far as they were navigable."   The administrative and military command of this region was to
depend from the Viceroy of Peru, and its bishop
was to be a suffragan of the Lima Archbishopric.
The Colombians deny the validity of this *cedula*
because it was never carried out, and so, in their view,
could not affect the *uti possidetis* of 1810, and they
show that Maynas and Quitos were in 1888 included
in Nueva Granada, and they base their claim to
ownership of the Putumayo on *cedulas* of 1717 and
1739, which define the limits of New Granada.
    The limit of the old kingdom of Quito to the
south, which Ecuador, pending other arrangements,
regards as belonging to the republic, cuts the
Marañon five leagues to the south of the mouth of
the Chamaya, or Huancabamba River, and then cuts
the Utcubamba, Chuchunza, Huallaga, and Ucayali
Rivers, and terminates with the course of the Yavari
in the mouth of that river, including, with the course

of the Amazon, a region of 107,200 square kilometres.[1] The western portion of this vast territory belonged to the old *Gobierno de Jaen*, and the eastern to that of Maynas, and at the present time it is occupied by Peruvians, who, from Chachapoyas and Moyobamba have advanced little by little to the edge of the Marañon, among the savage tribes that disputed their steps. It is to be noted, however, that all modern knowledge of that remote region, not only on the southern but on the northern bank of the Marañon and along the chief tributaries, is due to Peruvian explorers or to foreigners under Peruvian protection. Ecuador has done very little in this respect.

To the impartial observer it would seem that the boundaries of these countries—boundaries which have been so debatable and dependent upon somewhat obscure decrees—might be laid down now with some idea of proportion and stability. To give one nation a strip of land stretching arbitrarily behind or around another nation, or cutting such off from access to navigable rivers and coasts,[2] is irrational and unwise, and only lays the foundation for disturbance in the future. That one modern division of this formerly united Spanish territory should enjoy vast areas of territory entirely disproportionate to its population, whilst an adjoining one, of not greatly less population, is limited to a narrow zone is unnatural. Natural boundaries are best : a spirit of sane compromise would permanently establish good feeling between such nations, especially those which are in reality of the same blood and whose people are almost indistinguishable one from the other.

A natural boundary for Ecuador and Peru would seem to have been the Marañon River, the impartial geographer might, without offence, venture to think. It runs east and west, is navigable, and receives

[1] Wolf, *op. cit.*   [2] As in Bolivia and Chile.

from both countries great navigable affluents, in opposite directions—affluents in Ecuador coming from the north and in Peru from the south. It would be difficult to find a more natural line of demarcation, if it were possible to agree upon it. South of this line Peru enjoys enormous areas of rich and undeveloped territory, far greater than that of Ecuador. The important fluvial port of Iquitos, on the north bank of the Marañon, is of course indisputably Peruvian under any conditions. On the northern side of Ecuador is Colombia. The natural boundary between these two countries might seem to be the Putumayo River, at least for a portion of its course. This is the great navigable stream running into the Marañon or Amazon, and both republics should enjoy its advantages impartially. For Peru to control an almost isolated strip of territory on the Putumayo River, between Ecuador and Colombia, such as is claimed, seems to be striving to map out the land unnaturally and to sow upon it the seeds of future discord. Colombia possesses magnificent outlets to the sea, with a frontage on both the Pacific and Atlantic (Caribbean) Oceans ; she also possesses part of the great navigable Orinoco River. As regards Brazil, this republic possesses the greatest area of land on the continent, and to take possession of that angle of land which includes the mouth of the Putumayo and to own a further great angle of territory projecting into Peru (from 70° to 74° longitude W.) appears unnatural. A spirit of reasonable compromise ought to be capable of settling these South American boundary disputes. None of the countries involved can yet efficiently police or develop the vast territories they control, nor will they be able to do so until improved economic and political conditions prevail in South America.

CHAPTER VIII

THE COASTAL REGION

As already remarked, the territory of the republic of Ecuador is characterized by three great natural divisions : the coastal region, the upland region, and the eastern or Amazon region. It is necessary to consider each of these zones separately, and in detail, and in this chapter attention will be devoted to the littoral.

The coast region of this particular part of South America is of peculiar interest by reason largely of the changes consequent upon climatic phenomena. Its description may well begin with the southern extremity of the republic, upon the shores of the great Guayaquil Gulf, upon which lies its boundary with the neighbouring republic of Peru.

The form of this gulf, the largest opening in the whole of the South American coast, is triangular, the southernmost point being Cape Blanco, in Peru, below the fourth parallel of south latitude. Between this point and the sharp *Puntilla* of Santa Elena, above the second parallel, it is about 140 miles wide, with the Island of Puná as its inner delimitation. The boundary-line of Ecuador begins slightly to the north of the *ensenada,* or bay of Tumbez, the mouth of the Tumbez River, and encloses a group of islands, low-lying and covered with *manglares,* or mangrove swamp. The gulf penetrates inland to the east with a curve to the north at its upper portion for 100 miles, terminating in the Guayas River, or rather estuary, upon which lies the seaport of Guayaquil, more fully described elsewhere. The upper extremity of the gulf and its northern shores are broken by numerous small estuaries which penetrate inland for some distance, the mouths of streams descending from the highlands. These shores are generally fringed with mangrove swamps. The south-east part of the gulf, known as the Jambeli Channel, between the great Puná Island and the mainland, forms the entrance for vessels to the port of Guayaquil, and between Punta Salinas and Punta Jambeli is eighteen miles (nautical) wide, narrowing to six miles. The channel is somewhat dangerous to navigation by reason of shifting sandbanks, and steamers entering and leaving take on a pilot at or as far as Punta Arenas. The Morro Channel, the entrance north of Puná Island, is described later on. The Guayas River presents itself as a continuation of the gulf towards the north, and from the southern point of the island at Mondragon, where the gulf really ends, to the city of Guayaquil is a distance of thirty miles.

The sandy plain upon which Guayaquil is situated forms a neck of land dividing the Guayas River from the Estero Salado, a large estuary which in no very remote geological epoch formed the delta of the river, but which was filled up by the sands brought down by the current, which have now entirely separated the two waterways. The Guayas River descends from far beyond Guayaquil, as described in its place.

The island of Puná is of some interest. Its greatest length, from Punta Madinga to Punta Salinas, is thirty miles (nautical), and its width fourteen miles, with a total area of about 919 square kilometres. Its surface is undulating and of small elevation, the coast completely flat, with exclusive *salitrales* and *manglares*, or salt plains and mangrove swamps. A labyrinth of *esteros* divides the

GUAYAQUIL HARBOUR: RAFTS BRINGING FROM THE INTERIOR BANANAS FOR EXPORT TO PERU AND CHILE

[To face p. 164.

island almost into two parts. The general hydrographic and climatic conditions of the island are unfavourable for agriculture, and the principal industries carried on are cattle-breeding and the extraction of the excellent timber which is encountered therein. The densely wooded character of Puná is a striking contrast with the arid Peruvian shore to the south, the green of the exuberant foliage adding to the picturesque effect of the tropic coastal landscape. The small bluffs of the eastern shore rise above the general level, and the low mountainous ridge of the Zampo Polo runs through the island. There is only one *pueblo*, or village, on Puná, bearing the same name as the island, with a small population of about 200. This is a small shipping port and quarantine station for Guayaquil. The prevalence of yellow fever at Guayaquil has rendered necessary the establishing of an observation and quarantine station at Puná, and thither those of passengers or crew who might be within the period of infection are taken for the necessary number of days. The island is historically interesting, from the adventures of Pizarro and his companions thereon, as previously described.

Off the southern point of Puná, and about midway in the gulf of Guayaquil, a sterile, solitary island lies, known as Amortajada, or the Island of the Dead, also called Santa Clara. The name comes from the singular topographical form of this islet, which bears resemblance to a shrouded corpse lying upon the surface of the sea. This narrow crest of sandstone rock, two kilometres long, is crowned by a lighthouse.

Near the southern coast of the gulf the four principal islands are Payana, Tembleque, Pongal, and Jambeli. Off these islands to the west lies an area of dangerous shallows, known as the *Bajos de Payana*, uncovered at low water. These shallows, however, possess rich oyster beds, from which the Guayaquil market is provided, and certain Peruvian villages. To the north of the island lies a labyrinth of islets and *esteros*, to which the native fishermen are the only guide.

As a result of the great opening in the South American coast made by the gulf of Guayaquil, the sea approaches in this part of Ecuador much nearer to the Cordillera of the Andes, with a narrow littoral. Only from Tumbez southwards, and from the Island of Puná northwards, where the coast bends sharply to the west, do the littoral plains develop. The Tumbez River, in its upper part, belongs to the inter-Andine *hoya* or basin of Zaruma, elsewhere described, the rich gold-mining district of Ecuador. Leaving the mountains, the river enters upon the plain, and crosses the Ecuador-Peru boundary line. In its lower portion, or from about fifteen miles from Tumbez, the river is navigable for canoes. The land is gently undulating, and, in the rainy season, covered with vegetation and flowers ; but this character of landscape shortly gives place to the desert aspect, part of the melancholy wilderness of Tumbez, which occupies the northern part of Peru. The Peruvian town lies nine miles from the mouth of the river.

North-east of the Tumbez, along the coast, is the small Zarumilla River. This forms the boundary in part between the two republics (Wolf and others). The coast then bears away to the east, to the mouth of the small Arenillas river, which crosses lands still of a desert character. It is only near Santa Rosa, a few miles beyond, where the mountains approach the shores of the gulf, that the humid climate begins to develop itself, characteristic of the littoral zone of Ecuador.

The Santa Rosa River has several branches, one of which is crossed by the road from the port of Santa Rosa to Zaruma leading to the mines and to Loja. The river or *estero*, as its lower portion may be

termed, is navigable for canoes and *chatas* or sail-
less boats. The Jubones is a more considerable
stream. Its mouth lies north of the Santa Rosa
outlet, the coast of the gulf, or rather the Jambeli
channel as it has here become, curving sharply. The
Jubones River rises in the high *hoya* or inter-Andine
basin of the same name, between the two great Cordilleras of the Andes. The river breaks through the
western Cordillera. Upon its banks in this upper
portion exist extensive ruins of the Inca period, and
it is believed that these once formed the famous town
of Tomebamba, where Huayna Capac was born. On
one of the high tributaries of the river, upon the
conical hills near Pucará, are other old fortifications
of the Incas or Cañaris, at about 10,500 feet elevation
above sea-level. Still lower down, upon a small promontory overlooking the Jubones, is yet another
ancient fortress, that of Pitaviña, which was probably
the farthest outpost of the Cañaris towards the coast,
and this and the Pucará were doubtless defences against
the coast tribes defending the valley of Yunguilla.
A league below the Pitaviña ruins begin the plains of
Pasaje and Machala. The Jubones River, where it
crosses the littoral, appears to have changed its course
at one or more periods, and the Payana coast in this
district has a scarcity of water. The *pueblo* of
Machala, lying near the sea, does not enjoy a very
advantageous position on the border of the *salitrales*
and *manglares*, and lacks water. Its cultivated cocoa-
producing region is some distance away. From
Puerto Bolivar a short railway extends inland.

From Rompido to Naranjal, a distance of some
thirty-three miles, the coast is of a uniform character.
The Cordillera, which approaches nearest to the sea
here and so is seen from the gulf or from Puná,
presents a striking view with an elevation of 13,200 ft.

The littoral between Machala and Naranjal constitutes one of the most important cocoa-producing

districts of Ecuador. The region is uniform, and its
character may easily be observed from one of the
rivers that traverse it. Several rivers fertilize the
district. The first, north of the Jubones, is the Pagua,
which in its middle course receives as its tributary the
Machalera, also the Chaguana. All the lands adjacent to these three rivers belong to the great
hacienda of Pagua. Then follows the small Sielte,
rising near the conical Tenguelillo hill, and the Tenguel, which rises in the crest of the Cordillera in the
Nariviña lake, descending from that high elevation to
the plains, with a tortuous course reaching the sea.
Another stream of the district is the Gala, and all the
land between this and the Sielte, traversed by the
Tenguel, extending far up on tiie slopes of the Cordillera, belongs to the Tenguel *hacienda*, which is one
of the largest and most valuable landed estates in the
republic. The Balao River, following on the Gala, is
the largest as regards its volume, and whilst the upper
and middle valleys of the other streams are narrow
and without population, this is broad and well settled,
with *haciendas* and groups of dwellings as far up as
the *páramos*. A well-travelled road ascends thereby
to Cuenca, in the high Cordillera. Small steam-
launches and rafts reach Balao, the *pueblo* near the
mouth. The Jagua is the next stream, and various
smaller ones follow until the Naranjal is reached.
With this river the narrow littoral terminates ; the
plain widens considerably, marking the limit of the
gulf of Guayaquil and the beginning of the Guayas
River delta.

The Naranjal, known higher up as the Cañar, rises
in the great Azuay *nudo* or knot, and traverses in
its upper portion an uninhabited and little known
region, passing through tortuous defiles with frowning
porphyry crags on either hand. It has various
tributaries in its descent, one of which passes below
the ill-famed Pucatoma ridge, over whose crest, at

14,600 feet above sea-level, the old Inca road serpentined, a spot much feared by travellers by reason of the snow and the icy gales that beat upon it. Below the crest lies a beautiful lake served by a narrow channel, and a swampy and difficult valley, and near at hand are the Paredones, the ruins of a *tambo* or halting-place of the Inca period, elsewhere described. The town of Cañar lies above the river. Various streams join the Naranjal, among them the Chacazaen, upon whose bank is situated the *pueblo* of Naranjal. To the port of Revesa, at the confluence, the tide ascends, and the river or *estero* is navigable thereto for river steamboats.

As before remarked, the tract of the littoral between Machala and Naranjal, valuable generally for its cocoa plantation, is of uniform character. In ascending such a river as the Tenguel or Gala four zones are distinguished. The first is that of the *manglares*, along the edge of the gulf, about a mile wide and subject to inundation, and the flat craft known as *chatas* enter the stream on the flood tide. Second is the zone of the *sabanas* and *tembladeras*, with a variable width of one to three miles, a tract which does not lend itself to agriculture but is excellent for cattle. In winter it is almost entirely flooded, and the streams are tortuous. Third is the cultivated zone, the most important of all, extending between the *sabana* and the foot of the mountains, with a width of three to nine miles. This region is almost flat, formed of sandy soil overlaid by rich earth. In its natural state it is covered with thick and varied tree growth, in which is found much wild cocoa, showing the natural capabilities of the soil for the cultivation of that important product. In this zone all the conditions for *cacao*-growing are united, including a moist, hot climate, and a soil slightly sandy or gravelly but substantial. Other tropical products, especially coffee, bananas, and sugar-cane, yield equally well, and the region is one of the most fertile in the country, and far from being cultivated to its full capability. In this zone the streams are more stable, swifter and stronger, and not navigable even for small canoes. The fourth zone is that of the lower slopes and spurs of the Cordillera, up to about 3,300 feet elevation, to where the limit of favourable tropical cultivation is reached. The zone calls for more extensive cultivation ; it is generally covered with that majestic vegetation which characterises the foot of the Andes. The rivers are torrential, but form the fertile *bancos* and *vegas*, favourable for the cultivation of cocoa, coffee, bananas, tobacco, etc.

Beyond this district, along the littoral, begins, as before remarked, the delta of the Guayas and the rivers belonging thereto, which are separately described.

The Spanish topographical terms so freely encountered throughout the New World have certain special applications in different parts of North and South America, although with few exceptions they are general. In Ecuador, possibly, these exceptions are most numerous, following upon the exceptional climatic conditions which have given rise to peculiar topographical features. A few words of explanation regarding some of the terms thus employed in Ecuador will be of service.

The *manglares* are described in the chapter dealing with the plant life, as are the *salitrales*. The first named are the mangrove thickets, and the second are salt plains, lying generally behind the mangroves, the salt being formed by the alternate flooding and evaporating of sea-water. In these plains *pozos* are encountered, deep ponds where the sea-water, remaining and subject to a continual evaporation, forms thick beds of salt, as at Santa Elena, Puná, Payana, etc. This salt in many cases is a valuable article of com-

merce. The term *pampa* or plain is common to all
South America ; it is of Indian origin, and the word
has been incorporated into both Spanish and English.
The *sabanas* or savannas are grass-covered plains,
generally with isolated groups of trees or shrubs.
In Ecuador the *sabanas*, when free from flood, in
summer are known as *sartenjales,* and they are
cracked and dry, of clayey soil with grass tufts
isolated from each other rather than forming a continuous turf. Such areas are painful to traverse either
by man or beast, due to their hard, lumpy surface.
In approaching a coast, the *sabana, sartenjal, salitral,*
and *manglar* are generally passed in the order named.
Tembladeras are *sabanas* flooded throughout the year,
and are often of many square leagues in area. Giant
grasses and other plants flourish on these patches.
The water, however, is not generally stagnant, but,
lying to a depth of a few inches to several feet, is
generally the overflow of rivers which spread out in
this wise. The *sabanas* afford excellent forage-areas
for cattle. *Pajonales* are smaller *tembladeras,* found
mainly in the upper Guayas district, and are
generally situated between the *bancos* (later described). The name comes from the covering of
vegetation, the *pajon* plant, which differs from the
pajonal or grass of the sierra. *Esteros* (derived
from the Latin *æstuarium*) are small arms of the sea
subject to the rise and fall of the tide, but in Ecuador
the term is also applied to small rivers above the
tide-range, dry at times, or even old channels. Such
channels abound in Western Ecuador, where changes
in the watercourse of the alluvial coast plains have
so constantly occurred. At times the *esteros* form
means of communication between two river systems.

The running water of rivers gives rise to *playas,*
vegas, and *bancos.* *Playas* are flat beaches, at
water-level, of sand or pure gravel. They are not
fertile enough for vegetation to cover them and are

inundated at flood-time. In many instances in South America the *playas* are gold-bearing, like the bars of the California " creeks." *Vegas* are formed only in rivers possessing deep currents running strongly, and are deposits of vegetable earth mixed with mud and fine sand, which form on the eddy side of the stream opposite to the swifter current. They are movable and change their position frequently when the river rises or varies its course. Opposite the *vega* is generally a high *barranco* or steep verge, 'where the current carves out the border of the stream, depositing the material as a *vega*. Each turn of a river has its *vega* and *barranco*. The earth of the *vega* is extremely fertile, and the large deposits of this nature—which are well exemplified on the Daule (Guayas) River—yield a rich harvest in tobacco, rice, maize, and other annual plants. Still more important for agriculture are the *bancos*. It is upon the *banco* formation, in the provinces of Guayas and Los Rios, that the great cocoa plantations are made. What the " red earth " deposits are to the coffee-grower of Brazil, so are the *bancos* to the cocoa-growers of Ecuador. The material composing a *banco* is similar to that of a *vega*—a sandy but fertile earth, which permits roots to penetrate and expand with ease and yet retains the moisture well, whilst at the same time being compact. This rich soil, which is also known locally as *de pan sembrar*, forms the zone nearest to the course of the river, with a variable width from a few to many hundreds of yards. It is an alluvial product of the stream. The *banco* is a few feet higher than the *sabana*, which lies behind it, and tends to extend itself towards the *sabana* by fresh deposits, whether from its own side or that of the river, during inundations. The formation of a *banco* is not difficult to understand. The river, when a new opening in the bank occurs, runs into the *sabana*, and overflows at any slight rise of the stream, flooding it and depositing the material held in suspension by the water, whilst the very fine particles form a thin layer near the new border of the stream. With each rise the width of the layer grows, and in a few years a *banco* is formed, of greater or less width. Naturally *bancos* only form in districts where the necessary material is carried by the streams and where the topography lends itself thereto. It is due to the fact that *bancos* were extensively formed along the old *esteros,* as well as on the present rivers, that their number and area are so considerable. They exist in places, moreover, where no river course is visible, and so determine the course of streams long since disappeared. The *banco* districts, with their *cacao* plantations, are described in treating of the Guayas fluvial system.

The Estero Salado, mention of which has been made, is the direct continuation of the gulf of Guayaquil, and the pure water of the sea therein washes the back of the city of Guayaquil. The width of this waterway is three miles, between Punta Escalante and Boca de Sabana, but it narrows rapidly towards the head. Its channel is safe and deep, and large vessels may enter nearly as far as the *Baños del Salado,* close to Guayaquil. The *Canal del Morro,* between the island of Puná and the mainland, is only $1\frac{1}{2}$ miles wide, from Punta Trinchera to Punta Arena. North of the island the strait is dangerous and sown with islets and banks, and vessels avoid the passage in that direction. Here it is observed that the island was, in an earlier geological epoch, joined to the mainland.

From Punta Arena the Morro coast of the gulf trends with a uniform, unbroken character to the north-west, as far as the Puntilla or Cape of Santa Elena. This is the westernmost point of Ecuador, and, indeed, of South America, with the exception

8

of the Piura coast of Peru, to the south of Tumbez, which stretches a few miles farther into the Pacific. There are no harbours on this stretch of the Ecuadorian coast, beaten continually by the winds and waves from the south and made dangerous by sandbanks and *bajos* or shoals. It was anciently called the *costa mala* or bad coast. The Puntilla is a tongue of lowland, or sandy spit, about 2,000 metres wide, extending from the Salinas plain, which is almost at sea-level, but rising suddenly at the point to a scarped hill, with an elevation of 423 feet above the water. Geologically, this natural platform is composed of horizontal strata of clayey sandstone, and it sustains a lighthouse, whose rays dominate a wide horizon. The projection forms the southern side of the bay of Santa Elena, with the small port of Ballenita, a mile or so from which is the town of Santa Elena. This small port is open to the northern gales, but presents some conveniences for commerce, and large vessels find good anchorage outside it. Santa Elena is the landing-place for the west coast cable. An important petroleum-bearing formation is being developed here, as described in the chapter upon Mineral Resources.

The coast continues northward to Cape San Lorenzo, and various small streams descend thereto from the range of hills which run north-west from Guayaquil to the coast. This range is the Cordillera de Chongon, formed of cretaceous and porphyritic rocks, similar to those of the Andes. These hills mark the limit of the large *sabana*, or plain of Santa Elena and Morro, which otherwise contains only small elevations. Between Morro and Chanduy runs a small chain of low hills eighteen miles long and with a greatest elevation of 825 feet, except that the Altos de Chanduy at the east of the village of that name reach nearly 1,000 feet. The summit of these hills affords a fine view over

the whole of the peninsula. The peninsula, of diluvial
or Quaternary formation has but a light vegetation
and is without rivers, except in its northern part.
The principal of these is the Jabita, partly dry in
summer. This is followed by a series of streams,
generally short and torrential. The Chongon Cordillera, approaching the coast, creates a marked change
in the climate and vegetation even in this small area
—a humid region distinguished by vigorous vegetation. But where the hills again recede the aspect
of the coast takes on again its former dry character
and the humidity disappears. Near the mouth of
the above-described rivers small *pueblos* are encountered, consisting in general of a few houses,
the life of whose occupants is drawn mainly from
the possibilities afforded by the streams. Of these
the village of Manglar is the principal. This peninsula, composed of stony plains and undulations, with
a scanty and singular flora, is reminiscent of the
coast deserts of Peru. The cactus is one of the
principal plants, as are the algarrobos. Salango
Point, in the centre of Santa Elena bay, has in its
neighbourhood various small islands. One of these,
Salango, is two miles in circumference and rises
to a height of 524 feet. It is well wooded and
frequented by whalers in search of water and fresh
provisions. Near at hand is the small roadstead of
Machalita, where sailing vessels take on cargoes of
tagua or vegetable ivory, proceeding from the province of Manabi. Slightly to the north lies La
Plata Island, a few square miles in area, where
pearls and pearl-shell are obtained. The island rises
to a height of 790 feet and the anchorage is on the
eastern side. This island is of historic interest,
having been, it is said, used as an anchorage by
Drake in 1579 for the purpose of dividing the spoils
of the Spanish treasure-ship *Cacafuego*. Turning
again to the mainland, across the low Cordillera,

lies the watershed of the Guayas River and the streams which flow to that river. At Jipijapa, famous for its " Panama " hats, arises the Cerro Bravo, part of a group of hills, the highest of which, Montecristi, reaches about 1,500 feet elevation. At the foot of the hill is the *pueblo* of the same name. The prehistoric platforms and great sculptured stone seats or chairs found on Montecristi hill are described elsewhere,[1] and are among the marvels of Ecuador.

Beyond San Lorenzo cape and San Mateo point the coast bears sharply to the east, forming the Bay of Manta, similar in certain respects to that of Santa Elena ; and this bay terminates at Jaramijo Point. Its shore is, however, broken by several rivers, the principal of which are the Portoviejo and the Chones, which latter has its outlet in the smaller bay of Caráque, or Caracas. At the southern extremity of the bay of Manta is the small port of the same name. The broad valley of the Portoviejo River, which debouches in Manta Bay, separates two groups of hills. This valley or *ensenada* of Charapoto, as it is termed, has its source in the humid hills some considerable distance from the coast. The capital of the province of Manabi, Portoviejo, is situated some fifteen miles from the mouth of the river, and there are other *pueblos* in the vicinity. Portoviejo is an old city of about 6,000 inhabitants, with a cathedral and a High School, famed in the republic, a Governor's house, and a bishop's palace. The river is not navigable, due both to scarcity of water at seasons and to its torrential course. It is in this respect like the numerous streams that cross the Peruvian coast. Manta is the chief port of Manabi. Its early pearl-fishing industry was driven away by the depredations of buccaneers and by the ferocious *manta* sharks which

[1] In the chapter on Antiquities. These were earlier mentioned by Villavicienco, but the Savile expedition of 1907 fully describes them.

abound on the coast. The port has a custom-house and a lighthouse. A line of railway runs inland to the town of Santa Anna and Portoviejo, elsewhere described.

The bay of Caráques is formed by the wide river of that name, and penetrates some eight miles inland. The town lies at its head. The bay is a mile wide at the entrance, narrowing inland ; and were it not for the bar that extends across it, closing the entrance to large vessels, Caráques Bay would be the finest port on the Ecuadorian coast, as upon its waters might float the largest vessel built. By reason of this shoal steamers and large vessels are obliged to anchor outside. It is regarded as possible, without prohibitive cost, to open a channel through the bank, and when the construction of the railway, long projected, from this point to Guayaquil is made doubtless the operation will be carried out. The *pueblo* of Caráques presents a picturesque aspect, backed by verdure-clad hills, and it is the outlet to a fertile, productive country which lies at the back. The Chones River, which falls into the bay, has its rise in the hills beyond, and receives various affluents, among them the Garrapata and the San Lorenzo. The *pueblo* of Chone stands upon its bank. A line of railway runs from Caráques to Chone, the centre of a cocoa-growing district.

A few miles to the north of Caráques Bay the River Briseño falls into the sea. Rising in the neighbourhood of Chone, this stream is ordinarily of small volume, but in the rainy season it swells greatly and is scarcely fordable ; and this condition is common to some other rivers in the humid area.

North of Caráques Bay, and especially beyond Cape Pasado, twelve miles beyond, the aspect of the littoral changes greatly. Due to the greater humidity, the hills are thickly wooded, and numerous streams descend to the ocean. The cause of this phenomenon is not merely a local one, as in the case of the similar change occasioned at Manglar by the Colonche Cordillera. It is not due to the presence of the *montañas*, or hills, necessarily, for the plains also are forest-covered. The condition continues from Cape Pasado as far as the River Mira, on the border of Ecuador, and along the whole Pacific coast of Colombia. The cause is a deeper one—that of a change in the temperature of the ocean, due to the absence of the Peruvian or Humboldt current, as described elsewhere. Cape Pasado is but 0° 22' south of the Equator, and it takes its name from being the first cape passed after crossing the Line, as described in the explorations of Pizarro and Ruiz.

In the small *ensenada*, or bay, formed by Cape Pasado, lies the village of Canoa, and two streams, the Canoa and the Tabuchila, debouch at this point. The small Puntilla River also empties into the sea near by, and this, in common with the Briseño and the Puca, Colimes, and Magro, have the peculiarity that their waters, in the springtime, are brackish and non-potable. Eighteen miles north of Cape Pasado the mouth of the Jama River is encountered, a stream as extensive as the Chone, with various tributaries. A very similar fluvial system is that of Cuaque, whose mouth lies close to Point Pedernales. This small coast river has the distinction of running across the Equator, with its mouth almost upon the Line. The nomenclature of other small streams and capes between Pasado and Pedernales, such as Ballena or " Whale " Point, Camaron or " Prawn " River sufficiently indicates their origin.

Near Pedernales the hills begin to retreat from the coast, forming a great semicircle around the bayous of Cojimes and Portete, with some small islands. Here, as before observed, is encountered an extensive low region, with mangrove swamps, as in the Gulf of Guayaquil and the Puná Island. The mouth of the Cojimes *estero* is some three miles in width, divided into two channels by the island of the same name. Six miles inland the opening widens out into a lake form, of picturesque appearance, with three small islands. Unfortunately, this sea opening, which otherwise might form a good harbour for vessels larger than the small craft which use it, is obstructed at its mouth by a bar, an immense sand-bank known as the *bajos de Cojimes*. The southern extremity of the lake or fiord affords a good canoe route for trafficking between the Cojimes and Pedernales Rivers, paralleling the coast, and various streams fall into it. Following close upon this *estero* system is that of the Portete, with Zapotal Island, and others smaller ; and into this opening fall various streams which have their source in the high lands of Mompiche. The next opening is that of the mouth of the Muisne River. The course of this stream is tortuous, and three miles above the *pueblo* of the same name it begins to receive various affluents. It is bordered by immense mangrove swamps. The river is navigable for canoes for some distance, as are some of its tributaries. North of this district Capes San Francisco and Galera form the turning-point of the coast, from a northerly to an easterly trend. The town of Atacames, situated here, was the Indian place of importance seen by Pizarro on his voyage of conquest. A few miles beyond the last-named places the wide mouth of the important Esmeralda River, with the town of that name, is encountered. This river is not navigable for steamers, on account of its impetuous current rather than for scarcity of water, as it is full flowing at all seasons ; but canoes ascend it. The port of Esmeralda is similar to that of Caráques, in that steamers and large vessels are obliged to anchor far outside the mouth, due to the bar.

The Esmeralda is the largest and finest river of Ecuador which flows into the Pacific (excepting the Guayas). It rises under the names of San Pedro and Guallabamba, a few miles to the north of Quito, in the high Andean interior ; collecting the waters of that part of the *callejon*, or great upland valley-passage, the river breaks through the western Cordillera and descends to the coast, traversing in succession the various climatic zones of the republic. In the coast lowlands the traveller upon this river might imagine himself transported to the Amazon, due to the humidity, the dense tropic vegetation, and the absence of human beings. The littoral province of Esmeraldas has been described as " a jewel among the Ecuadorian possessions," but an unworked jewel, for, despite its beauty, and interest for the naturalist and the lover of scenery, and its agricultural possibilities, the population of the province consists of a few small villages on the coast. " The tiger is encountered where there should be herds of cattle, the gold deposits in its streams are neglected, and the savage Indian wanders with blowpipe and arrows almost in sight of the distant steamer." [1] Nevertheless, certain parts of the district are well populated, as on the Tiaone, a tributary of the Esmeraldas near the sea, where numerous *haciendas* exist. The Esmeraldas River is more fully described elsewhere. The distance from the town of Esmeraldas to Quito is forty-six leagues, of which twenty-two can be performed in boats up the river.

Passing the Rio Verde, the coastline to the east (nearing the Colombian boundary) displays the mouths of various rivers, with numerous *esteros* and islands : a broken character somewhat similar to part of the shoreline of the Gulf of Guayaquil. The fluvial system of the Santiago, which river debouches here, is composed of four large, torrential streams,

[1] Wolf, *op. cit.*

with numerous tributaries, the principal being known respectively as the Bogatá, the Cachabi, the Santiago, and the Cayápas. These streams rise at high elevation in the western Cordillera. They are navigable for canoes and steam-launches for some distance, but under difficulties in their more rapid reaches. Most of these streams are auriferous, gold being found in the alluvial deposits on their banks. Their headwaters are generally in almost inaccessible territory, and in some instances but little known. The bayous and natural canals ramificating among the islands at the mouth of the Santiago communicate with three or four large sea openings, the two largest of which are La Poza and El Pailon. If the entrance to these openings were not obstructed, they would form safe and commodious harbours. The principal islands are that of Tola, in front of the village of the same name, and those of Santa Rosa and San Pedro. La Tola, founded in 1741 by the Spanish Governor Maldonado, lies at the mouth of the Santiago, and earlier was a flourishing town. The neighbourhood is rich in prehistoric relics, as mentioned elsewhere.

From the mouth of the Santiago system wide maritime plains extend to the River Mira, and in this low region, largely covered with *manglares*, the *esteros* form a veritable labyrinth. At the south of La Tola is an extensive swamp, reaching to the sea, inhabited by vast numbers of aquatic birds. The region between the mouth of the Santiago and Point Manglares, which point is on the boundary-line with Colombia, is known as the Bahia de Ancon de Sardinas. It is full of sandbanks and shoals, like Cojimes and Payana, to the south, and difficult of access by vessels. As its name implies, the bay is a fishing-ground. All these shoals and islands are of fluvial rather than maritime origin, material brought down by the rapid streams which cross the littoral from the hills beyond. The coast is not yet well marked or stable. In some places the sea encroaches, in others the land, and the mangroves are a factor of some importance in the building up of the latter. The River Mira, forming in its lower portion the Ecuador-Colombian boundary, has its rise, like the Esmeraldas, in the great inter-Andean valley, and breaks through the western Cordillera to reach the Pacific. The delta-channels of the Mira are navigable, and are tributary to the Colombian port of Tumaco. The river is more fully described elsewhere.

With its large coastal rivers the littoral of Ecuador is a region well favoured by Nature. The fertile, well-watered plains, the undulating lands, covered with rich alluvial soil, the dry, healthy districts, alternating with the moist forests or *montañas*,[1] and the majestic vegetation, crossed by numerous navigable streams, form a possession of great value, and should be more rapidly developed in the near future.

[1] It should be noted that the word *montaña* in South America does not necessarily mean "mountain," but "forest," or broken forested land.

CHAPTER IX

THE GUAYAS AND ESMERALDAS RIVERS

THE Guayas River, and the fluvial system of which it is the outlet, is one of the most valuable and interesting in South America, and its economic importance to Ecuador is very considerable. The system drains and irrigates the extensive region lying between the Andes and the low hills of the Pacific coast—a zone varying from ninety miles wide upstream to five or six miles wide near Guayaquil, covering an area of some 14,000 square miles, and forming the richest and most fertile belt of tropical territory in western South America.

The system comprises several long rivers which flow from north to south in roughly parallel or fan-shaped form. The rivers comprise, in the aggregate, waterways navigable for over 200 miles, an important series of natural canals. The bordering country for a long distance inland is flat, and has been formed by the silt brought down by the rivers, as Quaternary alluvials. Portions of this huge plain are flooded during the rainy season. The soil is perhaps the most favourable in the world for the cocoa-tree, which, originally growing wild, is extensively cultivated in the numerous *haciendas* served by the rivers, and the district forms an important source of the world's supply of cocoa and chocolate. The region is tropical, contained between latitude 0° 30′ and 2° 30′ south. Alligators of large size inhabit the rivers, and are frequently shot from the steamboats, or at times from the train on the Guayaquil-Quito Railway, which follows the lower part of the valley. Opposite Guayaquil, below the confluence of the various streams whose united waters form the Guayas, the river is 6,600 feet wide, and higher up, near Los Calis, it is still 4,600 feet wide.

The Guayas loses its name a short distance above Guayaquil, where the long Daule affluent enters it, and is knows as the Bodegas, after the town of that name upon its banks.[1] The Daule is the most important stream of the system, and forms with the Bodegas the River Guayas. The Yaguachi or Chimbo enters on the eastern side of the Bodegas, some fifteen miles above Guayaquil. Next, on the right, is the River Vinces or Quevádo, with a labyrinth of several mouths emptying into the Bodegas, and lastly the Caracas or Sapotal River. The Daule higher up becomes the Balzar River, and these three, the Daule, the Vinces, and the Caracas, flow from the north. All these streams are navigable on their lower courses, regular steamboat traffic being maintained on the Guayas and Bodegas with the river port of that name eighty miles above Guayaquil and for forty miles on the Daule.

The Bodegas River, otherwise known as the Babahoyo, is tortuous, curving constantly from north to east. Navigating from Guayaquil for six miles to the north, the island of Mocoli is reached, and thence, seven or eight miles to the east, the mouth of the Yaguachi or Chimbo. This river is crossed by the Guayaquil-Quito railway by an iron bridge.

The Chimbo River forms a wide curve, flowing from the Cordillera southwards, westwards, and finally north-west, falling into the Guayas. It is

[1] Here, as throughout Ecuador and the greater part of Spanish America, is to be noted the system, exceedingly troublesome to the geographer, which the Spaniards introduced of giving different names to the same river in different parts of its course.

COCONUT-PALMS NEAR YAGUACHI, GUAYAS VALLEY

To face p. 124

joined in its westward portion by the Chanchan. The Chimbo valley ends at the bridge of the same name, where the river leaves the *montañas* and enters on the plains. Both the Chimbo and Chanchan have repeatedly changed their courses in the district, as evident by the old channels and *esteros*. The land is not here very favourable for agriculture, although there are extensive *bancos* of good soil. About eighteen miles west of the bridge the Chimbo and Chanchan unite, and approach near to the Boliche River, which flows in a similar direction, and in winter the waters of the one escape to the other. Near the Chobo *hacienda* the river takes the name of the Yaguachi, and at this point, nine miles from its mouth, it is subject to the tide, and is navigable, although in summer steamboats ascend only as far as the *pueblo* of Yaguachi, situated upon the right bank. For a few miles above and below this place the river on both sides is covered, in a narrow zone, with *bancos*, but elsewhere traverses the *sabanas*. One of the main affluents is the Milagro, upon whose banks is situated the flourishing *pueblo* of the same name surrounded with coffee plantations and fruit-trees. The headwaters of the Chimbo come from the great tableland surrounding Chimborazo, and the river, in its upper torrential portion, flows past the town of Guaranda, capital of the province of Bolivar, in the high Andine uplands. The Chanchan rises in the Alausi *hoya* and its surrounding Cordilleras, and above its banks lies the town of Alausi, 8,100 feet above sea-level. Ascending the valley of the Chanchan, the Guayaquil-Quito railway takes its difficult course. These high districts are far removed from the fluvial district of the Guayas.

As far as the Yaguachi confluence the Bodegas is from 2,000 to 1,500 metres wide, but from that point it narrows considerably and turns due north. A short distance up-stream the river bifurcates, forming an island, and beyond this one of the mouths of the Vinces is passed. The river has changed its course within the last half-century in this portion of its course, and what was formerly a small *estero*, navigable only for canoes, now forms the main steamboat channel. About twenty-one miles from Guayaquil the village of Zamborondon is reached, the steamboats performing the journey on a flood tide in three or four hours. To this point the tide carries up salt water, but, although the tide influence is felt beyond Bodegas, still higher up-stream, this is only the reflow of the fresh water of the river. Due to this circumstance, a notable difference is observed in the landscape as seen from the deck of the steamer. From above Zamborondon the land, which hitherto consists of *sabanas* or plains, with cattle-ranches, becomes of the *vega* and *banco* formation, with cocoa and coffee growing *haciendas*. The *sabanas* region is non-agricultural, but pastoral ; the other combines both industries. Between Guayaquil and Zamborondon the river banks are open, the open *sabanas* extending away on either hand, terminating farther inland in *tembladeras*. The land does not lend itself to planting, as the river does not carry in suspension here the necessary material to form the *bancos* as before described ; and when the stream overflows the turgid waters deposit a fine mud such as forms the *sabanas* and *sartenjales*. In spite of some monotony in appearance this district is not lacking in picturesque views, especially when in winter the *sabanas* are covered with a green carpet, and the cattle, which at that season prefer the river banks to the *tembladeras*, appear by thousands thereon. The groups of coco-palms, with their graceful columns and feathery foliage, and the sombre mango-trees, which flourish around the *haciendas*, complete the pleasing picture, and the relative poverty of the *sabana* plant life is forgotten. The only highland

BANANAS AT THE WHARF FOR EXPORT.

[To face p. 120

encountered near the river is the *cerrito* or small hill of Calentura, near Guayaquil.

Continuing' the journey up-stream, the River Bodegas soon becomes half its width, with a constant direction to the north-east. On the left hand—that is, on the right bank of the river—another branch of the Vinces is passed, and various islands, one of which, the island of Flores, is six miles long. Various *esteros* enter the main channel. At Cabonda the river curves markedly, and receives the Baba, another mouth of the Vinces. Near the *pueblo* of Pimocha the river has of recent years changed its course, as in the case before described. Pimocha is twelve miles from Zamborondon, and two miles beyond Bodegas is reached. The stretch of river between these two last-named places is again characterized by the *bancos* formation, giving rise to a beautiful and exuberant vegetation along the margin, in which the natural decorative scheme continually offers new forms. The boat passes among *cacaotales*, or cocoa plantations, *cafetales*, or coffee plantations, and *cañaverales*, or cane-covered areas, and past *vegas* sown with tobacco and rice and with fruits of all kind, belonging to the numerous *haciendas*. Open *sabanas* alternate with planted areas reaching to the river verge. These *sabanas* extend behind the plantations, especially on the eastern side, and the *bancos* comprise only a narrow zone. The land partakes of the character of that below Zamborondon. The western part, from the mouth of the Baba upwards, is also crossed by the *bancos* which accompany the network of streams and *esteros*. The region is absolutely flat except for the Zamborondon hill, surrounded by *tembladeras* and *sabanas*. The summit of this conical hill reaches 884 feet above sea-level, and although small in comparison with the Andes mountains, the hill, by reason of its isolation, stands up prominently. The *pueblo* itself is surrounded with many traditions and fables, and the hill summit is of value as a landmark for twenty miles around.

The town of Babahoyo, or Bodegas, is the capital of the province of Los Rios, and the principal port for the interior of the country. It lies thirty-six miles up-stream from Guayaquil, on the left bank of the river, facing the mouth of the River Caracol, which is a large stream descending from the north. The old part of the town is subject to floods, and is being replaced by the new. The ebb and flow of the tide is strongly marked, and upon the flood river steamers from Guayaquil ascend even in the dry season, the journey occupying eight hours. Such navigation beyond Bodegas, or upon the Caracol, is only possible in winter, when the rivers are in flood. From Bodegas the journey by land into the interior or mountain provinces begins.

The Caracol or Zapotal has its origin far off in the Cordillera of Angamarca, in the province of Leon. It receives a number of small tributaries from both sides. The river is navigable for canoes throughout the year as far as Zapotal, but river steamers can ascend only in winter (*invierno*) as far as Ventanas with facility, the course being difficult above, due to the strong current in places. From Bodegas to Caracol the distance is nine miles, from that point to Catarama six, and from Catarama to Ventanas six more, and thence to Zapotal twelve miles. At Zapotal the river has already left the mountains and entered upon the plains. Below that point from Catarama to Bodegas the region traversed is one of *bancos* and cocoa plantations, and from Catarama to Bodegas the land is *sabana* and pasture. From Caracol downwards to Bodegas the land is subject to flood, and the town, like Bodegas, has the appearance of being surrounded by a lake. In summer the waters retire to the swamps, and the *sabana* is covered with abundant pasture. A low hill at Cachari, on the left side of the river, is noteworthy—it is but a rock of syenite 90 feet high rising from the swamps—as a remnant of the formation when in earlier geological times the waters of the gulf of Guayaquil washed the base of the Cordillera.

The Pueblo Viejo River is a tributary of the Bodegas, running parallel with the Caracol, and emptying into the main stream below Bodegas, near Pimocha, after a course some thirty miles long. This river formed the ancient course of the Zapotal, but was cut off therefrom by the formation of the *bancos* near Ventanillas. Due to this natural change, the town of Pueblo Viejo, which stands upon it, the chief town of the canton, decayed, and the flourishing *pueblo* of Catarama arose on the new channel, as the old stream became dry in summer, and navigation was no longer possible. The whole district above described, of the Bodegas and Caracol, etc., forms one of the richest parts of the territory of the republic, and, as before remarked, is the centre of the cocoa cultivation. Among the principal *haciendas* and plantations, are those of Ventanillas, San Juan, Juana de Oro, Santa Rita del Convento, and Pechiche Dulce, and there are many others not less fertile, although smaller, adding to the importance of the cocoa-producing industry. This district, with the adjacent ones of Baba, Vinces, and Daule, produce the *Cacao de Arriba*, which is superior in quality, and fetches a higher price in the market, than the *Cacao de Abajo* of Machala and Naranjal, on the coast below Guayaquil. The cocoa gardens or plantations which occupy the *bancos* along the river form a network following upon the natural configuration of these important deposits.

The Vinces River, with the Palenque and Quevado, by which latter name the upper courses are designated, is one of the largest tributaries of the Guayas system. It flows roughly parallel with the Caracol or Zapotal last described, considerably to the west. The furthest source of this river is near Santo Domingo de los Colorados, distant about 110 miles from its confluence with the Bodegas at Zamborondon, and with the exception of a small upper portion, the Pilalo, in the Andine region, the river belongs to the lowlands. Its general course is from north to south, varying somewhat to the west. The Palenque rises on the highlands which separate the Guayas system from the Esmeralda system (in latitude 0° 15' south of the Equator) to the *pueblo* of Quevado, traversing an uncultivated and little known mountain region. It is navigable for canoes to the *puerto de Ilo* near the Indian *pueblo* of San Miguel, and is quiet-flowing from very near its source. The Pilalo forms almost a right angle with the above, descending from the Cordillera, with a spacious basin. It rises near the Toachi River, part of the Esmeraldas system, and some of its affluents descend from the volcano Quilotoa. The upper valley, partly Andine, is well populated, with numerous *haciendas*. From Quevado to Latacunga runs one of the bad mule-roads of the mountain regions, almost the only " road " in that part of the country. From the confluence of the Pilalo with the Palenque, near Barro, the character of the river changes, with great bends and extensive *playas* or flat shores. The region between Quevado and Vinces at both sides of the river is a combination of *lomas* or hills, and *sabanas*, generally covered with brushwood, but near the river there are also large stretches of *bancos* planted with *cacao* and other fruits. An uninterrupted series of fine *haciendas* on both sides attest the fertility of the land. The *pueblo* of Palenque, which is some twenty-four miles from Quevado, lies a mile from the stream, and is a much older place than Vinces and Quevado. Vinces is the chief town of the canton, situated about nine miles to the south of Palenque, on the eastern bank of the

THE GUAYAS VALLEY : COCOA GATHERING.

[To face p. 150.

river. It presents an extremely picturesque appearance with its background of dark cocoa plantations and the slender stems of its coco-palms. The place was named after a priest, the owner of a near-by *hacienda,* and who, about the middle of the eighteenth century, caused a change in the course of one of the rivers, due to the opening of an aqueduct. The Baba, Arenal, Macul, and Garrapata *esteros* at one time formed the courses of the Vinces River, and with others constitute a network of channels, falling into the Bodegas, some of them navigable in the wet season. The flood tide in the Bodegas ascends the Garrapata for some six miles, and small river steamers easily enter it to the port of Arenal, a mile from the *pueblo* of Baba. The Baba River is lined with *bancos,* and consequently with cocoa plantations throughout its length, whilst the Arenal is so cultivated only in its upper part. The Macul is lined with *bancos* and plantations only in its lower part, and these are well cultivated. The *bancos* of the Vinces River reach only as far as the " California " plantations ; below that the land is low and flooded, and near the *pueblo* of Salitre begin the *tembladeras.* From the summit of the Zamborondon hill an interesting view of the district is obtained, which appears in winter, due to the floods, like an inland sea, sown with small islands and woods. At that season of the year navigation in all directions is easy, within or without the ordinary courses of the river, but in summer, in spite of the abundance of water, navigation is difficult. If all the backwaters and *esteros* were united in a single course, a strong river such as the Bodegas would be formed, navigable for steamers in the driest season, but under existing circumstances these smaller streams are not navigable in summer. Small canoe traffic upon some of them is possible as far as Quevado. In winter steamboats generally ascend to the port of Palenque, and at times as far as Moquique. This region is therefore mainly suitable for cattle-ranching, the cultivable land being limited in extent, due to the changes in the course of the streams and the instability of the land.

The River Daule is the westernmost and largest of the four main waterways of the Bodegas and Guayas systems. It receives no water from the Sierras, and belongs entirely to the lowlands. The length of this river is about 130 miles, without taking into account the numerous windings of its course. The general direction is from north to south, and the many small tributaries, traversing level land, are often navigable for canoes. In the upper system the principal tributaries are the Grande and the Peripa. The last named rises in the flat land of Santo Domingo, and runs parallel with the Palenque River. Six miles from the *pueblo* it receives various tributaries, and begins to be navigable at the port of Capelé, whose elevation is 214 feet above sea-level. Navigation to this point, however, is difficult in the dry season. A large number of small *esteros* enter lower down, such as the Cocoya, Congoma, Armadillo, Chaune, the last named being navigable for some distance. Then follow the Damas, Gualipe, Pajarito, and Guayabo, and from the left side the Pocachi, Quita-Palanca, Salapi Grande, Salapi Chico, both navigable, and the Mono, Achole, and Muricumba. The Peripe is a placid stream, its banks covered with dense vegetation, presenting a monotonous appearance. The Grande rises fifteen or twenty miles to the east of the *pueblo* of Chone, which lies at the head of the river of that name, running into the Pacific at Bahia de Caraques. It receives various tributaries, of which the Pupusa is one of the principal, the confluence being at an elevation of 195 feet above sea-level. From this point a trail leads to Santo Domingo de los Colorados, two days' journey on foot over flat land. From the mouth of the Pupusa to that of the

Peripe the distance is about thirty miles ; the journey by canoe is made in twelve hours. From the Peripe confluence downwards to Colimes the river is known as the Balzar, or, properly, the Daule. Between the two points the distance is thirty miles, or forty-five with the windings of the current. The journey is made up-stream by canoe in three days, rowing eight hours a day, and down-stream in twelve or fourteen hours. The main affluents between the Grande confluence and the Colimes are the Conguillo, Comipaga, Tigre, Zapatilla, Zapata, Jemu, and Congo, with others lesser in size. The last named is the most important and is navigable in canoes. The other tributaries are mainly *esteros*. A few miles above Balzar begins the inhabited *montaña* or wooded lands, covering the whole district on both sides of the river, a territory gently undulating, with *colinas*, or low hills, 70 feet to 120 feet high, unclothed by vegetation.

The town of Balzar, at the edge of this *montaña* region, marks the beginning of a changed landscape as a down-stream course is pursued. A notable succession of curves form the course of the stream, surprising and agreeable in their variation, revealing an uninterrupted series of *haciendas* and groups of dwellings on both sides, converting the district into a continuous garden of fruits and flowers. The *banco* and *vega* formation of the land is largely the cause of this change. Among the rivers of Western Ecuador the principal in point of scenic beauty is adjudged to be the Daule, from Balzar downwards, and the traveller who desires to form an idea of the resources of the province of Guayas, such as cannot be acquired from a visit to the neighbourhood of Guayaquil, may profitably ascend the river by steamboat in winter as far as Balzar, and one of the most picturesque countries within the tropics will have been surveyed.

The above described region extends from Balzar to Daule, a distance of some thirty miles in a straight

line. There are few affluents from the left or eastern
bank. In front of Colimes, which place is nearly
midway between the above-mentioned points, *sabanas*
and *lomas* lie behind the narrow *bancos* formation,
extending to the Bobo River, running parallel some
miles to the east. This river falls into the Daule much
lower down. The *pueblo* of Santa Lucia lies on this
part of the river. From the western side three large
tributaries enter the Daule—the Puca, the Colimes,
and the Magro. These streams rise in the low chain
of hills near the Manabi coast, which rises near Jipijapa to 1,000 feet. In summer they have but little
water, but in winter they are navigable for canoes
and rafts to the beginning of the *montaña*. Their
waters are brackish and non-potable, due to the
character of the ground at their sources.

The lower course of the Daule, between the *pueblo*
of that name and the confluence with the Guayas, near
Guayaquil, is distinguished from the upper course by
its width and the great curves of the channel and by
the lack of high banks at the verge. It is full-
flowing and placid. The aspect of the landscape also
changes notably nearer Guayaquil by reason of the
hills which arise on either hand. The town of Daule
is situated twenty-one miles north of Guayaquil on the
left bank of the river. Below, the River Bobo or Macul,
before mentioned, enters ; a stream with some curious
characteristics. It rises between the Palenque and
Peripa Rivers, and traverses the *montaña* region, afterwards the *lomas*, and lastly the *sabanas*, almost equi-
distant between the Vinces and Daule. From the
confluence of this stream as far as Guayaquil the
Daule has no further tributaries, but is fringed by
hills, rising to about 1,000 feet in some cases. The
Daule is navigable for canoes to its headwaters as
described, for river steamers at all times to the town
of Daule, and in winter as far as the mouth of the
Congo, six miles beyond Balzar. The tide is felt as

far as Colimes, but the salt water ascends only to the mouth of the Bobo.

The products of this important fluvial system of the Guayas have their outlet at Guayaquil, whose advantages as a port are elsewhere described.

The Esmeraldas fluvial system lies in the north of the republic, and rises in the snows of the great peaks and volcanoes of Cayambe, Antisana, Sincholagua, Cotopaxi, Iliniza, Atacazo, and Pichincha, draining all the Cordillera Occidental between Quilotoa and Cotacachi. Throughout this vast stretch of mountains innumerable small rivers and streams rise, forming the upper portion of the system. It is calculated that the area drained covers 21,060 square kilometres, or 680 square leagues, of which 11,860 square kilometres belong to the Andine portion and 9,200 to the littoral portion of the territory traversed.[1] In this respect the system differs much from the Guayas, whose largest drainage area is that of the littoral.

The largest and longest tributary of the Esmeraldas is the Guallabamba. This river gathers all the waters of the inter-Andine valley of the province of Pichincha, and breaks through the western Cordillera some twelve miles north of Quito, flowing between immense rocky walls in the deep valleys of Puellaro, Perucho, and Niebi. Throughout the whole course between the chasm in the chain whence it issues and its emergence upon the low region of Esmeraldas the margin of this river is almost inaccessible by reason of scarped mountain sides, and the fall of its bed is so rapid and irregular that navigation by canoes is impossible.

The fluvial system of the Quito *hoya*, or basin, which forms the farthest sources of the Guallabamba, and so of the Esmeraldas, has many ramifications.

[1] Wolf, *op. cit.*

The most remote streams are those which descend from Cotopaxi and Iliniza. Others descend the Chillo valley between Pasochoa and Sincholagua, forming the Pita and Pedregal Rivers. The Guapal tributary, draining Sincholagua, has in part a subterranean course, due to a lava flow which covered the stream in the middle of the eighteenth century. This eruption dammed up the valley, but the water found way beneath the obstruction when the lava cooled, and now issues as a beautiful spring. The wide Chillo valley and the Machache plain give rise to various streams, which unite in the San Pedro, flowing north. Here the Chillo *altiplanicie*, or plateau, is nearly nine miles wide, and its elevation above sea-level 8,250 feet. The small plain upon which Quito is situated is separated from the San Pedro by low hills. The Italo mountain has various mineralized hot springs, and the San Pedro River, having passed this point, enters the valley of Tumbaco, leaving on its right the spacious plains of the same name, with others. From the right it receives several tributaries, such as the Tumbaco, the Guambi, and the Quinche. Near the right bank of the Guambi are the pyramids or trigonometrical points which mark the baseline of the French surveyors in the eighteenth century, in the geodesic operations of the famous arc-measurement. The Caraburo cairn is at an elevation of 2,368 metres above sea-level, and that of Oyambaro 2,637 metres, and the distance between the two points, forming the baseline, is 12,228 metres. After its confluence with the beforenamed streams the San Pedro becomes the Guallabamba. The *pueblo* of the same name lies half a league from the river, and is situated on a plain at an elevation of 1,000 feet, enjoying a medium temperature, with a fertile soil and subtropical vegetation. But the intermittent fevers, which there are endemic, cause the place to be feared, and act against agriculture on a larger scale. Slightly to the north of the town of Guallabamba, and precisely upon the Equator, the last large tributary from the Quito *hoya* enters, that of the River Pisque, which flows practically along the Equator from its source, the beautiful, snowy Cayambe, itself upon the equinoctial line. From this confluence the Guallabamba begins to turn upon its western course, and enters the great opening in the western Cordillera, which gives it passage downwards to the lowlands. In its middle course, below the mountains, the Guallabamba receives the Llurimagua, upon its right bank, a little-known stream which rises in the snows of Cotacachi, in the Intac valley. From the left side it is further swollen by the Alambi, the Bota, and the Pitsara, flowing from desert regions. The Guallabamba is difficult for canoe navigation, and only expert native boatmen are able to ascend it in times of high-water. Frequent portages are necessary as far as Agua Clara, a small affluent in this part of its course. The rapids are dangerous, and the river runs in a wide valley with many windings and frequent gravel shoals. The margins are not of a character to attract settlers, nor of pleasing appearance in this district.

The Guallabamba becomes the Esmeralda at the point of its confluence with the Blanca, the river bearing the name to its mouth on the coast. The Blanco rises on the western slopes of the Cordillera below Quito. A large tributary of the system, the Toachi, comes from farther south, draining the Cordillera of Ilinazo. The Blanco receives a number of streams on its southern side, some of which rise in little-known regions. The Toachi is larger than the Blanco, and several streams fall into it, but near Santo Domingo it begins to flow slowly to its confluence with the Blanco, which point lies within the low regions. Lower down the Quininde enters, from the south. These affluents of the Blanco, with the

Toachi, drain the region north of the water-parting of the Guayas basin, the tributaries of which system approach near to the above. Among the tributaries of the Blanco below the Toachi confluence are the Canoni, and its arm, the Silanchi, both navigable for canoes. On the left side of the last named is the " port of Quito," and on the right bank of the Canoni is another " port." These so-called ports are only landing-places for travellers who journey from Esmeraldas to Quito through the *montañas* of Mindo, on foot. There is a similar " port " on the Blanco. Another tributary of the Blanco is the Inga, along whose bank passes an old road to the port of Guachala, on the Guallabamba. The Quininde is the tributary third in importance of the Esmeraldas, and its course through the plain is easy for canoe navigation. The vegetation upon its shores is rich, and often majestic in appearance, fine timber and rubber being contained in the woods, a circumstance which has attracted travellers and others. Similar advantages are enjoyed by its tributary streams, such as the Platano, Dogola, Arenanga, and the Mache, which is almost as large as the main stream, and which lends itself to navigation to the neighbourhood of Santo Domingo. The Quininde falls into the Blanco, nine miles above the confluence of that river with the Guallabamba.

The Esmeraldas, formed by the above-described waterways, is some thirty-six miles long in a straight line, with a general direction to the north-north-west. It is very rapid down to its mouth, and so is not navigable by steamboat, although the volume of water is more than sufficient for such. The journey in canoes up to the Guallabamba against the current takes six or seven days, and the return journey only as many hours. The valley is narrow, fringed by hills somewhat less than 1,000 feet high, and the river serpentines through rocky walls, distinguished

by this circumstance from all the other large rivers
of the Ecuadorian littoral. If from this reason the
surrounding region is not readily cultivable, there
is some recompense in the beauty and grandeur of
the scenery which opens to the view at each turn
of the course. This varied and attractive scenery
has no rival in the country, and is worthy of the
attention of the artist.

The tributaries of the Esmeraldas are generally
navigable in their lower third portion, but are small
and short, the Sade and Caninde, on the right, and
the Viche and Tiaone, on the left, being exceptions
in point of size. The Cole, which joins the river
half a league below the Guallabamba confluence, is
placid, flowing from the plains ; the Caninde is long
and rapid, and from its head the *caucheros*, or
rubber-gatherers, cross to the Rivers Onzola and
Grande, of the Santiago system.

The settlements along the Esmeraldas are mostly
concentrated at the mouths of these streams, as
generally the valley widens at such points, and small
groups of houses are encountered. On the right the
montañas interlace with those of the Rivers Muisne
and Cojimes, which run to the coast south of
Esmeraldas. The Viche enters the Esmeraldas about
midway in its course, at some twenty-one miles from
the coast. Its volume is considerable, and it is
navigable for canoes for two days' journey up-stream
to the Bamba affluent. Its banks are overlooked in
places by hills, similar in aspect to those of the
Esmeraldas, with the lower part of the valley of
some width. The rubber-gatherers pass from one
to other of the headwaters of these various rivers.
At one time considerable quantities of rubber were
obtained from the Viche forests, as also from those
of the Quininde. The Tiaone, the last of the
Esmeraldas tributaries, is similar to the Viche in its
configuration, with a winding course. But its

margins are well populated and cultivated, and the river is, in this respect, one of the best in the province,· and provides the town of Esmeraldas with many necessary articles of life. In its lower portion the banks appear like a continuous garden, and at each turn the traveller has in view a *hacienda*, or group of dwellings. The river is navigable almost up to its source, which lies in the *montañas* which fringe the Upper Muisne.

The Esmeraldas widen considerably at its con-fluence with the Tiaone, and in the wide elbow at this point the Pueblo Viejo, or ancient town of Esmeraldas, lies, in a very picturesque position, but a less healthy one than that of the newer town. The estuary, or broad part of the river, which extends six miles inland, is full of islands, some of which are large and cultivated. The Esmeraldas has no delta, however, and its current falls with great force and rapidity into the sea. The tide ascends scarcely more than $1\frac{1}{2}$ miles up-stream from the mouth. Thus serious obstacles exist against steamboat naviga-tion, and only with difficulty do large craft ascend to the town, the capital of the province, only half a league from the mouth.

A geographical peculiarity of the rivers forming the Esmeraldas system is that the large streams, the Guallabamba and Blanco, whilst they enter at the foot of the Cordillera upon very extensive plains, almost similar in character to the littoral plains, again pass through a mountainous region before reaching the sea, a condition unknown elsewhere in Ecuador, and, indeed, uncommon. Thus the traveller who ascends the Esmeraldas is surprised to observe that, after passing the mouth of the Quininde, and thread-ing the high hills on either hand, a great plain opens out, and the rugged surroundings, instead of increasing and forming part of the Andine spurs, as might have been supposed, fall away into the level horizon. Similarly marked is the effect in descending the river, where the high hills seem to shut off the valley entirely from the sea, the opening between them not at first being visible. The middle part of this great plain is at an altitude of some 230 feet above sea-level, and from it on a clear day the great peak of Pichincha and other high points of the Andes are seen.

The Santiago River system differs from that of the Esmeraldas. It has no tributaries in the Andine basins. Its most remote source, however, is on the slopes of Yana-Urcu, one of the high peaks of the Western Andes. With its numerous affluents the system covers a considerable area of territory, between the Cordillera and the sea. Of the four principal streams, the Bogota (not to be confounded with the same name in Colombia), the Cachabi, Santiago, and Cayapas, the two first-named unite with the third near the *pueblo* of Concepcion, eighteen miles in a direct line from the sea, and the last, the largest of all, joins some six miles lower down, where the delta of the Santiago begins. The Santiago and Cayapas form at their confluence a right angle, coming respectively from the east and the south, and fall into the main stream near the *pueblo* of La Tola. In this delta islands are constantly forming. The most thickly populated island is that of La Tola. Between the mouth of the Cayapas and the sea several tributaries enter. The *esteros* of this delta are wide, deep, and placid, the only motion of the water being due to the tide. The principal arm presents a majestic aspect, and lends itself to navigation by small steamers, after the manner of the Guayas. The vegetation that fringes the island is pleasing ; the monotony of the *manglares*, such as elsewhere obtains, especially on the lower Guayas, is absent ; and the sombre sapotillo-trees, with their huge aromatic flowers, the climbers, and bamboos, and, above all, the groups of small, graceful palms, form the most pleasing features in these almost impenetrable woods.

The Cayapas carries a large volume of water, but is placid and favourable for navigation by steamboat and canoe. As far as the *pueblo* of the same name, and somewhat beyond, the river preserves the width it possesses at its mouth, 330 to 800 feet, with a considerable depth. The tide reaches Herradura, a day and a half's journey by canoe from La Tola, and only higher up, above the mouth of the Sapayo, is a strong current encountered. This does not offer much difficulty to the expert native rowers, and within three days the ascent may be made to the most remote points inhabited by the Indians, a league above the mouth of the Barbudo. From this point, however, navigation is difficult, dangerous, and in places almost impossible, due to rapids and cascades in the deep, dark ravines traversed by the stream. Here the foot of the lateral spurs of the Andes is reached. The Cayapas flows almost north. The tributary nearest the mouth is the Pagola, entering on the west side, and upon its margin white and mestizo settlements terminate, the first Indian habitations, those of the Cayapas Indians, being near the mouth of the Onzole, half a league higher up the river. The Onzole is well populated with Indians throughout. It can be ascended in canoes by poling in six or eight days. Its source is near the Sade lagoon, and it receives a number of tributaries. Above the Onzole is the Herradura, into which the Camarones enters, navigable for a day's journey. Up to this point the whole region traversed is a flat plain, in which no eminence is seen, the banks of the river being some six or nine feet high, according to the state of the tide, and covered with a layer of extremely fertile black soil. Above the Camarones the country is traversed by low hills, and the vegetation, consisting of palms of different species, is of beautiful type. The great, sombre Chipero trees form, with their hanging branches along both edges of the stream, a shady covering, high enough for canoes to pass beneath. Parrots and monkeys are encountered. An occasional Indian dwelling is seen, surrounded with banana-plants, and the inhabitants, almost naked, lie idly at ease. The Indians also live in communal houses. The whole river presents at each turn scenes of extreme picturesqueness, and " might seem to water a veritable paradise." [1] The Cayapas is also gold-bearing. The Sapayito, another tributary, is navigable to its source. Following is the small Telembi stream, and also the Sapayo Grande, with gold-washings, both entering on the right side. On the left side is the Mafa, rich in gold, and the Grande, a full-flowing affluent. This last, like the Onzole, is populated by Indians, and can be ascended by canoes for five days' journey to its source. Lastly is the Barbudo, and at a point a day's journey up this stream begins a road used by the Indians, which, crossing the Santiago River, leads to the *páramos* of Piñan and thence to Ibarra, in the high Andine *hoya*. The source of the Cayapas and that of some of the tributaries in the Cordillera are but little known. Due to the numerous bends and doublings, the distances for navigation are great, but in a straight line are very much less.

The Santiago itself is of a different character, with a swift current throughout the greater part of its course, full of rapids, narrowing and widening alternately, sown with gravelly islands and having inaccessible banks. Beyond La Concepcion the river is not navigable, except for small canoes and under dangerous conditions. The course from the mouth to the town of the same name lies for six miles to

[1] Wolf, *op. cit.*

the east, and is wide, deep, and placid. The tide
ascends to the confluence with the Bogotá, and the
river there is navigable for small steamboats. La
Concepcion occupies a curious but picturesque
position between the Bogotá and Santiago. The
upper course of the Santiago, above Playa de Ora,
is less known. The Indian tribes inhabit the higher
portions, the middle being occupied by blacks,
descendants of slave times. The tributaries are small,
except the Uimbi, which is navigable to the *pueblo*
of that name, and its gravelly banks are gold-bearing. The Cachabi, which falls into the Bogotá near
La Concepcion, partakes much of the character of
the Santiago, being swift and dangerous for navigation by the small canoes which ascend it, and frequent
portages are necessary. The whole river is gold-
bearing. From the *pueblo* of the same name, inhabited by a few blacks, a trail ascends to the
province of Imbabura, San José, somewhat lower
down, being more thickly inhabited. The Bogotá
is somewhat similar to the Cachabi and Santiago,
serpentining through a flat region, but it is navigable
for launches and canoes. Its tributary the Tululbi
brings from the north a considerable volume of water
and is navigable. The Bogotá is auriferous only
in its upper reaches.

The River Mira, which empties into the Pacific
in the northernmost portion of the republic, constituting in part the boundary with Colombia, forms
a delta of some size, and its upper tributaries cover
a considerable area of mountain territory. The
system is one of those which drain an inter-Andine
basin, that of Ibarra, breaking through the western
Cordillera to gain the coast lowlands after the
manner of the Esmeraldas. The principal of its
upper tributaries are the Blanco, the Chota or
Chamchan, and the Apaqui. Lower down the Lita
and the San Juan and others enter, and from

Colombia come the Guaiquer and Nulpe. The
Blanco rises on the slopes of the great Mojanda
peak and in the San Pablo lake, the various streams
which form it uniting near the town of Otavalo at
an elevation above sea-level of 8,500 feet. The
Otavalo or Blanco runs about north, and flows past
the large *pueblo* of Cotaccachi, whose snows feed
some of its lesser tributaries. The Yana-yacu lake,
in this district, is elsewhere described. It is joined
by the Taguando, which flows past Imbabura. The
famous Yaguarcocha lake of Huaina Capac's victory
lies near the town of Ibarra on the course of
this stream. The plains between the Blanco and
Taguando, on the broad base of Imbabura, form the
best agricultural part of the district. The above-
named streams unite with the Chota, forming the
River Mira. Above this confluence the Apaqui enters
the Chota, which, coming in a south-westerly direction from the highlands of Boliche, rounds the foot
of the "knot," receiving various streams. From
the Apaqui confluence to that of the junction of
the Ambi—the former at 5,250 elevation—extends
the deep, hot valley of Chota, known for fertility
of its soil wherever artificial irrigation is possible,
as also for its subtropical vegetation and its insalubrity, due to intermittent fevers. This province
is of peculiar character, with a very broken surface,
the rivers running enclosed between long, rugged
ridges, with naked peaks and volcanic wastes on
every hand, and in the depths where the valleys widen,
oases of sugar-cane, coffee, banana, and fruit plantations. The Angel or Mira, which enters the right
bank of the Chota, is of some considerable size.
To this stream the French surveyors extended their
geodesic measurements in the eighteenth century.

The Mira flows across the littoral in a general
north-west direction to the sea, and off its mouth lie
a complicated network of islands, surrounded by
10

manglares, reminiscent of the regions of Payanas and the Estero Salado of Guayaquil. This system extends to the mouth of the Santiago River, as before described ; on the northern side of the Mira delta is Punto Manglares, on the frontier between Ecuador and Colombia.

The littoral province of Esmeraldas, like those of Manabi and Guayas, enjoys a rainy season. In Guayas and Manabi the vegetation loses its beauty during the dry season, but this does not take place in Esmeraldas. The humid atmosphere conserves a perpetual verdure. The plains and the mountains, the majestic woods, with their corpulent trees or slender palms, overgrown with climbers and parasites, shade the land from the slopes of the Cordillera to the broad plains of the Pacific coast. The province rivals, in respect of its climate and products, the Oriente and the Amazon territories, but gains greatly upon these by reason of its proximity to the sea, which affords a ready means of transport for such products. Whilst it is not remarkable that the remote Amazon regions are still unpopulated by the white race, it is a matter for surprise that the province of Esmeraldas should so far be so slightly settled.

CHAPTER X

THE HIGH ANDES AND VOLCANOES

THE extensive mountain range of the Andes, as previously observed, reaches its greatest development in Ecuador, as regards the number and height of its snowy volcanoes. The general formation of the Andes throughout Chile, Peru, Bolivia, Ecuador, and part of Colombia presents a certain uniform structure, perhaps more symmetrical than is exhibited by any other mountains on the globe. In southern Peru and Bolivia the Andes reach their greatest width, forming three roughly parallel ranges, two—and in places three—of which continue throughout northern Peru, through Ecuador, and into Colombia. One main range (with a lesser parallel range) runs through Chile, the whole continuous system from the southern extremity of the continent at Cape Horn to Panama and the Caribbean Sea being, approximately, 4,400 miles long. This continuous chain of highlands parallels the entire western coast of South America, its average height being 13,000 feet above sea-level.

The highest peaks in the Andes, beginning at the south, may be briefly named. Aconcagua, in Chile, is the leader, its elevation being 23,393 feet above sea-level ; with Tupungato, 22,329 feet ; and others in Chile between 19,000 and 20,000. In Bolivia are Sorata or Llampu, 21,490 feet ; Illimani, 21,190 feet ; and many others from 18,000 to over 20,000 feet. In Peru are Coropuna and Huascaran [1]

[1] Partially ascended by the Author.

above 22,000 feet ; and there are others of 19,000 and 20,000 feet. In Ecuador the highest points are : Chimborazo, 20,498 feet ; Cotopaxi, 19,613 feet ; and others, later enumerated. In Colombia, Tolima reaches 18,400 feet, with others slightly less. The perpetual snowline in the Andes is highest in Peru, where it lies at about 16,500 feet. Thus this vast range unfolds itself throughout an entire continent.

In Ecuador, as in Peru, the eastern chain is known as the Cordillera Oriental and the western as the Cordillera Occidental. The eastern chain is also specifically termed the Andes of Ecuador, or Cordillera Real.

The great longitudinal depression which runs between the two Ecuadorian Cordilleras also forms the boundary between the ancient rocks of the eastern part of the country and the Mesozoic beds which form the greater part of the western territory. The eastern Cordillera is of gneiss, mica, and chlorite schist, and other crystalline rocks of ancient date. The western Cordilleras, on the other hand, is composed of porphyritic, eruptive rocks of the Mesozoic Age, together with sedimentary deposits containing cretaceous fossils, and the range of hills running north-west from Guayaquil is of similar porphyritic and cretaceous character. Near Loja, in the great longitudinal depression between the Cordilleras, recent deposits with plant remains occur, and northeast of Cuenca a sandstone formation with cinnabar or mercury ores, somewhat like that in Peru. The great volcanoes of the north, of Tertiary and recent formation, stand variously upon the folded mesozoic beds of the western Cordillera, or on the ancient rocks of the eastern Cordillera, or on the floor of the great inter-Andine depression between the two ranges.

The hydrographic system of the Ecuadorian Andes is one of peculiar interest. It embodies a series of

hoyas or basins, drained by rivers which break
through the eastern and the western Cordillera
alternately, finding their way respectively to the
Atlantic (Amazon) or to the Pacific, as described
in part of the foregoing chapter. The northernmost
of these river basins is that of the Pasto, flowing into
Colombia and thence through the western Cordillera
to the Pacific ; the second the Mira, to the Pacific ;
the third the Guallabamba or Esmeraldas, to the
Pacific ; the fourth the Pastaza, to the Atlantic
(Amazon) ; the fifth the Chimbo, to the Pacific
(Guayas) ; the sixth the Cañar or Naranjal, to the
Pacific (Gulf of Guayaquil) ; the seventh the Paute
or Santiago, to the Atlantic (Amazon) ; the eighth
the Jubones, to the Pacific (gulf of Guayaquil) ;
the ninth the Zarumba or Tumbez, to the Pacific ;
the tenth the Zamora, to the Atlantic (Amazon).

The two Cordilleras, starting from the somewhat
confused mass near the Peruvian border, run nearly
north by east to Colombia. The parallel ranges,
as in Peru and Bolivia, are joined transversely by
nudos, or knots, the articulated system forming the
well-defined *hoyas*—basins or plateaux which have
their hydrographic outlets to the Pacific or Atlantic
as described. There are nine such *nudos* in the
Ecuadorian Andes, with their corresponding *hoyas*.
The system may be more broadly described as forming an elevated plateau, whose length is some 300
miles and width twenty to thirty miles, divided into
three great shallow basins or plains by the main
transverse ridges, or knots, of Tiupullo in the north
and Azuay in the south. The dividing high ridges
are also known as *páramos*, the word in Ecuador
and Colombia denoting the high, bleak uplands. The
three basins thus defined are those of Quito, Ambato,
and Cuenca respectively. The general elevation of
these three basins descends towards the south, that
of Quito having an average altitude of 9,500 feet

above sea-level, of Ambato 8,500 feet, and of Cuenca 7,800 feet. They are also characterized climatically by the increasing aridity towards the south, the Quito plain being fertile and vegetation covered and the others barren and desolate except in certain sections, this barrenness being influenced partly by the volcanic character of the region.

Rising from both the eastern and western rims of this elevated plateau are the higher Cordilleras, their main summits culminating far above the perpetual snowline, which in Ecuador lies at about 15,750 feet above sea-level. As before remarked, due to their peculiarly symmetrical arrangement and spectacular appearance, such an assemblage of snow-clad peaks is not found in any other part of the world. Not only for their height are the Ecuadorian peaks noteworthy, but for their peculiar occurrence in parallel lines, sometimes in pairs facing each other across the " cyclopean passage " or avenue formed by the long plateau. There are twenty-two of these great peaks, several of which are actual volcanoes, grouped along the central plains almost within sight of each other. Built up by subterranean fires, the great mountain edifices of Ecuador are sculptured by glacier streams and perpetual snows. The volcanoes of Ecuador have rendered the country famous among geologists and travellers of all nationalities. They were the terror of the primitive Indian, and objects of awe and worship by the semi-civilized peoples of the land, and have been at various periods terrible scourges and engines of destruction.

The largest number of high peaks and the greatest average elevations occur upon the eastern Andes, or Cordillera Oriental, whilst the western or Occidental is distinguished by having the highest individual elevations. The altitudes given by various authorities of these peaks differ somewhat, and the measurements of later investigators vary considerably, from those of Humboldt in some cases. Humboldt was the first to study and measure the Ecuadorian volcanoes, and La Condamine measured them in 1742. The more modern investigators were Drs. Reiss and Stübel, who spent four years, from 1870 to 1874, in the study, and in 1880 they were the subject of Edward Whymper's famous travels. The alleged remarkable condition of the sinking or rising of various of these summits and localities may account, it has been stated, for the variation found in measurements made at different times. It has been estimated that a considerable decrease in the elevation of the Ecuadorian Andes in the region took place during last century. Quito has sunk, it is stated, 26 feet in 122 years, and Pichincha 218 feet in the same period. The farm at Antisana, where Humboldt lived for some time, has sunk 165 feet in sixty-four years. On the other hand, two of the active volcanoes, those of Cotopaxi and Sangay, have increased in altitude since they were measured by La Condamine, it is asserted. Underlying seismic disturbances have doubtless been the cause of these movements.

Following are the elevations of the principal peaks as given by Reiss, Stübel, and Whymper, together with their position on or nearest the eastern or western Cordillera respectively :—

EASTERN CORDILLERA.

	Feet.
Cotopaxi (Whymper)	19,613
Antisana „	19,335
Cayambe ,, ...	19,186
Altar, or Capac Urcu (Reiss and Stübel)	17,730
Sangay (Reiss and Stübel)	17,464
Tunguragua (Reiss and Stübel)	16,690
Sincholagua „ „	16,365
Quilindaña „ „	16,235
Rumiñahui „ „	15,607
Sara-Urcu (Whymper)...	15,502
Cerro Hermoso or Llanganati (Reiss and Stübel)...	15,070

WESTERN CORDILLERA.

	Feet.
Chimborazo (Whymper)	20,498
Iliniza (Reiss and Stübel)	17,405
Carahuairazo (Whymper)	16,515
Cotocachi „	16,301
Pichincha „	15,918
El Corazon or Chamalari (Whymper)	15,871
Atacetzo (Reiss and Stübel)	14,892
Mojanda	14,088

The volcanic territory extends from beyond the frontier of Colombia—in which country there are also volcanoes—as far south as Loja, in Ecuador, covering four and a half degrees of latitude. Its western limit is the Cordillera Occidental, upon whose outer slopes the volcanic material rapidly disappears, except where it is carried down as a secondary deposit by the streams. In the Esmeralda and Mira valleys secondary deposits of volcanic material are found even near the sea in places. Towards the east the volcanic territory occupies the Cordillera Oriental from Cayambe as far as Sangay, covering all the interior and western slopes and the central crest as far as the valley of the River Pastaza. In the province of Chimborazo, from Tunguragua, the covering is not continuous, and is limited to the environs of the eruptive centres. In all parts of the district, in the valleys and ravines below the volcanic flows, are to be observed the ancient crystalline schist formation lying at the surface some distance from the volcanoes. From Sangay to the south the eastern Cordillera is free from volcanic effects. In the Cuenca basin a 'large area is covered by volcanic material, although there are no active volcanoes : old andesite alone is encountered, not recent lavas. In the Loja province, the southernmost of Ecuador, there is no vestige of volcanic action, which appears again, only many degrees to the south, in Peru. The volcanic belt in Ecuador is therefore well-defined.

The northernmost group of volcanoes is that comprising Cumbal and Chiles, both of which are quiescent. They have large craters and are surrounded with recent lava flows, but their latest eruptions must have been before the Spanish advent. Hot gases and vapours, however, proceed from the solfataras of Cumbal, around whose mouths native sulphur is deposited. Chiles is on the frontier line with Colombia. A further group of extinct and ancient volcanoes in this region is that of Imbabura and Mojanda. The crater of Imbabura is well preserved, and it is celebrated for its destructive eruptions of mud and water. It has been asserted by some explorers—principal among them being Humboldt—that great quantities of hot mud have been thrown from the mouth of this volcano, and furthermore, that in an eruption of 1691 the mud contained great quantities of fishes of a species known as *preñadillas* (*Pimelodus cyclopum*) which "fell so plentifully on the surrounding country that their putrefaction brought about fevers among the inhabitants." This story, however, is repudiated by Wagner, also by Wolf, who visited the crater in 1871, and who states that, as the crater is open at one side, it could not contain a lake of water, and moreover that fish could not live at such an elevation above sea-level as that of 13,200 feet. This elevation is slightly less, however, than that of the great Lake Titicaca in Peru and Bolivia where fish are caught. That subterranean lakes exist in the volcano has not been proved. Imbabura is the highest of the northern peaks, and stands midway between the two Cordilleras at the northern end of the plateau, and belongs to the *nudo* or transverse ridge. Its name is derived from the words *Imba*, meaning fish, and *bura*, mother, resulting upon the legend of its casting forth of the *preñadillas*. In the neighbourhood of Mojanda is the beautiful San Pablo lake, half a league in diameter, and at 8,800 feet elevation, and near Ibarra lies Yaguar-cocha, the " lake of blood," so named from Huayna-Capac's massacre of the Caranquis.

Cotacachi is the only snowy peak found between the valleys of the Guallabamba and the Mira Rivers. It is a volcano of exceedingly picturesque aspect, with a great glacier upon the eastern side of the summit, and rises to 16,300 feet elevation. At the foot of the south-east slope is the lake of Cuicocha, in an ancient crater, with two islets therein. Two leagues to the north is the volcano Yana-urcu, otherwise known as *cerro-negro* or " black hill," due to the contrast presented by the black rocks of its summit with the white of its snowy companion. It reaches somewhat over 15,000 feet. The town of Cotacachi lies at an elevation of 8,100 feet, and near at hand are various hot springs highly charged with carbonic acid and bicarbonate of iron and lime. The Yana-yacu or Tinte spring is the best known, and its waters are used for dyeing cotton textile fabrics black.

Perhaps the best known of the volcanoes of Ecuador is Pichincha, otherwise the " boiling mountain." This is the only active volcano in the western Cordillera, and its destructive eruptions and proximity to Quito have caused it to be regarded with dread. At the time of the Spanish conquest the volcano was quiescent, but thirty-two years after the foundation of Quito a severe eruption, in October and November of 1566, terrorized the inhabitants of the city. In 1575 followed a still more severe eruption, with another in 1582. After a period of activity lasting for sixteen years, a quiescent period of seventy-eight years followed, but the mountain suddenly broke out again in 1660 with the most frightful eruption known in history. The eruption of 1575 covered Quito three feet deep with stones and ashes, but the three later outbreaks were regarded as the most destructive.

The last eruption broke down the western side of the crater, and this was a favourable circumstance for the safety of Quito, as it is believed that any eruption will thus be directed from the city in a future outbreak. The volcano appeared to have exhausted itself, for no eruption has taken place since. However, since the earthquake of 1867, it has sent forth dense masses of black smoke and great quantities of fine sand. The crater is in a state of solfatara, sending forth sulphurous and aqueous gases and vapours, and at times a column of dense smoke rises over its summit. The ascent of the two Pichincha peaks is easy, and to visit the edge of the crater is one of the pastimes of the people of Quito. This may almost be reached on horseback, and even the descent of the crater, 2,540 feet deep, is not a difficult performance, and has been carried out by various scientific parties. It is stated that the red-hot lava bed in the crater may be observed rising and falling.

To the south of Pichincha lie the volcanoes Atacazo, Corazon, and Iliniza, also Ilato, Pasochoa, and Rumiñahui, all quiescent, and in some cases having fine craters, easy of access. Iliniza is composed of two distinct hills, the northern of which appears to be the older, and the saddle between them is covered by a glacier which descends therefrom. The mountain occupies an advanced position in the western Cordillera, analogous with that of Cotopaxi in the eastern, which it rivals in respect of its majestic and powerful appearance. The eastern slopes, scarred by deep and inaccessible *quebradas* or ravines, fall towards the plains of Callo and Machache. The two pyramidal peaks are marked features of the landscape, and Iliniza is regarded as one of the most interesting mountains of Ecuador. Bouger, the French Academician, who was at the head of the scientific commission sent in 1736 to measure a degree of the meridian on the Equator, measured the height of the peak trigonometrically. Chamalari, or El Corazon, is, like Iliniza, without a crater, and lies near the last named, overlooking the basin of Quito.

Passing the peaks which fringe the eastern slope of this great basin, the majestic Cayambe is seen. This for many centuries has been quiescent, and even the form of its crater has disappeared. Cayambe rises in beautiful pyramid form, covered with its shining snowcap. This, the second highest peak in Ecuador, has the distinction of standing almost upon the Equator. Its base covers a large area, and, as seen from Quito, with its square top rising far above the snowline, the mountain is a splendid sight for the people of the capital.

South of the foregoing lies the interesting group of which Antisana is the monarch. Antisana is of historic activity, and cannot be considered as altogether extinct. The mountain is crowned with a double dome, and presents an imposing sight. It was ascended in 1871 by Dr. Stübel, and ten years before by Señor Espada,[1] a Spaniard. Whymper ascended it in 1880. La Condamine and Humboldt speak of early eruptions of the volcano, and the last named saw smoke issuing from the crater in 1802. The *hacienda*, or farm, at which Humboldt stayed, 13,306 feet above sea-level, is on the western slope of the mountain. Three great lava flows surround Antisana, and the rocks in its vicinity are of much interest to the petrologist. Besides pumice-stone, obsidian is encountered, a mineral which was used by the Indians before the conquest of Peru in the manufacture of instruments and utensils (as in Mexico). In many parts of the Andine region arrow-heads, knives, and fragments of this volcanic glass are encountered, even near the coast, where they were doubtless carried

[1] Wolf, *op. cit.*

as articles of primitive merchandise. Sincholagua and Quilindaña, lying farther to the south, are both extinct.

The great Cotopaxi, with its unrivalled cone, is the most terrible and dangerous in Ecuador, and the highest active volcano in the world. From its summit smoke curls upwards unceasingly, and knowledge of its activities begins with South American history after the conquest. The first eruption experienced by the Spaniards was in 1534, during the attempted conquest of the ancient native kingdom of Quito by Alvarado. The Indians regarded the terrible outpourings of the volcano, which coincided with this foreign advent, as a manifestation of Nature in aid of the invaders and against themselves, and this was a factor in breaking down their opposition. But the rain of ashes from the burning mountain greatly troubled the small army of Alvarado for several days, as before described. After this outburst Cotopaxi remained quiescent for more than 200 years, until 1741, when it broke out with extraordinary force, and became for twenty-six years the scourge of the districts of Quito and Latacunga. The province of Leon and Latacunga, which formerly had been among the most beautiful and fertile, became poverty-stricken by reason of the eruptions. These outbreaks generally consisted in a great rain of sand and ash, followed by vast quantities of mud and water, which were thrown over the valleys and plains, destroying whatever lay in the way. Between 1742 and 1768 there were seven great eruptions of this character, and it is noteworthy that none of these were accompanied by earthquakes. The thunderings were heard at Honda, in Colombia, 500 miles away, it is recorded. Cotopaxi then remained quiescent for thirty-five years, until 1803, when Humboldt heard the detonations of a new outbreak, like discharges of a battery, from the gulf of Guayaquil, where he was on board a vessel for Lima. A number of lesser outbreaks occurred during the nineteenth century, but comparatively little record has been kept of them. There were streams of fresh lava, columns of black smoke, and showers of sand sent forth at various periods, and in 1877 a further memorable eruption took place, followed by others up to 1880. It would appear that since the volcano of Tunguragua entered again into action Cotopaxi has been less vigorous. Cotopaxi is regarded by various travellers as one of the most beautiful mountain peaks in the world, its symmetry of out-line rivalling the famous Fuji-yama of Japan, which it overtops by more than 7,000 feet. This Ecuadorian volcano is 2,000 feet higher than Popocateptl, the "smoking mountain" of Mexico, and more than 15,000 feet higher than Vesuvius, and 7,000 higher than Teneriffe. It rises in a symmetrical cone, with a slope of 29° or 30°. Its height, as before given, is 19,613, according to Whymper, and the crater varies from 2,300 feet to 1,650 feet in diameter, and is 1,200 feet deep approximately, bordered by a rim of trachytic rock. The summit of Cotopaxi is generally shrouded in cloud masses, and only visible for a few days even in the clearest season of the year. The volcanic cloud reached a height of 28,000 feet above sea-level. The mountain lies thirty-five miles south-south-east of Quito. In 1802 Humboldt made an unsuccessful attempt to ascend the cone of the volcano, but pronounced the ascent impossible. Boussingault attempted it in 1831, and Wagner in 1858, with a similar result. But the view that Cotopaxi was unconquerable was erroneous, and in 1872 Dr. Reiss reached the summit, followed next year by Dr. Stübel, and by Dr. Wolf in 1877, by Thielmann in 1878, and Whymper in 1880. It is noteworthy that all these ascents were made by foreigners;

indeed, nearly all scientific and exploratory work in Ecuador has been so performed, the native Ecuadorians lacking the initiative or powers to perform such. The gases escaping from the fumaroles of Cotopaxi were closely studied by Wolf.[1]

Quirotoa is an extinct volcano in the western Cordillera, which does not reach the snowline, but its crater encloses a lake of considerable size, of salt water, with an island in its centre, the water being of a temperature of 61° F., much higher than the surroundings. It has been stated by some who observed the crater that the waters of the lake have at various times risen and fallen, covering and exposing the island alternately. Among these was La Condamine. This was, however, doubted by Reiss, who examined the crater, whose steep walls descend for over 1,000 feet, although the surface was found to bubble with the escape of carbonic acid gas, whose effects destroyed animal and vegetable life in the vicinity.

Cerro Hermoso or Llanganati lies in the eastern Cordillera, in a region the least known of any in the republic, its melting snows forming the headwaters of the Curaray and some affluents of the Pastasa River. The altitude is given as 17,843 feet, the highest of a group of summits of which it is the chief. In a lake upon the slopes of this mountain, tradition states, the treasures of the Inca were secreted. Parts of the mountain are impregnated with pyrites, and great mineral riches have been claimed—doubtfully—for it. The western side is said to be as inaccessible as a great wall.[2] An enormous glacier covers this in part.

Chimborazo is the monarch of the western Cordillera, the highest point of the Ecuadorian Andes, reaching to 20,498 feet above sea-level, according to Whymper, or 20,703 according to Reiss and

[1] *Ecuador, op. cit.*   [2] Reiss.

Stübel.   The beautiful form of this mountain rises majestically from the plain and surrounding ridges, and it was long believed to be the highest peak and culminating point of the whole chain of the Andes throughout South America until the Chilean, Bolivian, and Peruvian peaks, before enumerated, were found to be of greater elevation.   The name " Chimborazo " is derived from the Indian designation— *Chimpu-raza,* or the " mountain of snow." The term *raza,* or snow, is also encountered in the Indian name for the high Huascaran peak in Peru of *Mataraza,* or " snow forehead."   The first attempt to ascend Chimborazo was made by Humboldt in 1802, but it was unsuccessful.   All attempts of others failed similarly, until in 1820 Edward Whymper successfully reached the summit.   Chimborazo stands seventy-six miles north-east of Guayaquil, and at times the snowy cone, half-hidden in the clouds, may be seen from the steamer's deck, although this is comparatively rare.[1]   From almost any point of view the mountain is imposing, although from the Pacific slope it can be most fully appreciated, the base being covered with forest up to the snowline, above which the pure white dome rises for a further 5,000 feet. But the view of the mountain is rarely unobstructed, due to the mists and clouds that hang upon it.   Chimborazo is an extinct volcano, and due to the deviation of the plumbline, from only $7''$ to $8''$, it is deduced that the mountain is hollow.   Whymper believed that the craters were of considerable size, although they were not visible.   Formerly this volcano and some others of Ecuador were believed to be homogeneous uplifts, but Whymper observed the lava and andesite strata as built up by successive outpourings. The façades of its precipices are described as presenting a large number of parallel bands, horizontal in the lower part and distorted above, tinged with

[1] So seen by the Author.

CHIMBORAZO, SEEN FROM A HIGH ELEVATION.

[To face p. 182.

bright colours when sunlit, present an attractive appearance. Beds of lava and hot springs at the base appear to confirm the belief that Chimborazo is an extinct volcano.

Immediately to the north of Chimborazo, and separated therefrom only by a narrow valley, arises Carahuairazo, with its triple summits, the centre one of which reaches 16,515 feet. The natives term this volcano *Chimborazo-embra*—that is, " Chimborazo's wife." This peak presents a weird and picturesque appearance with its hollow cone. This collapsed in 1698, it is stated, due to a great earthquake, leaving the present jagged rim. It has been affirmed by early writers that Carahuairazo was originally of greater altitude than its mighty consort, but other writers deny this, and state that the present curious form is the primitive one, which has not suffered any alteration. Notwithstanding its lower elevation, this volcano, due to the conditions attending its western slope, carries an immense quantity of ice and snow, which it is affirmed is greater in volume than that of any other peak of the Ecuadorian Andes. The summit was reached by Whymper in June, 1880, all previous attempts at its ascent having failed.

Tunguragua, the " modern competitor " of Cotopaxi, stands opposite Chimborazo, rising from the eastern Cordillera. It has a cone-shaped summit, somewhat like that of Cotopaxi, with a slope of 38°, and, rising from a plain of somewhat lesser elevation than that of the surrounding central plateau, and standing away from the other eminences, is of exceptionally imposing appearance. Tunguragua, in spite of certain traditions of activity in the eighteenth century, was generally regarded as an extinct volcano, until a frightful eruption in 1886 banished the sense of security. A very old Indian of over a hundred years had informed La Condamine of an eruption

11

in 1641, and there were chronicles of other activities in 1773, when smoke was observed. But from 1781, when the municipality of Riobamba recorded in the archives of Quito that a *gran reventazon,* or bursting out of the volcano had taken place, Tunguragua was silent for more than a hundred years. Suddenly, in January, 1886, the sleeping volcano broke out with terrible fury, and devastated the valley of Baños and its surroundings. Enormous quantities of liquid lava were for months vomited from the crater, forming great fiery currents, which invaded and destroyed the beds of the Patate and Chambo Rivers, damming up their waters into an extensive lake, which, filling up to the brim, overflowed and formed a new channel. A characteristic feature of Tunguragua is a cataract fed by the melting snow which lies upon it, the water leaping in three great cascades over a height of 1,500 feet. The fertile, cultivated valley of Baños below, with its thermal springs, accentuates the aspect of Tunguragua, which has been described by some as the most beautiful of all the snowy peaks of Ecuador. The first to ascend to the crater of this volcano was Dr. Stübel in 1873, and soon afterwards a North American artist passed a night there, taking views.

Some four leagues to the south of Tunguragua lies El Altar, otherwise known by the natives as Capac-Urcu, or the " king-mountain." The term " capac " is familiar to the student of early Peruvian history as having been the designation of the first and succeeding Inca monarchs, such as Manco Capac, Huayna Capac, and others. The broken cone and impressive outline of El Altar render it one of the most picturesque mountains in the country. Stübel termed it " the masterpiece of volcanic creation." It was stated by Humboldt that a tradition existed among the Indians to the effect that the mountain was once higher than Chimborazo, but that a series

of eruptions caused the cone to collapse, lowering
its elevation and giving the present jagged appearance. This event took place—according to the
alleged tradition—fourteen years before the invasion,
near 1460, of the Inca Emperor Huayna Capac.
This falling in of the crater is, however, denied by
other authorities. The summit comprises a group
of eight snowclad peaks, and rises to a greatest
elevation of 17,730 feet. The mountain has a further
name, that of Collanes, which is not a Quechua word,
but belongs to the Aymará language of Bolivia, and
signifies magnificent or sublime. This more ancient
word—for, as described elsewhere, the Aymará preceded the Inca or Quechua—serves to show how
widespread also was the pre-Inca influence in Western
South America. There are many other words and
place names belonging to the Aymará linguistic
region, showing the remote antiquity of intelligent
man in the Andean regions. There have been no
signs of activity in the Altar mountain since the
discovery of America.

Sangay is the southernmost of the active volcanoes
of Ecuador, and is at the same time one of the most
active in the world. Fortunately, the region surrounding it is sparsely populated. According to La
Condamine, its modern activity began in 1728, and
since then manifestations of unrest have never been
entirely interrupted. An outburst of 1739, observed
by the last-named explorer from the *páramo* of Zula,
and described by him, " seemed to set on fire the
whole mountain and its crater, and a burning river
of sulphur and bitumen took its course in the midst
of the snowy slopes." This " burning river " was
doubtless of red-hot lava, however, it is objected by
Wolf. Reiss states that for four years without intermission a stream of incandescent lava flowed from
the western slope, and the engineer Wisse counted,
in 1849, 267 loud explosions in an hour. The

roarings of the volcano were frequently heard in Guayaquil, and the showers of ashes vomited from the crater are at times wafted out upon the Pacific Ocean, as in the case of Cotopaxi and Tunguragua. The eruptions, though frequent, are not of a very severe nature generally, but the volcano is one of peculiar interest to scientific investigators, due to its unceasing activity and by reason of its peculiar position in the Andean system. Surrounded, however, by difficult approaches and broken country, Sangay is but rarely visited. It rises from the eastern Cordillera, and below it to the east is the wild territory at the head of the Amazon affluents.

The volcanic territory south of the above region is very ancient. The *nudo* of Azauy forms an enormous mass of mountains, lying between the eastern and western Cordilleras, and extends its ramifications on all sides. The centre of the mountain knot at Quimsa Cruz reaches 14,200 feet elevation, and is covered with perpetual snow. It is a high, cold *páramo* region, the birthplace of many rivers, and forms the water-parting of the continent, some of the rivers flowing west to the Pacific, others east to the Amazon and the Atlantic.

In Ecuador the numerous earthquakes, known in Spanish as *terremotes* when severe and *temblores* when only of light effect, have rarely been found to have any connection with the eruptions of the volcanoes. None of the great shocks or earth movements in the country's history had any coincidence with the volcanic outbreaks, according to various writers. Nevertheless, there is no doubt that some relation exists between the two phenomena, where both occur together. It has been shown that the Tertiary and Quaternary alluvial deposits which compose the littoral of Ecuador may contain elements conducive to earth unrest. They embody great quantities of substances subject to mechanical and chemical alteration, such as clays, which become softened, lime, salts, and bituminous substances whose volumes may diminish due to solubility, and the resulting tendency to equilibrium may bring about earth-movement. Such operations are exemplified in the peninsula of Santa Elena, where hot springs highly charged with salt exist. From this point alone it has been calculated [1] that with a base of $13\frac{1}{2}$ grammes of salt per litre of water which results from the analysis of the spring water, some $31\frac{1}{2}$ millions of cubic metres of water annually would be discharged, with 8,500,000 quintals of salt, from a relatively small area of land. Such is an example of the possible cause of sinkings in land of this character, giving rise to earthquakes. In the Andes, moreover, the strata in some cases stand almost vertical and exposed, and the heavy rains of the uplands entering therein may influence by their subterranean currents the lower lands of the littoral, where their exit may occur. The presence of the Andes, with its enormous mass and elevation, rising from the depths of the Pacific shore—for in places the sea is very deep in proximity to the coast—is such as would give favourable conditions for setting up tectonic strains and other causes resulting in the almost continuous earth-movements encountered along the several thousand miles of the South American littoral.

The first recorded earthquake in Ecuador was a severe one in the spring of 1541, which took place in the neighbourhood of Antisana, terrifying Gonzalo Pizarro and his companions, who at the time were on their expedition through Canelas to the Napo River. In 1587 Quito was partially destroyed, on the last Sunday in August, by a frightful earthquake in the night, which threw down the houses and strewed the city with dead, affecting the country

Wolf, *op. cit.*

for twenty leagues around. This was followed by a less severe shock in 1628. In 1645 the town of Riobamba was partly destroyed ; buildings were wrecked and numerous persons buried beneath the ruins. In 1651 a series of shocks again afflicted Quito, and, according to the usual custom in Latin American cities during such occurrences, the mayor organized a procession, carrying the image of *Nuestro Señora de Guadalupe*, the saint whose special protection was customarily invoked in times of earthquakes. In 1686 the shocks continued, and another patron saint was chosen ; *San Miguel Arcangel*. In 1660 there was a great eruption of the Pichincha volcano, and from the west side of Sincholagua an enormous fragment of the mountain exploded or fell away, causing in Quito the most terrible earthquake ever experienced at that time. Whether the rockslide caused the earthquake or the earthquake the slide it was impossible to say. From 1661 to 1662 the shocks scarcely ceased, and many buildings and churches were ruined, and again in 1678 a severe shock was experienced. In 1687 the towns of Ambato, Latacunga, and Pelileo suffered, and in 1687 the same towns, with Riobamba, were again visited with shocks, Ambato being completely destroyed, with its surrounding villages. According to a royal *cedula*, 6,500 persons perished in those towns as a result. In 1703, 1736, 1741, 1749, 1755, 1757, and 1786 earthquakes of varying severity visited the same places, leaving a trail of ruined churches and houses and many dead. From April to June of 1786 as many as 110 shocks were recorded. In 1797 Riobamba was completely ruined by a shock. The ruins were visited by Humboldt five years afterwards, and it is recorded that 6,000 persons perished. Great exaggerations of deaths were commonly made during these occurrences, estimates rising to 40,000. In 1802, 1803, and 1840 other shocks occurred in various places, and the newly built town of Riobamba experienced such. In 1859 Quito was again visited; all the churches were ruined; their towers toppled to the pavements. In 1868 the earthquake of Tulcan took place, and a terrible catastrophe rendered desolate the province of Imbabura. Ibarra, the capital, Otavalo, and other flourishing places were converted in a minute of time into heaps of rubbish, and thousands of their inhabitants were crushed in the ruins, the number of bodies having been estimated as 15,000 to 20,000. Nearly all these disasters occurred in the higher places, for, due to the light construction of dwelling-places on the tropical coast, where houses are of wood, the numerous earthquakes caused but little damage. In the records of Guayaquil no such terrible occurrences are noted. Moreover, the earthquakes on the coast have been more of the nature of *temblores* than of the more disastrous *terremotes*. This catalogue of earth-movements—which is more than duplicated in Peru, to the south—seems to show the unstable conditions of the Andean territory and the risk to human life and property therein from causes of earth unrest. Although a low type of construction prevails, it is plain that the inhabitants of such regions have not yet evolved earthquake-proof houses, and there is undoubtedly room for experimental science in this field.

There may be some material advantages for the future in the peculiar topographical configuration which the high countries of the Andes embody, with the advance of physical and engineering science, matters perhaps little suspected hitherto. The opinion may be ventured [1] that science may reveal sources of power or other economic advantage from the vast differences of elevation such as are encoun-

---

[1] This point was enlarged upon in the author's *Andes and the Amazon, op. cit.*

tered in the Andine (or other mountainous) countries. It may be that some " difference of potential,"
due to the reaching up so far into the ether as do
these mountain uplands, will yet be evolved. There
may be hidden agencies, powers, and natural influ-
ences, hidden sources of fertility or mineral uses,
or of electric, hydrographic, or gravitational phenomena which may yet come into the scope of everyday
life to the benefit of humanity—sources and agencies
still concealed in these dreary *páramos* and lofty
ridges of the Andes. Volcanic energy, moreover,
may yet be used in the service of man. Hydraulic
power is, of course, abundant, and electricity in the
atmosphere very marked at times.

The effect of the high elevation on man, and also
upon animals, is noteworthy. On the human
organism it gives rise to various disorders, among
which is that known in the Andes as soroche, or
mal de montaña. This is a troublesome, painful,
and at times dangerous malady, taking the form of
very severe headache and vomiting, with palpitation,
weakness, and even heart failure, among those who
suffer from it.[1] Some persons, however, are by
nature immune from soroche. Whymper made a
special study of mountain sickness as experienced in
Ecuador.[2] There are other effects of high environment of some interest. It is established that the
pugnacious instinct, the predatory and quarrelsome
character, both of men and animals, is greatly
weakened at these elevations. The inhabitants of
high mountainous regions are hardy, but at the same
time patient and long-suffering. This is well typified
in the Andes. The great mountain empire of the
Incas was the most beneficent that history has produced, and the evolved arts were perhaps the most
remarkable in early America.

[1] See *The Andes and the Amazon*.
[2] *The High Andes of Ecuador*.

CHAPTER XI

THE ECUADORIAN ORIENTE

HAVING examined the coastal and mountainous regions of Ecuador, a description must now be entered upon of the Oriente, or eastern portion of the republic, embodying an extremely wild and savage territory. The Andes, in their northern development in Ecuador and Colombia, throw off numerous great spurs and ravines north of the *nudo* or knot of Loja, with rapid-flowing rivers descending the slopes, crossing the country and the plains on roughly parallel lines as navigable waterways from north-west to south-east. These great streams fall, one after the other, into the Amazon. Enumerated in their order from west to east, these rivers are : the Chinchipe, the Santiago, the Morona, the Pastaza, the Chambira, the Tigre, the Nanay, and the Napo. Several smaller streams follow, and continuing the same parallelism is the Putumayo, and beyond it the Yapurá or Caquetá, as also the Negro in Brazil. The series of rivers forms an important topographical feature of this part of South America, constituting the north-west periphery of the great Amazon basin.

The principal rivers of this system rise in the Ecuadorian Andes and flow for long distances through the Ecuadorian Oriente—a territory in part claimed by Peru and in parts by Colombia, as before remarked. Considerable economic value attaches to these rivers by reason of their navigability, giving access by steamer, and beyond that in boats and canoes, to the

enormous areas of forest and plain which they traverse. The Morona, the Pastaza, the Tigre, the Napo,
the Putumayo, the Caquetá, and the Negro, are
generally full-flowing rivers, navigable for great distances into this north-west territory.

The Chinchipe rises to the south of Loja in an angle
formed by the Cordillera Real, or eastern Cordillera,
with the Cordillera of Condor on the Sabanilla *nudo*.
It rises under various names and receives a number
of tributaries and flows in a general direction nearly
south, crosses the (provisional) Ecuador-Peru frontier
and falls into the Marañon, somewhat below that point
where the Marañon, leaving its long, non-navigable
north-westerly course, parallel with the great ranges
of the Peruvian Andes, turns to the north-east to enter
upon the Amazon plain. Below the confluence of the
Chinchipe and the Numbala the river carries a considerable volume of water, and the *pueblo* of Zumba
is found lower down. It is shortly joined by the River
Canches, which descends from the Cordillera, a considerable stream which forms the provisional Peru-
Ecuador frontier line.[1] The river is crossed by the
road from Zumba to Huancabamba, and near this
point lies the *pueblo* of Chito. Below the large San
Francisco tributary enters from the east, a little-known
stream, rising in the Cordillera of Condor. The Chinchipe is further swollen by numerous small streams,
in whose valleys various *haciendas* exist but at an
elevation somewhat above the general level of the
Chinchipe, which has a reputation for being unhealthy.
Along the left bank runs the road or trail leading to
Zumba, to Jaen de Bracamoros, San Ignacio, and
Chirinos. To the south the little-known Chirinos
tributary enters from the west, and the Tabaconas,
which was formerly confused with the Huancabamba,
which enters the Marañon more to the south of Jaen.
From its confluence with the Tabaconas, the Chin-

[1] "*La frontera pretendida de parte del Peru.*" Wolf, *Ecuador*.

chipe is broader and navigable to its junction with the
Marañon. The Huancabamba runs in the valley
formed by two ranges of the Cordillera, and the
pueblo of the same name is situated on its upper
portion, with that of Chamayo near its mouth in the
Marañon. This region is occupied by Peru. At an
elevation of 3,200 feet above sea-level lies the town
of Jaen. The original place of this name was
destroyed by savages.

The Santiago River (not to be confused with that on
the coast) rises near the town of Loja on the Zamora
River, and passes through the Cordillera Oriental,
flowing east and then south-east. The region included between the two Cordilleras and the two
" knots " is the valley or basin of Loja, and the town
and capital of the province of the same name lies
at 7,300 feet elevation. Many streams fall into the
Zamora, and, with the Gualaquiza and the Paute, the
Santiago River takes on its considerable volume. The
Gualaquiza, descending from the high Cordillera,
flows between deeply scarped valleys surrounded by
high peaks, and upon its banks various *pueblos* are
found, among them that of Rosario. Some ten
leagues from the Cordillera the valley widens and
forms what may be regarded as one of the largest
Oriental plains of the country. It is joined by the
Bombisa, and five leagues below enters the Zamora.
The Paute has as its main upper tributary the Matadero River, rising in the Western Cordillera. Its
source lies among some small lakes, and flowing thence
through the picturesque valley of Quinuas, it breaks
through the Cordillera. Its upper tributaries drain
the Cuenca *hoya* or basin, and break through the
eastern Cordillera north of the Zamora break. This
river is topographically distinguished by the fact that
its source is nearer to the Pacific Ocean than any
other river which flows to the Atlantic, its headwaters
being only some thirty miles in a straight line from

the gulf of Guayaquil. Here the remarkable hydrographic conditions of this part of South America are
seen. The Yanucay and Tarqui affluents join the
river near Cuenca. From the Tarqui *llanura* or plain
on its northern edge, and on the left bank of the
Tarqui River, arises a small conical hill known as *el
cerro de la pyramide* or pyramid hill, from the small
monument erected on its summit, which was the terminating southern point of the French triangulation
in the arc-measurement to determine the form of the
earth in the eighteenth century. Near the triple confluence of the Tarqui, the Matadero, and the Yanuncay,
forming the River Paute, is situated the beautiful
capital of the province, the town of Cuenca, at an
elevation of 8,500 feet above sea-level. Cuenca is
the third city of importance in the republic. Numerous
streams fall into the Paute, among them the Azogues,
near the town of that name, and the Gualaceo, above
which are some gold placer mines. Gualaceo is a
pretty town at 7,650 feet elevation, in a beautiful
valley, and is surrounded by fruit-trees. Various
streams of considerable size swell the Paute before it
breaks through the Cordillera on its eastward way,
such as the Dudas and others which flow from inaccessible and uninhabited regions. The Yanguay hill,
11,000 feet elevation, the crowning-point of the chain
near by, affords a wide view, with an immense horizon,
especially towards the eastern Cordillera and over
the Cuenca valley, as upon a map stretched out below.
To the east is seen the Paute, and on its banks the
old lazarette known as " Jordan " and the Santa Rita
hacienda, almost the last outpost of civilization towards the east. Below this the river takes a great
turn and suddenly rushes through the profound opening in the Cordillera. The remarkable Allcuquiru
promontory, forming the bend in the river, exhibits a
crest of " peaks, horns, needles, and teeth," whose
Quechua name is expressive of its appearance. To

the north lies what is almost a deserted and unknown world, the ranges that go out from the Azuay heights. Beyond, arising as the background of this strange amphitheatre, is seen the Cordillera Real of the Andes with its high snowy crest. Upon the water-parting of the Cañar River—which flows to the Pacific —standing upon a promontory, lies the ancient fortress of the Incas known as "Incapirca," at an elevation of nearly 10,800 feet, whose ruins, elsewhere described, are one of the most interesting monuments of pre-Hispanic times in the history of Ecuador.

The Santiago River, whose affluents traverse the interesting region of eastern Ecuador above described of the Cuenca and Loja basins, is called by the *infieles* or savage Indians, Canusayacu, and is not much better known than its upper affluents. After passing the Cordillera, it is joined by the Zamora, which river enters upon the plains and joins the Gualaquiza, the valley of which may be considered the beginning of the great eastern plains. The Santiago, running south-south-east, falls into the Marañon, near the celebrated Manseriche *pongo* or rapids. These rapids and the Marañon River are described elsewhere. Near this point at one period existed the town of Santiago, which shared the same fate as the town of Borja, in having been destroyed by the savages. The Santiago is described as being navigable as far as the confluence with its principal tributaries.

The next river of this group, which descends from the north to the Marañon, is the Morona. Its tributaries rise in the eastern Cordillera. One of these, the Manguasisa, has its source on the north-east of Sangay, at 13,200 feet elevation, and the other, the Cangaima, on the north of the Azuay knot, at 14,200 feet. Above the confluence with these tributaries the system enters upon the plains, and the Morona continues its course through the plains in a general south-east direction, with a very tortuous

course, falling into the lower Marañon in (about) latitude 4° 46' south, and longitude west (Greenwich)
7° 00'. From the point of union with the large
tributaries above named it runs for 300 miles, and is
swollen by many lesser affluents, some of which are
navigable by canoes, such as the Rarayacu, the Yarina,
the Tacshashi-Nuasi, the Shihuasi, Sicuanga, the
Pushaga—which communicates with Lake Rimachuna
or Rimache-cocha—and, lastly, the Maruzaga. The
Morona is navigable for steamers of 2 ft. to 4 ft.
draught at high-water period, as far as the Manguasisa, or 300 miles, and at low water as far as
Rarayacu, nearly 200 miles.[1] The Manhuasisa is
navigable for craft of the same size for about
seventy-five miles, and the Cangayma for fifty-five
miles from the confluence with the Morona.

Due to the tortuous course of the Morona the navigable stretches of 300 miles represent about 120
miles in a straight line. The first recorded navigation
of the river was made by the Ecuadorian General
Victor Proaña in 1861, and in 1874 a Peruvian Commission in the steamers *Napo* and *Mayro* ascended the
river to the confluence of the Cusulima and Manguasisa.[1] At the period when all this part of the
country was covered by flourishing missions the town
of Sevilla de Oro existed where now lies the *pueblo*
of Macas. This village is upon a plain on the Upano
River, which rises in the high Cordillera north-east
of Azuay, at an elevation of 3,470 feet. The Upano,
with its various tributaries, forms the higher portion
of the Morona. The destruction of a Peruvian outpost near the Morona, in February, 1913, is mentioned elsewhere.

The great Pastaza River has its rise between the
eastern and western Cordilleras, near the Equator,
in the *hoyas* of Latacunga and Riobamba, at

[1] *El Peru en* 1906. Garland : Lima.
[2] As recounted in Raimondi's book.

more than 14,800 feet above sea-level. It breaks
through the Cordillera to the north of Tunguragua,
leaps the Argoyan falls, and entering its cañon at
5,100 feet elevation, debouches thence upon the
plains. This district is but little known, but the
distance from the pass through the Cordillera to
the confluence with the Bombonazo is some sixty
miles. Flowing thence with a southern course, with
bends to the east and west, the river reaches the
lower Marañon in latitude 4° 53′ 40″ south. Its main
tributaries are the Lusin, the Palora, the Puque, the
Bombonaza, the Pinche, the Upiazaco, the Huasaga,
the Viluyacu, and the Copalyacu. At high-water
periods the river is navigable for steamers of two
to four feet draught, as far as the Huasaga,
120 miles, and for 30 miles at low water.
Canoes navigate the river for 200 miles beyond
Hausaga.

This interesting fluvial system of the Pastaza,
draining the Latacunga, Ambato, and Riobamba
basins, has as its main upper sources from the north
the River Cutuchi, which becomes the Patate below
Latacunga, and the River Chambo and its tributaries
from the south. The Patate rises on the western
slopes of Cotopaxi, and the Cutuchi on the southern
slopes of Iliniza, the great snowy peaks before
described. The chief tributary of the Cutuchi is
the Ambato River, united with the Panchalica, and the
Ambato rises among the snows of the western slopes
of Chimborazo and its consort Carihuairazo. The
Salazaca, a tributary which descends from Carihuairazo, passes the *pueblo* of Mocha, famous in
Inca history as a strategic point. The Chambo
drains the Riobamba *hoya*. Its headwaters are
known as the Yaguar-cocha, by reason of its
passage through the lake of that name. It unites
with the Guamote, which is fed by a subterranean
outlet from the Colta lake. This is one of the

largest of the inter-Andine lakes, about $1\frac{1}{4}$ miles long, standing 10,850 feet above sea-level. But the arid slopes and the entire lack of trees form a landscape among the most melancholy and unattractive. From the confluence of the Guamote with the Cebadas the river takes the name of Chambo, which it maintains to where it falls into the Patate. The Chambo receives tributaries which descend from the snows of the high Altar, and before its confluence with the Patate it curves round the base of Tunguragua. The largest tributary of the Chambo on the western bank is the Chibunga, which rises in the snows of Chimborazo. The town of Riobamba, capital of the province, lies a few miles from the river at an elevation of 9,240 feet above sea-level, and is elsewhere described.

The Pastaza, below the confluence with its tributaries, at an elevation of 5,940 feet, cuts the eastern Cordillera from west to east by a deep valley, which extends for some twenty-four miles between the spurs which are thrown off from Tunguragua and the Cordillera of Llanganates. Here the Pastaza is also known as the Agoyan River, as far as the great cataract of that name. At this point the river, narrowed between sombre precipices, leaps downwards for 190 feet at a bound, a spectacle of much grandeur, especially when beheld from the lower side, the immense quantity of falling water being transformed into white foam. This is one of the most picturesque places in the Andes, its appearance heightened by the vegetation, which, at this elevation of 5,120 feet, takes on a tropical character. A number of streams fall into the Pastaza below the falls from its northern side, some of which have been named above. The Verde is long and comes from the *páramos* of Llanganates and Cerro Hermoso, and the Nieve from Altar. From the confluence with the Bombonaza a *varadero*, or portage-trail for canoes, runs to the Tigre River and to Cononaco on the navigable Curaray and thence to San Pedro on the Aguarico. The Bombonaza affluent rises near the village of Canelos, the old mission centre, running for a long distance parallel with the upper Pastaza, a few miles to the north. Its course is tortuous but quiet, flowing through a flat region and navigable for canoes. Near its confluence with the Pastaza is the *pueblo* of Andoas, which in the history of the missions was more important than at present. There are various miserable *pueblos* of Indians on its banks. Lower down the Sugachi and two other streams enter the Pastaza, and this first-named is long and navigable for some distance. On the right bank of the Pastaza below this point there are some large lakes, communicating with the river by the natural *caños* or canals which are a feature of the hydrography of the Amazon plains. Among these is the Rimachumac lake, some eight leagues in length, lying between the Pastaza and the Morona, communicating with both by means of the *caños*. Near the confluence with the Marañon the Huarama enters the Pastaza, also the Mahuaca, on the eastern banks, said to be equal in size to the Bombonanza.

The Pastaza was navigated by Don Pedro Maldonado during his journey in the Amazon in 1741, and his map formed the basis of knowledge about it. In 1845 and 1848 Fray Castrucci ascended it in mission to the savage Indians of Canelos. In 1873 the Peruvian steamer *Mayro* ascended for a few leagues, the captain being Mr. Butt, an Englishman, who described the river as being as wide as the Marañon, but with a channel very difficult for navigation in times of low water, due to sudden rise and fall, the steamer having shoaled various times. These irresistible floods are the result of suddenly swollen mountain torrents from the Andes, and the silt brought down by the current form shoals. This

12

difficulty of navigability is questioned by Raimondi,[1] who states that the river is navigable at all seasons for canoes, and that at earlier periods a fortnightly " mail " service was kept up with Andoas. But undoubtedly the fury of the river in flood times is great. The ancient name of the Pastaza was the Sumatara. The river crosses the provisional Ecuador-Peru boundary.

The River Tigre differs from the foregoing in belonging altogether to the plains region, but its remotest affluents rise in the eastern Cordillera. It is an important stream, although its volume is not comparable with the Pastaza and the Napo, lying to the west and to the east respectively. Its mouth lies forty-two miles west of the confluence of the Ucayali, the great tributary belonging to Peru, coming from the south with the Amazon or Marañon. The Tigre is navigable for steamers of four to eight feet draught[2] for over 400 miles from its mouth ; and at high-water period, and for the same distance at low-water period, for a draught of two to four feet, up to the confluence of the Cunambo and Pintuyacu. To this is added 100 miles under the same conditions for its tributary the Corrientes and forty miles for the Pucasuro, and with a further 1,260 miles of tributaries, navigable by canoes, reaches a total length of available waterway of 1,800 miles. Being navigable at all stages to the Cunambo-Pintuyacu confluent, the Tigre forms an extremely valuable river route for Ecuador. In 1873 the steamer *Mayro*, under Captain Butt, ascended the river for 104 miles, and the channel is described as wide and deep at all seasons. Until recently little more was known about the river, but the region traversed is a rich one in natural products. The Pintuyacu and Cunambo sources lie between the left

[1] Raimondi, *El Peru.*
According to A. Garland, *El Peru in 1906.*

division of the Upper Pastaza and the right of the upper course of the Napo. The river takes a general course to the south-east and passes the ravine of Hunguraque, and before emptying into the Marañon in latitude 4° 26' south, receives 109 tributaries. The principal of these tributaries are the Pucacuro and the Corrientes. The first-named flows in the same general direction as the main stream, entering on the north bank. At its upper end the Pucacuro is crossed by the *varadero*, before mentioned, from Andoas, on the Pastaza. The Corrientes comes in much below this point on the south bank, draining the broad territory between the Pastaza and the Tigre. A small tributary, the Puma-Yacu, flows in upon the same side below the Corrientes. The Tigre crosses the provisional Ecuador-Peru line.

The course of the Marañon and the Tigre form a vast semicircle, and within this flows the Nanay. This river belongs altogether to the plains region, and its course is very tortuous, with a slow current. The channel is narrow, in places widening out so as to form what is in appearance a chain of lakes. It was ascended by the *Mayro*, under Captain Butt, for 105 miles, from its confluence with the Amazon to near its source. Its volume is due to the drainage or overflow in flood-times of the large region traversed, whose numerous lagoons overflow into it. In spite of the abundance of water the banks of the river are high. The climate of the district is described as healthy, with an almost entire absence of malaria. The Nanay falls into the Amazon close to Iquitos, slightly below that port, and lies outside the Ecuador-Peru (provisional) line. The Itaya River is a much smaller tributary of the Marañon, entering near the Nanay somewhat up-stream of Iquitos. The *Mayro* entered for thirty-eight miles, to where the course is obstructed by masses of drift-wood.

The River Napo is an important waterway as regards the economic regimen of the part of South America it traverses, and as set forth elsewhere, it is politically important as forming the (provisional) boundary-line of the republic on the north-east. Historically the Napo is of much interest as having been the route by which the South American continent was first traversed. The exploits of Orellana, the lieutenant of Gonzalo Pizarro, who reached the Atlantic from Quito by floating down the Napo to the Amazon, and of Pedro de Texiera, who ascended it, are famous in the history of exploration. Orellana's voyage has been described in the historical section ; that of Texiera is mentioned later on. The Napo was for a long time considered to be the *rio madre*, or longest tributary of the Amazon fluvial system, until further exploration determined the existence of the more extensive affluents of the Amazon in Brazil and Peru.

The Napo has its sources on the slopes of the Ecuadorian volcanoes Cotopaxi, Antisana, Sincholagua and Quilindaña, part of the group of peaks of the colossal Cordilleras, which form the water-parting of South America. These streams are fed by the perpetual snows of the volcanoes, the principal being the Antisana River, that of Valle-Vicioso, that of the Juntas, and that of Chalupas, and there are others coming from the south. These high regions or *páramos* are of the bleak and inclement character common to the Andean uplands, descending rapidly, however, to the *montaña* or thickly wooded regions. The small village of Napo lies at the verge of this region at the foot of the Cordillera, about 108 miles from the source, and it is at that point that canoe navigation begins, the upper reaches being too swift and obstructed for such purpose. The river at Napo is about 1,500 feet above sea-level. From Napo to the confluence of the Coca is a distance of

some sixty miles or more. From the south side enter
the Ausupi, the Arazuni, and other smaller streams.
In addition to the village of Napo are those of
Aguano, Napotea, Santa Rosa — the largest — and
Suno, on the left bank. The Coca descends from
the north, rising in the profound gorges of Cayambe
and the slopes of Sara-Urcu. There are other
affluents in this region, both from north and south,
some of them of considerable size, which flow through
extremely broken territory, access to which is difficult
owing to the dense vegetation and the precipitous
character of the territory. The Maspa, coming from
the south-west and having its source in the *páramos*
around Antisana, is one of the principal of these.
The northernmost tributary of the Coca crosses the
Equator not far from its source. Near the confluence of the Maspa and the Coca are the old ruins
of Baeza, and higher up the road from Quito to Napo
crosses the Maspa. The Papallacta is a tributary
of the Maspa, and upon its banks is the *pueblo* of
that name. At the confluence of the Coca and the
Napo the river is some 860 feet above sea-level.
From Napo to this point three considerable streams
enter the Napo River from the north—the Hollin,
the Suno, and the Payamino, with other smaller
ones, and from the south the Arayuno and others.
The region lying between the Maspa, Coca, and
Napo formed in colonial times the provinces of
Quijos and Avila, and at present forms the Napo
misiones or missions. This particular section is
described as "a beautiful region long since known
and visited by botanists and zoologists, and of much
importance for Ecuador, but of which no exact plan
or topographical data exist." [1] It is in these regions
of the *montaña* in Ecuador, as in Peru far to the
south, that the influence of the Romish Church and
of the *Cristianos* ends, and that of the *salvajes* or

[1] Wolf's *Geographia del Ecuador*, 1892.

infieles, the aborigines of the Amazon valley, begins. The Coca was the route followed by the expedition of Gonzalo Pizarro.

United with the Coca, near the village of that name, the Napo flows south-eastwardly to the confluence of the Aguarico, the river at this point being about 590 feet above sea-level. The Aguarico is a large, powerful stream, similar in size to the Napo, rising near Cayambe and near the frontier of Colombia. It 'flows for a considerable distance parallel with the Coca, some fifty miles to the north, crosses the Equator near longitude 77°, and receives a number of tributaries which swell its volume. It is described as being navigable for seventy miles from the confluence with the Napo, slightly below the Equator, such as the Cuyabeno and the Zancudo on the left bank and the Hena and the Cavinayacu on the right. At the confluence with the Aguarico is the *pueblo* or village of San Pedro, which at one period of its existence was destroyed. From San Pedro runs the *varadero* or portage, practicable to the Curaray River. This river is an important tributary of the Napo, entering the right bank from the east. At this point the river is 500 feet above sea level. The Curaray rises in the Cordillera of Llanganates, but little is known about it. It is, however, given as being navigable for steamers of two to four feet draught for 275 miles as far as Cononaco. Its current is swift, its mouth at the confluence wide, with three or four fathoms of water. Somewhat below this confluence the Napo approaches nearest to the Putumayo, a distance of some fifty or sixty miles intervening, and by means of intervening tributaries and a *varadero* communication between the two rivers is obtainable. By a route of this nature the rubber-bearing region of the Putumayo is accessible from the Napo, which route is a shorter one to the important Peruvian town of Iquitos than that of the Putumayo River itself. From the Putumayo to the Napo, below San Pedro, passage is also possible by means of a *varadero* to the Santa Maria, a long tributary of the Napo, entering upon the left bank. Such routes are, of course, only practicable for canoes, and are used by the rubber-gatherers. Below the confluence of the Curaray the provisional line of the Ecuador-Peru boundary is encountered at Huiririma Chico.

The Napo, from its confluence with the Coca, runs through flat, forest-covered plains, and from the river not a hill is to be seen. The banks are uniformly level, their monotony relieved only by the mouths of entering tributaries, or lagoons and swamps. In that portion of its course described as lying provisionally in Peruvian territory there are various tributaries entering on either hand. The general course is south-east. As regards the conditions of navigability of the Napo and other rivers of the Oriente, it is to be recollected that there is a tendency to the exaggeration of the mileage over which craft may journey in all the Amazon tributaries. It is often the case that during the high-water periods streams are navigable for small launches but impossible when the current is low in the dry season. Canoes and rafts, moreover, may be forced with difficulty among shoals, rocks, and rapids, and this constitutes "navigation" to a certain extent. The Napo, however, is navigable from the Amazon up to the confluence of the Curaray, about 216 miles,[1] and perhaps a few miles farther. Another authority [2] states that it is navigable at high-water periods as far as Aguarico, 900 kilometres, or 558 miles, for river steamers drawing four to eight feet of water, and at low-water periods for 800 kilometres. Other writers describe journeys wherein sandbanks were

[1] *Encyc. Brit.,* "Amazon."
[2] Garland, *El Peru en 1906.*

encountered, and also speak of small steam-launches reaching Santa Rosa on the upper Napo.[1]

One of the principal authorities on Ecuador [2] states that the Napo presents no difficulty for navigation up to the mouth of the Curaray, and probably up to the mouth of the Coca. On a recent map [3] the limit of steam navigation is shown as beyond Santa Rosa on the Coca, and near the Equator on the Aguarico, and considerably beyond Cononaco on the Curaray. Between the Coca and the Curaray there are snags, and sandbanks, and islands covered with dense jungle, and numerous backwaters, and natural canals or *caños*. In the rainy season these are partly covered by the rising flood, which greatly increases the width of the river. Santa Rosa may be reached by canoe, often with difficulty, and at this point the traveller who has descended from the uplands of Quito embarks to reach the Amazon. Canoes may ascend the Coca as far as its deep canyon between the mountains, where falls occur.

In a Peruvian account of the Napo made in 1902 [4] it is stated that this river has been an " apple of discord " between Ecuador and Peru. The river is there given as navigable for steamers drawing a fathom of water as far as the mouth of the Aguarico, and from that point to the Coca of launches drawing three feet. The channel is stated to be very irregular and tortuous, offering no small difficulty to navigation. The numerous islands formed by the river are a further cause of obstruction, but nevertheless the river is described as a " magnificent means of communication with Ecuador and Colombia."

In the times of the missions, in past centuries, numerous journeys were made up the Napo. Among

[1] Orton.   [2] Wolf.
[3] By the Sociedad Geografica de Lima, Peru.
[4] *Documentos oficiales del Departamento de Loreto.*

the explorers of the river in the nineteenth century.
were Osculate in 1848 and Orton in 1867, who descended from Quito to the Amazon by this route.
In 1875 the steamer *Mayro*, under Señor Raygada,
ascended it to the confluence of the Curaray, 216
miles up-stream, calculating the actual traverse of
the vessel among the windings of the stream. This
voyage was followed by that of other steamers. The
plan of the river and its affluents is very imperfectly
surveyed.

The Putumayo River, paralleling the Napo on the
east, traverses territory whose ownership, as before
remarked, is debatable, but upon some maps it is
shown as within Ecuadorian territory. It is scarcely
necessary to describe the river here in detail. It
rises near Pasto in the Andes of Colombia, and
flows for nearly a thousand miles, largely through the
territory claimed by Colombia and Peru, entering the
Amazon in Brazil. The river crosses the Equator in
its upper portion, and is navigable for canoes above
that point and for steamers for a vast distance above
the confluence with the Amazon. The tract of territory lying upon the river and some of its larger
tributaries was the scene of the terrible atrocities
practised upon the Huitoto Indians [1] by the rubber
merchants. These agents worked under the auspices
of a company of Peruvian origin floated in London
with a capital of £1,000,000, having a British board
of directors. The inquiry which took place before
a committee of the House of Commons [2] in 1913
resulted in the censure of the British directors, and
the company was wound up.

The River Marañon, whilst it is not generally shown
as belonging in any part to Ecuador, is shown on

[1] See *The Devil's Paradise*, by W. E. Hardenburg. T. Fisher
Unwin : London, 1913.

[2] The Author was called as a witness before the Committee to
give evidence on the sociological condition of the Peruvian Indians.

various maps [1] as forming the boundary of that country with Peru, and is claimed by Ecuador in this connection. Some account of the Marañon is necessary to a proper understanding of the eastern river system of Ecuador. The river, where below latitude 6° south it crosses the boundary line of the old kingdom of Quito, has a course in a direction south-south-east to where it reaches Jaen (new) in latitude 5° 36′. In this stretch it receives from the west side the Huancabamba and Chamaya Rivers, and thence the Marañon flows past the *pueblo* of Bellavista to the north-east. The elevation of the river hereabouts is 1,450 feet above sea-level. Some seven miles lower down the Marañon is joined by the Utcubamma on the right bank, and a short distance beyond by the great Chinchipe, and falls in a distance covering three leagues of latitude some 260 feet, showing the rapidity of its upper course. This rapid fall is demonstrated by a series of rapids, from the mouth of the Chinchipe to Borja, which point is below the mouth of the Santiago. The current runs between high walls, which narrow the stream, forming rapids dreaded by canoe navigators, and known as *pongos*. The first of these is the Retema *pongo*, which had never been passed by any craft until the engineer Wertheman and his companions, at great risk of life, descended it in 1878, and passed the successive, dangerous rapids which exist as far as the confluence of the Chuchunga, some thirty-five miles beyond. Only the strength of the raft in which the adventurous voyagers made the passage prevented their destruction. Raymondi's account [2] states that the raft was carried along at frightful velocity, thrown into whirlpools and against rocks, where a halt was im-

---

[1] Among them, that of the *Bulletin* No. 64 of the Bureau of American Republics (Pan American Union), Washington, 1894. The *Bulletin* describes Ecuador as extending to 5° 30′ south lat.

[2] Raymondi, *Peru*, vol. iii.

possible until a quieter portion of the current was entered. This was only the prelude to a worse passage, for, immediately afterwards, the voyagers heard the roar of a cataract, the current quickened and narrowed again, running in a deep, rocky chasm with vertical walls, at whose end the river appeared to vanish from view. Suddenly the raft dashed upon the edge of a cascade, from which arose a dense mist from the falls, which fell with a thunderous sound below. So great was the force of the current and the volume of water that the raft was carried down on the curving surface of the river and flung over the falls, where fortunately it fell flat and continued to float in the rapids, the occupants escaping with their lives. This cascade is known as the Pongo de Mayasi.

Below this point the river widens, and the valley of the Chuchunga is approached. Here M. Condamine embarked on his journey down the Amazon in the eighteenth century. Various other *pongos* and narrows are encountered, but much less dangerous than the above, and the hills retire, an immense *pampa* opening to the view, limited only by the horizon. The river is sown with islands, dividing it into many branches, the current has a velocity of three miles per hour, and the low banks are covered with impenetrable woods. The course from the Chinchipe lies to the north-east, turning more to the east as the confluence of the Santiago is reached, below which the formidable *Pongo de Manseriche* lies. This *pongo* or rapids is the gateway of the upper Marañon, and lies between the Santiago mouth and the old town of Borja, and is generally described in all geographies of the country. The chasm which the Marañon here traverses is a natural cutting through the easternmost Andine chain. It has always been feared by voyagers but was passed by Wertheman, who afterwards endeavoured to ascend it in a steam-launch. With a

Peruvian Commission on board the *Napo* steamer,
Wertheman ascended the Marañon from Iquitos, and
reached the foot of the rapids with ease. Slightly
below Borja, which *pueblo*, founded in 1619, was at
various times destroyed by the savages of the region,
the river runs in a single channel with a velocity of
four miles an hour, and has a width of 1,000 feet,
enclosed by a high chain of hills. Above Borja the
natural canal is a perfect cutting effected in the Cordillera to a depth of nearly 2,000 feet ; the current
increases to from six to twelve miles an hour, and the
channel narrows to 100 feet. The rock walls arise
vertically, and by an optical illusion seem almost to
meet overhead, and the daylight is obscured, giving a
singular and menacing aspect to this gargantuan
throat of the Andes. The *Napo* arrived midway in
the passage when a great wall of rock was observed
in mid-stream as if the passage were closed, whilst
the current formed a powerful whirlpool at the point
of its division by the crag. Under full steam and
with the greatest difficulty, the boat passed this dangerous point, but not without severe damage caused
from striking against the rock. Having passed the
dreaded *peña* or rock, the voyagers thought the
passage accomplished, but a mile above it the current
became still swifter, and the utmost efforts of the
vessel were unable to overcome it. The *Napo* then
returned down-stream, past the dangerous rock. The
commandant of the *Napo*, Señor Carbajal, and
Wertheman, calculated the difference of level between
the rock and Borja as twenty-eight feet in two miles,
and arrived at the conclusion that only a steamboat purposely constructed could ascend the stream, and that
the passage must in general be regarded as imprac-
ticable. Otherwise it was shown that the Marañon
can be navigated without danger, and for nine months
in the year, by river steamers of considerable size
from Iquitos to Borja, and for the three remaining

months of the dry season from Calentura, near the mouth of the Morona, not far below, for smaller steamers. Consequently, Borja is the westernmost river port, and the highest, of the Marañon or Amazon, its elevation being 650 feet above sea-level. The distance of this place in a direct line across the Andes to the Pacific Ocean at Payta is only about 250 miles, whilst the navigable Amazon below it extends for some 2,500 miles to the Atlantic. The Peruvian Government have long had under consideration a railway from Payta to this point, which line would be of much strategic and commercial value to Peru,[1] and, indeed, to the whole Amazon basin.

From Borja, over a vast stretch of country to the mouth of the Ucayali, the Marañon takes a general easterly course over four degrees of latitude, although there is a bend towards the south near the confluence with the Huallaga. The channel of the river, which in this region is not bordered by hills, is of variable width, divided in places by the numerous islands which stud it. The rivers falling into the Marañon from the Ecuadorian side have already been described, and from the Peruvian bank the principal are the Huallaga and the Ucayali, draining enormous areas of territory in eastern Peru, and flowing with a northerly course. At the confluence of the Napo with the Marañon the Largartos Island divides the two streams. The width of the two channels together of the Marañon, measured by La Condamine, was 6,000 feet, and of the Napo, 4,000 feet. The points of confluence of the Amazon, with its great tributaries, such as the Napo, Pastaza, Morona, etc., look almost like open seas of fresh water, and for so vast a distance inland are remarkable. Between the Ucayali and Napo confluence the Marañon turns and runs sharply to the north, again serpentining, at the last-named point, to

[1] The author was requested by the Government of Peru to undertake a reconnaissance for the line in 1906.

the east. Below Omaguas, near the Ucayali confluence, the width further increases and high waves form during storms. Near the confluence of the Yavari lies the Peru-Brazil frontier line, Peru extending to Tabatinga.

The voyage of Orellana down the Amazon after the discovery of the Napo has been described elsewhere. The river was given its name by Orellana, who believed himself attacked at one point of the journey by a tribe of female warriors or "amazons." But although there are records or traditions of a tribe of women warriors in South America, doubtless Orellana and his men were deceived by the long hair of the Indians and the cotton shirts or *cushmas* which they wore into thinking these were women. But the tribe which attacked Orellana were the Tapuyas, and their women as well as their men fought. In 1638-9 the journey of Orellana, but in an inverse direction, was repeated by Pedro de Teixeira, whose famous voyage up the Amazon gave the world important knowledge of the great river and its tributaries. At that time (Philip IV being King of Spain and Portugal) the Dutch had made an attempt to colonize the lower Amazon, but they were driven out by Teixeira. The voyage up-stream to Ecuador was a very great feat. A band of Franciscan missionaries from Quito had been massacred by the Indians of the Napo, only two escaping. In a small boat these two survivors drifted down the Napo to the Amazon, and miraculously escaping the dangers of the voyage, arrived at Pará or Belen. As a result of the sensation caused thereby, Teixeira, with 1,200 Portuguese and Indians, set out, and the flotilla, voyaging for many months, ascended the Amazon and Napo and reached the mouth of the Aguarico. Leaving the bulk of his people there, the leader proceeded to Quito, whence he returned by the same route in 1639 with two Jesuit fathers, nominated to accompany him by the Peruvian

Viceroy.   The discoverer of the lower Amazon was
Vincent de Pinzon, who ascended it for fifty miles, and
in connection with whom it was called the Marañon.
From that period began the ill-treatment, flight, and
diminution of the Amazon Indian tribes, which may
said to have culminated in the Putumayo atrocities of
the last few years.

It should be remarked that the low-water period of
the series of rivers entering the left bank of the Marañon and Amazon is in the months of February and
March. On the contrary, the low-water period of those
great affluents which enter on the right bank, flowing
from the south-east through Peru, is in August and
September.   This affords some measure of equilibrium
in the hydrographic regimen of the Amazon, tending
to ensure a greater constancy in the volume of that
river.   The difference of level, however, is at times
considerable, and a source of some inconvenience to
navigation.

CHAPTER XII

CLIMATE, SEASONS, PATHOLOGY

As earlier remarked, the climatic conditions of Ecuador depend more upon the topography of the country than upon its latitude, a condition it shares with other Spanish-American countries which lie within the tropics.

Ecuador is included between latitude 2° north of the Equator and 6° south, being consequently traversed by the equatorial line and lying entirely within the torrid zone. In spite of this, there are few countries in the world presenting such climatic and meteorological changes, for, within a relatively small extension of territory and within a few hours' journey, all the climatic zones of the earth, from torrid to glacial, may be encountered. These changes are due to local agencies : first, the orographical formation, and second, the conditions attending the temperature of the sea which washes the coasts.

Throughout the whole of South America there is to be observed an eastern and a western climate, corresponding to the eastern and western side of the Cordillera of the Andes. This is very pronounced in Peru [1] and northern Chile. The great Pacific littoral is dry and its territory arid, whilst the eastern plains and valley are humid, subject to heavy rainfall, and covered with dense vegetation. This is primarily due to the prevailing or trade winds, which

[1] See the author's *Republics of Central and South America*, Dent and Sons, 1913 ; also his *Peru*, T. Fisher Unwin.

blow continuously from the east, from the Atlantic, and across Brazil, and which, charged with aqueous vapours, deposit their moisture in the form of rain, hail, ice, and snow on the summits of the Andes. Thus the moisture is intercepted or " blanketed " by the Cordilleras and so fails to reach the Pacific coast, which, in consequence of this and another cause, becomes in Peru and northern Chile of Sahara-like aridity. So great is the barrier imposed by the mountains that the winds are encountered by vessels only far out on the Pacific, away from the South American coast.

The cause of the peculiar conditions on the Ecuadorian coast, of alternating barren and forest-covered districts, long remained a problem for those travellers and scientists who had observed it. The arboreal vegetation, so abundant and luxuriant on the Ecuadorian coast, ceases at the south of Tumbez near Cape Blanco in 4° south, and only appears again south of Valparaiso, in 33° south, in the thick woods resulting from the humid climate of Valdivia and Chiloé. The whole intervening space, covering twenty-nine degrees of latitude, is, as before observed, arid and treeless. It was long believed that the aridity was due to the lack of vegetation, when in reality the last condition is the result of the first. The earliest to make a study of the condition was Bouger, in the middle of the eighteenth century, who held the above erroneous opinion. Raimondi, the well-known Peruvian naturalist, in the middle of the last century believed the effect was due in part to the sandy nature of the littoral, upon whose hot surface the watery vapours could not condense to form rain. But if such were true for Peru it would also have been true for Ecuador. For the formation of clouds from moisture-bearing sea winds a point of colder contact is necessary. But in Peru the temperature of the land was found by Humboldt,

13

who was the first to study the temperatures of the
region, to be higher than that of the sea. Thus the
great importance of the Antarctic or Humboldt current upon the climate of the region was shown ; but
although Humboldt made these observations he did
not arrive at their ultimate consequence or regard
them as largely the cause of the aridity of the
Peruvian littoral. The true conditions later educed
is that the cold current bathing the shore extracts
from the sea winds their humidity, and so prevents
the formation of rain on the coast-zone. That the
same condition does not obtain north of the Equator
is due to the outward trend of the current, caused by
the bulging South American coastline, the current
being deviated towards the Galápagos Islands, where
its effect is also notable, as elsewhere described.

Due to the absence of the current on the northern
part of the Ecuadorian shore the sea remains at
its normal temperature, which is higher than that of
the land, with the result that rain is formed, often
in greater quantities than necessary. The Peruvian
coast, thus deprived of moisture by the absorbent
character of the current, receives, however, a light
mist-drizzle, known as *garua*, when the winter has
somewhat diminished the heat of the land due to cool
winds, and this permits a scanty vegetation and
pasture to come to being on the foothills, of short
duration. The greater the difference between the
temperature of the sea and the land the purer and
clearer is the atmosphere upon the coast. The season
of the mist-drizzle or *garua*, which is so notable and
often disagreeable a feature of the Peruvian coast
towns—especially in Lima, where chill and damp
occurs in the evenings—coincides with the winter
or *invierno* in the southern hemisphere from May
to September. This lowering of temperature in the
atmosphere on the coasts is brought about in the
uplands by their elevation, and so clouds and rain

are encountered in the Cordillera also, in the summer. Thus when on the coast the clearest skies and highest temperatures are seasonable, in the Cordillera and uplands the period of most frequent and constant storms occurs. But in the upper region on the western slopes vapour in the atmosphere is equally scarce, with the result that the vegetation is scarce and the countryside generally presents a sterile and melancholy appearance. It is only north of the fourth parallel of (south) latitude, in Ecuador, that these conditions change. It may be said that without the influence of the Antarctic current the arid Peruvian and Chilean coast, which strikes the traveller with surprise as its deserts unfold to the view from the steamer's deck, would rapidly become forested and overgrown with the dense vegetation that covers the littoral of Ecuador, Colombia, and Panama.

The general temperature of the Ecuadorian littoral between the Andes and the sea is 82·4° F., ranging in its extremes from 66° to 95°. There are variations due to local causes, such as the approach of hills to the coast and to the impingement on the coast of a branch of the Antarctic current. In Guayaquil the average temperature for the year is given by some authorities as 80° F. and by others 76° F., the highest being in February and March. The heaviest rainfall is in the same months, and in 1911 was 2,289 litres per square metre. The climate is influenced by the fresher breezes from the sea and also by the lower temperature of this. Farther inland towards the mountain few observations of temperature have been made. In general terms it may be said that the temperature decreases in proportion with the height at the rate of 1° C. to every 200 metres of elevation. Beginning with a temperature of 26° C. (79° F.) upon the plains at the foot of the Cordilleras, there would be reached at an altitude of 1,000 metres 21° C., at 2,000

metres 16° C., at 3,000 metres 11ᵁ C., and at 4,000
metres 6° C., or, say, 43° F. at 13,200 feet above sea-
level. In practice this calculation is very nearly
borne out, especially in the higher elevations. As
regards the atmospheric pressure, the barometer in
Ecuador is of little use in indicating changes of
weather as employed in countries outside the tropics ;
but, on the other hand, its results are excellent in
determining altitudes above sea-level,[1] due to the
absence of variation.

In Ecuador the terms *verano* and *invierno*, or
summer and winter, do not coincide with the astronomical summer and winter as generally understood.
The *verano* or summer is the cool season, whilst the
invierno is the warm or rainy season. All the regions
have a dry and a wet season, but this varies in
different zones. As before described, the three main
zones are those of the coast, the highlands, and the
Amazon forests. In the forest or Oriental zone
summer reigns whilst in the other two it is the
winter season, and vice versa. The inter-Andine
region participates in the *invierno* of the western
and not of the eastern region, because the eastern
Cordillera is higher and wider than the western and
does not present any breaks or gaps, such as is the
case with the latter, or to a much less degree.
In western Ecuador the summer or *verano* is
from the middle of May to the middle of
December, with some slight variations. The
nearer the foot of the Cordillera the shorter is the
summer and the longer the winter. The prevailing
wind in the *verano* is from the south or south-west,
generally from midday until early morning. The
contrary direction is held in winter. Hurricanes
are almost unknown in western Ecuador. In winter,
however, the atmosphere is highly charged with
electricity, and severe thunderstorms occur. The

[1] Wolf, *op. cit.* ; also Whymper.

rainy season cannot be described as of continuous rainstorms, for the *aguaceros* or downpours are intermittent. These periods are, however, very severe : the streams overflow and traffic is suspended, and the air, drenched with moisture, is oppressive and often pestiferous.

The descriptions of the bad climate of Guayaquil—or rather, the hygienic conditions attending it—whilst generally exaggerated, contain a good deal of truth. All seaports where yellow fever prevails have an unenviable reputation, and in the case of Guayaquil the authorities have lagged greatly in the exercise of modern methods of sanitation, such as in a few years have effected favourable changes at Panama, Rio de Janeiro, and elsewhere. Taken as a whole Ecuador might without exaggeration be termed the healthiest tropical country in the world, but the special insanitary spots of its seaports and in its interior rob it of any advantage in this respect in foreign estimation. The climate of the coast region generally is cool and agreeable, rendered temperate by the sea, and in the coast towns and villages diseases are perhaps rarer than in the *sierra* or upland region. Longevity is a common condition, not only in the dry coast regions such as Puná, Chanduy, Morro, Santa Elena, Colonche, Manta, and other villages or towns of Manabi, but also in the humid and hot section of the littoral, including those from Machala to Naranjal, that of Manglar Alto, and the province of Esmeraldas. It is true that in certain humid localities, as in the valley of the Esmeraldas River, there are *calenturas* and intermittent fevers, but these are not necessarily pernicious or endemic. The humidity does not necessarily create insanitary conditions, nor the presence of mangrove swamps of sea-water an unhealthy climate. More inland, on the central plains of the littoral and primarily at Guayaquil and on the fluvial system of the Guayas, the climate is good, and even agreeable in the dry season, notwithstanding that the temperature is higher than at the coast. The death-rate is not greater than in the uplands or in extra-tropical countries. If in Guayaquil the number of deaths and burials seem large, this is mainly due to the fact that people arrive there from the country, seeking medical advice for their infirmities, often when too late. In the *invierno* or winter season sanitary conditions change little in the small towns and villages but considerably so in the larger, show-ing that it is to the people rather than the climate that disease is due.

In the Andine region the *verano* or summer is from June to November and the *invierno* from November to May. A short period of dry weather known as the *veranillo* or "little summer" occurs in winter, soon after the December solstice, and con-versely an *invernillo* or "little winter," a short rainy spell breaks the summer, following the September equinox. Thus in the uplands no month is com-pletely free of rain, and in summer in the highlands and plateaux of the Andes formidable snowstorms and hailstorms are encountered, which destroy the young crops. The thunderstorms which in the *sierra* or high regions arise generally between one and three in the afternoon, and especially during the September equinox, are most frequent in summer. The days are generally calm until one or two o'clock, with a brilliant sun and clear sky and atmosphere ; but about that hour vapour begins to arise, which shortly covers the whole heavens with black clouds, from which proceed furious tempests of thunder and lightning, making the very rocks tremble, bursting into torrential downpourings, and the streets of the villages become rivers and the *plazas* are converted into lakes. This continues perhaps until sunset, when the sky again clears and the storm ceases. Very similar conditions obtain throughout the Andes generally ; and in Peru, as in Ecuador, the cautious traveller, if his way lies across the Cordillera, will see that he crosses the range before the sun passes the meridian.[1]

Whilst the annual rainfall varies for different places in the Andine regions, at Quito it has been shown to average somewhat over forty inches, with from 150 to 185 rainy days and 100 to 110 thunderstorms. The mean annual temperature of Quito, 9,343 feet above sea-level, is 58·8° F., and the diurnal variation 10° F., the annual maximum 70° F., and the annual minimum 45° F. At elevations of about 9,200 feet are the towns of Riobamba, Latacunga, and Calacali. The temperature of the two first is 57° and 58° F. At 9,900 feet Angamarca has a temperature of 52° F. Local variations are influenced by the surroundings to some extent, whether of sandy plains, whether of cold *páramos*. In the localities belonging to the cold *páramos*, with a temperature below 50° F., cereals do not grow, and the thermometer goes down at times below freezing-point. The region of the *páramos* is taken as beginning at the general elevation of 11,500 feet above sea-level, with a mean temperature of 47·5° F. The greater part of the inter-Andine population is found at an elevation 7,250 to 9,200 feet, with an average temperature of 55° to 61° F. Only above this last named elevation does the thermometer descend below freezing-point at night. In the Ecuadorian Andes some plants are found above the line of perpetual snow on the slopes of the peaks, but generally the *páramo* vegetation ceases at 13,800 feet.

Although the word *páramo* has in reality a topographical application, it is also used by the dwellers of the fell in a meteorological sense, expressing the peculiar conditions of the highlands, such as describe

[1] See also the Author's *The Andes and the Amazon.*

storms of hail, snow, and wind, with alternate sun-
shine.   The word *paramear* is applied by the *serrano,*
or upland dweller, to a peculiar formation of fog also,
such as in these high places on occasion covers the
landscape as with a transparent veil, through which
objects such as rock, trees, animals, and so forth are
fantastically augmented, but which the strongest wind
cannot disperse.   This apparent immovability of the
neblina or fog is explained by its formation in place
rather than being wind-borne.   The spectacle offered
by such mists, with the sun upon them, is often
extremely curious.   Elsewhere occurrences of mist
are often of strange appearance in the Andes.   Dense
banks of such lie along the valleys, or rise menacingly
like the waves of the sea.   The phenomenon of the
anthelion is witnessed on occasions.   In summer the
ascent or passage of the *páramos* is not without
danger for the traveller.   The wind at times blows
with hurricane force, and whistles through the grass
or scanty herb as if it would tear out even these by
the roots.   It is almost useless to seek shelter behind
a rock, for the wind and storm seems veritably to
come from all quarters, as if purposely descending
upon the head of the traveller who has the temerity
to invade this roof of the world.   Although the temperature may still be a few degrees above zero,
the cold occasioned by the wind and the peculiar
fog is so keen that it seems to penetrate to the
very marrow of the traveller's bones.   To build a
fire is impossible, as it is, indeed, to plant a tent.

The perpetual snowline in the Andes of Ecuador
rises considerably in elevation, depending upon local
conditions and not entirely upon altitude above sea-
level or geographical position.   The dryness of the
climate at any given point is a factor determining
the elevation.   In the Andes of Peru and Bolivia,
where it might have been supposed that the snowline
would be lower than in Ecuador due to the distance

from the Equator, the reverse is the case, the line being somewhat higher. This is doubtless due in some cases to the arid climate of the plateaux from which the snowy crests or peaks arise. The snow-line, of course, corresponds with that elevation in which the annual snowfall is equivalent to the mass of snow thawed or evaporated, and thus the permanent snowline depends not only on the average temperature but also on the dryness of the air. There are in Ecuador, apart from smaller patches, sixteen *cerros nevados*, or snowy peaks, whose names are given elsewhere, and observations have been made of all except Sangay, principally by Drs. Reiss and Stübel. Several of the Ecuadorian peaks, as Pichincha, Rumiñahua, and Imbabura, are snow-covered only for certain months of the year. The average limit of the snowline, calculated by the above named explorers, is, for the western Cordillera, 15,650 feet above sea-level, and for the eastern, 14,060 feet. The glaciers on certain peaks descend much below the snow-level. Thus the perpetual snowline on Antisana begins at 15,500 feet elevation, but the glacier from the crater descends to 13,900 feet. Eleven glaciers observed in the western Cordillera descend to an average elevation of 15,000 feet, and nine in the eastern Cordillera to 14,200 feet. One of the glaciers of Cayambe descends to 13,600 feet, and that of Sara Urcu is a little higher. The highest snowline is found on Chimborazo, due to its dry surroundings, and lies between 15,840 feet and 16,500 feet. It is observed that the higher line faces the *Callejon*, or inter-Andine valley, where the climate is dry, and the lower the outside slopes, where it is humid. Thus, on Cotopaxi, the western snowline is at 15,500 feet, and the eastern 14,850 feet. It is seen that no two peaks have their snowline at the same elevation. On Cotocachi, according to Whymper, the permanent snowline was at 14,500 feet, whilst Imbabura was free of snow to its summit, which reaches 15,033 feet. The permanent line on Antisana was at 16,000 feet, whilst Sara Urcu, near by, rain-drenched from the Amazon valley throughout the year, has its snowline at 14,000 feet. The eastern range receives the heaviest snowfall. These singular conditions in the permanent snowline are also very marked in Peru, in the White Cordillera and the Black Cordillera, bounding the *Callejon* or valley of Huaylas.

The climate of the Ecuadorian uplands must in general be considered healthy, like that of the corresponding regions in Peru, Colombia, and Bolivia. Humboldt characterized the climate of certain parts of the inter-Andine valleys of Ecuador as the finest in the world. The atmosphere is bracing. Pulmonary tuberculosis is said to be unknown at these elevations, but catarrhal complaints are common. The people of these regions rarely use fires or stoves for heating purposes in their dwellings, regarding artificial heat as liable to provoke pulmonary complaints, and when it is especially cold they wrap themselves in *ponchos* or overcoats. This condition is observable throughout all the Spanish-American countries, whether in Peru, whether on the highlands of Mexico, and the foreigner, accustomed to the interior warmth of his dwelling, office, or hotel, shivers uncomfortably in the low temperature. Whether the custom really embodies a wise precaution or is due to an unfounded prejudice it is difficult to decide. The relatively high death rate among the working population and Indians is due, not to the climate but to the poor condition of their life, as elsewhere discussed. Leprosy, one of the most terrible and incurable diseases, is found with some frequency in the *sierra* or upland region, and is known as *elefancia*. It is propagated only by contagion, and has no special origin in the climate, although possibly. this favours its development. Leprosy is found in most Latin American countries, including the warm lowlands, such as those in Paraguay, as well as the highlands. Malaria, that scourge of the tropic lowlands, is by no means unknown in the highlands. It might have been supposed that the high elevation and cool atmosphere would have rendered the propagation of *tercianas*, or tertian fevers and agues, impossible, but in various districts of the Andes, throughout Peru, Bolivia, and Ecuador, it is encountered. It is probable that the disease has its origin in the lowlands, and is acquired by persons who ascend to the higher regions rather than having any origin in the latter. It has been proved of late years in medical research that the origin of malaria is in the mosquito, and it is in the lowlands that these pests abound. But in the Peruvian *sierras*, even at elevations of 16,000 feet,[1] malaria attacks the employees of mining and other *haciendas* at times, and large quantities of quinine are consumed. In the form of a liqueur, consisting of native *aguardiente*, or cane alcohol, in which the quinine bark has been steeped, the febrifuge is also taken.

The region of the Ecuadorian *sierra*, or interAndine districts which are generally regarded as least healthy, are those of the valley of Catamayo, in the province of Loja ; Yunguilla, in Azuay ; Guallabamba, in Pichincha ; and Chota, in Imbabura. The altitude of these districts lies between 4,000 feet and 6,600 feet above sea-level, with a mean temperature between 63° and 68° F. The common characteristic is the dryness of the atmosphere and the sterility of the soil, with an absence of vegetation and trees except where cultivated. The sandy plains and naked, stony hill-slopes are heated under a burn-

[1] The men employed by the author were severely attacked by malaria at these high elevations in some cases.

ing sun to such an extent that the thermometer may
mark 86° F. in the shade during the day and fall to
43° F. at night—a very wide diurnal range. Although
this may have some effect in the insalubrity of the
districts, there are doubtless other unstudied causes.
In such valleys the *calenturas*, or malarious fevers,
are endemic, and neither the white nor the Indian race
can resist these attacks, whilst even the negroes and
mulattoes, who form *peon* labour in the *haciendas*,
suffer greatly.   Persons predisposed to such attacks
suffer in these districts from exceedingly refractory
malaria, and even the traveller who passes a single
night therein, or who may have crossed them in his
journey, may be attacked.[1]   Beyond these places and
some others of similar character the Ecuadorian inter-
Andine region generally enjoys a good climate.   The
sierra in reality is regarded as a species of sana-
torium, and with the growing population and means
of access the Andine regions are likely to acquire
wide fame.   Valleys at certain elevations in the
mountainous parts of South America often merit the
name of " zones of eternal spring," such as enthusiastic native writers are fond of conferring upon them.
Sheltered from the cold winds of the uplands, and
free from the humidity of the lowlands, their climate,
vegetation, and general surroundings are pleasing
and healthful.   Among the localities in Ecuador
which answer this pleasing description are Ibarra,
certain points in the valley of Tumbaco, Chillo, Baños,
at the foot of Tunguragua, the valley of Gualaceo,
Paute, Loja, and places near the upper limit of the
banana and palm zone.
   The seasons in the Amazon region are variable
and at times opposed, according to their distance
from the Andes, and this is exemplified upon the
Napo River.   In the Ecuadorian Oriente or Amazon
region two wet periods may be distinguished,

[1] The Author found similar conditions in Peru, to his cost.

although rain falls during every month. The principal rainy season is from the end of February to the middle of June, and the lesser from the middle of October to the beginning of January. The first period produces the greatest flood heights on the Amazon, and the second, according to Bates,[1] is only one-third as severe. But in the higher part of the watershed, upon the slopes of the Andes, the distribution of the season is different, with defined wet and dry seasons, the latter of which, the *verano* or summer, or *estacion de secas*, lasts from November to April. This is the most favourable period for the naturalist or traveller.

[1] *A Naturalist on the Amazon.*

CHAPTER XIII

GOVERNMENT AND TERRITORIAL DIVISIONS

ECUADOR is a centralized as opposed to a federated republic, with powers defined by a written Constitution. The government is therein described as popular, representative, and republican. The Constitution has been changed eleven times since 1830. The centralized form of republican government is that adopted by most of the Latin American nations, the exceptions being Mexico, Brazil, Argentine, and Venezuela, which are federal republics, after the model of the United States. The government of Ecuador, like those of the other Latin American republics, and following after the United States model, comprises three main sections—the legislative, the executive, and the judiciary.

The legislative power is vested in the Congress, consisting in a Senate, or *Cámara de Senadores*, and a Chamber of Deputies, or *Cámara de Diputados*. The Senate is composed of thirty-two members, or two from each province, who are elected for two years, one-half being renewed every two years. There are forty-two deputies, also elected for two years, on a basis of proportional representation of one representative for each 30,000 of the inhabitants, and one supplementary for an additional 15,000. A senator must be over thirty-five and a deputy over twenty-five years of age. The elections are direct. The exercise of the vote, whilst it is termed

" universal," is limited to persons of the male sex who can read and write, are over twenty-one years of age, and are or have been married. As by far the greater bulk of the population are illiterate, the suffrage is in practice of limited range. But there is no legal obstacle to the acquisition of the vote by the lower classes and the aboriginal races, under education.

The executive power is vested in the President and Vice-President, elected by direct vote of the people for a period of four years. These officials cannot be re-elected for a second consecutive term. The President has a limited veto power ; he can convene special sessions of Congress, and appoints diplomatic and consular representatives and the governors of the provinces, and exercises some control over the administration of justice and education, by the appointment of officials, and is also chief of the army. His salary is 12,000 sucres per annum (£1,200). A Cabinet of five Ministers assists the President—those of Interior and Public Works, Foreign Relations and Justice, War, Finance, Public Instruction, Posts and Telegraph. There is also a Council of State to assist the executive authority of fifteen members, including the Cabinet Ministers, with important advisory functions.

The judiciary consists in a Supreme Court, at Quito, of five judges and a *fiscal*, or public prosecutor ; six supreme courts, established in the larger towns, with a total of nine judges ; a *Tribunal de Cuentas*, and various municipal courts, or *alcaldes*, in the chief towns ; also civil courts of first and second instance in the larger towns, with justices of the peace, and so forth. The laws of the republic are based on the old Spanish codes and procedures, and embody civil, criminal, and commercial codes. The provinces are administered by governors, named by the executive, the departments by *jefes politicos*, or political chiefs, and the municipalities by *tenientes politicos*, or political lieutenants.

Thus the machinery of government is well established, in theory, and were its administration but effected in the spirit in which it is drawn up on paper, order and progress could not fail to result. In that, however, lies the fatal rift in all Latin American Governments.

Ecuador is divided into fifteen provinces and one territory, with the Galápagos Islands as a second territory. These provinces, with their area in square miles, capitals, and approximate populations, are as follows :—

Province.			Area.		Population.		Capital.
Carchi	...	...	1,495	...	40,000	...	Tulcan
Imbabura	...	...	2,416	...	68,000	...	Ibarra
Pichincha	...	...	6,219	...	205,000	...	Quito
Léon ...	...	...	2,595	...	110,000	...	Latacunga
Tunguragua...		...	1,686	...	103,000	...	Ambato
Chimborazo...		...	2,990	...	122,000	...	Riobamba
Bolívar	...	...	1,260	...	43,000	...	Guaranda
Cañar	...	...	1,519	...	64,000	...	Azogues
Aznay	...	...	3,874	...	133,000	...	Cuenca
Loja ...	...	...	3,707	...	66,000	...	Loja
El Oro	...	...	2,340	...	33,000	...	Machala
Guayas	...	...	8,216	...	100,000	...	Guayaquil
Los Rios	...	...	2,296	...	33,000	...	Babahozo
Manabi	...	...	7,893	...	64,000	...	Portoviejo
Esmeraldas ...		...	5,465	...	15,000	...	Esmeraldas
Oriente	...	...	territory unknown	—	—		—
Galápagos Islands ...			2,865	...	2,000	...	—

The above areas and populations are in some cases approximate, as certain boundaries of the republic are not definitely fixed, and the census is only an estimate. The provinces are subdivided into cantons, and these into *parroquias*.

The province of Carchi lies on the frontier with Colombia, formed by the river of the same name,

and the San Juan, a tributary of the Mira. Its
southern boundary is the Imbabura province, with
the Chota and Mira Rivers, and to the east are the
montañas, on the headwaters of the Rivers Cofanes
and Aguarico. The province is very mountainous,
and is traversed by the great *nudo* forming the
Altos de Boliche (Nudo de Huaca) and the Angel
páramos. The other rivers are the Apaqui and the
Angel or Mira. The principal resources are the
good upland pastures, cultivation of cereals in the
temperate districts and of sugar-cane and other sub-
tropical products in the Chonta lowlands. There is
little commerce. The chief town is Tulcan.

Imbabura is bounded by Carchi on the north,
Pichincha on the south, Esmeraldas on the west, and
the Oriente on the east. Its very broken territory
includes the greater part of the inter-Andine *hoya*,
or plain of Ibarra, and the Cordillera that overhangs
it. The principal mountains are Imbabura, Cusni,
Mojanda, Cotacachi, Yana-urcu, Cerros de Ango-
chagna. It contains the lakes of San Pablo and
Yaguacocha, and the principal rivers are the Blanco,
Taguando, Chamachan, Pisco, Chota, and Mira.
The principal resources are in agriculture, the growing of cereals, sugar-cane, cotton, also cattle, textile
industries, and salt extraction. There is some commerce with Pasto and Quito. The capital of the
province is Ibarra, a pleasing town, founded in
1606, and named after the Spanish President of
that period. The province is divided into ten cantons
of Ibarra, Otavalo, and Cotacachi, with chief towns
of the same names respectively.

Pichincha has at the north Imbabura, at the south
Leon, at the west Esmeraldas and Manabi, and at
the east the Oriente. It extends over the great
inter-Andine basin of Quito, with the adjacent Cordillera, and is very mountainous. Within it lie, as
principal mountains, Pichincha, Pululagua, Atacetazo,

14

Corazon, Rumiñahui, Pasochoa, Sincholagua, Antisana, Guamani, Puntas, Pambamarca, Sara-Urcu, Cayambe, and, in part, Mojanda. The Guallabamba, with its inter-Andine tributaries, and the system of the Blanco and part of the Toachi are its principal rivers, with the Peripa and Palenque. The principal resources are agricultural and pastoral, and there are some small textile industries. A brisk commerce is carried on with Pasto and Quito. The railway from Guayaquil to Quito traverses the southern part of the province. Pichincha contains the capital of the republic, Quito, and is divided into three cantons, those of Quito, Cayambe, and Mejia, the chief towns of which are respectively Cayambe and Machachi.

Leon is bounded on the north by Pichincha, on the south by Tunguragua and Bolivar, on the west by Los Rios, and on the east by the Oriente. It is throughout very mountainous, and includes the northern frontier of the great inter-Andine *hoya* of Latacunga. Its principal peaks are the great Cotopaxi, Quilindaña, Iliniza, and Quilotoa, which are elsewhere described. The main river is the Cutuchi, and on the west the province occupies territory traversed by the Toachi, Pilalo, and Angamarca. On the east are the headwaters of the Napo. The principal resources are agricultural and pastoral, with some textile-making, and sugar manufacture in the lowlands. The province is traversed by the railway. There are two cantons, those of Latacunga and Pujili, with chief towns of the same name.

Tunguragua lies south of Leon, with the province of Chimborazo on its southern side, Bolivar on the west, and the forests of the Oriente on the east. Its mountainous territory includes the southern part of the Latacungua *hoya*, and contains the great peaks and volcanoes of Carihuairazo, Casaguala, Cerro Hermoso, and the formidable Tunguragua, elsewhere described, and its principal rivers are the Ambato,

A STREET IN RIOBAMBA

To face p. 216.

the Panchalico, the Patate, and the Pastaza. Agricultural and pastoral industries are carried on, with viticulture and small manufacturing. There are three cantons, those of Ambato, Petito, and Pillaro, with chief towns of the same names.

Chimborazo lies south of the above, with the province of Cañar as its southern boundary, Bolivar on the west, and the Oriente on the east. Like all the inter-Andine provinces, it is mountainous, but contains the Riobamba *llanura*, or plain, and the smaller one of Alausi. Chimborazo, Igualata, Altar, Cubillui, and Sangay are its principal peaks, and the rivers form the system of the Chambo, the tributary of the Pastaza, and the Upper Chanchan. The resources are similar to the other provinces above described. There are four cantons—Riobamba, with its chief town of the same name upon the Guayaquil-Quito Railway, Guano, Colta, Alausi, and Sangay. The last-named extends to the eastern versant of the Cordillera Real, with undefined frontiers, and the missions, tribes, and lands included in the old *gobierno de Macas* are comprehended therein. The province is traversed by the Guayaquil-Quito railway.

Bolivar lies west of the Chimborazo province, with Leon on the north, Guayas on the south, and Los Rios on the west, and contains, in its mountainous territory, the *hoya* of Chimbo. Its resources are similar to those of its neighbours. There are three cantons—Guaranda, with the pleasing town of the same name, Chimbo, and San Miguel.

Cañar lies south of the Chimborazo province, with Azuay on the south, Guayas on the west, and the Oriente forests on the east. It includes the great knot of Azuay and part of the western Cordillera ; its central river is the Cañar, and it touches the Azogues River and other tributaries of the Paute. The cantons are Azogues and Cañar. The old quicksilver mines which gave their name to the province

are near the chief town, but they appear to be exhausted. Great quantities of *huacas*—Inca antiquities
—have been encountered in part of the canton. A
few miles from the town of Cañar are seen the ruins
of the old fortress of Inca-pirca.

Azuay lies to the south of the last-named province,
with Loja on the south, Oro on the south-west,
Guayas on the west, and the Oriente on the east.
It occupies the inter-Andine *hoyas* of Cuenca and
Jubones, with their surrounding Cordilleras, and is
watered by the rivers which form the Paute and
others, and the sources of some of the western
streams. In addition to agriculture and cattle, there
are some gold-washings, also hat-making. The
cantons are Cuenca, Gualaceo, Paute, Jiron, and
Gualaquiza or Sigsig, with chief towns of the same
names.

Loja lies partly west of the Cordillera Real, and
partly east thereof, in the *hoyas* of Zamora and
the Chinchipe, but its total area depends upon the
settlement of its boundary with Peru, forming the
frontier on the south. On the north is the Azuay
province, on the west Oro, and on the east the
Oriente. It is mountainous, but extremely varied
as to temperature, with some cold regions and others
hot, according to elevation. The principal rivers
are the Catamayo in the centre, the Zamora on the
east, and the Chinchipe on the south. There are
five cantons—of Loja, Zaraguro, Paltas, Celica, and
Calvas.

The foregoing, it is seen, are mainly mountainous
regions, with the agricultural and pastoral industries peculiar thereto. Some of them contain pleasing
towns and fertile lands, others inclement areas and
bleak, broken ridges, interspersed among which are
miserable hamlets of the Indians. Others have as
undesirable neighbours the forest Indians. Cut off
as they are in most cases from the outside world,

ALAUSI. A TYPE OF UPLAND *PUEBLO*.

[To face p. 240.

the resources of these districts are small and their civic life backward. Many of them contain points of special interest, others are of that melancholy, and uninteresting character which is so marked a feature of the small places of the Andine uplands throughout thousands of miles of territory in Ecuador, Peru, Bolivia, Colombia, and elsewhere. The European race and traditions become attenuated in the remoter regions, although at least the influence and authority of Church and State are established. These regions must be regarded as lying fallow for future development, containing possibilities of progress and inviting encouragement from the outside.

The coast provinces are not in general much more advanced, excepting certain districts, but their greater accessibility by reason of the sea renders them of more economic importance in certain respects.

The province of Oro is bounded on the north by Guayas and Azuay, on the south and east by Loja, and on the west by the Pacific Ocean. The eastern half of its territory is mountainous, comprising the Zaruma *hoya*, and the western half consists in the littoral plains, crossed by *esteros* and the River Jubones. The coastline is that of the gulf of Guayaquil and the Jambeli Channel. The principal resources are the mining industries in the mountains, sugar-cane growing and sugar-making in the temperate valleys, and the cocoa plantations on the littoral. There are also fisheries on the coast, and some timber extraction. The three cantons are those of Machala, Santa Rosa, and Zaruma, with chief towns of the same name. At the mines of Zaruma, which are elsewhere described, there is some resident foreign population, attracted by the mineral industry.

Guayas is bounded on the north by the Manabi province, on the east by Los Rios, Cañar, and Azuay, by Oro on the south, and by the gulf of Guayaquil

and the Pacific Ocean on the west. Its territory,
is generally flat or gently undulating, broken here and
there by isolated groups of low hills. The only
Cordillera of any importance is that of Chongon and
Colonche. The province is crossed by the fluvial
system of the lower and middle Guayas, and by the
Daule in part. The coastline forms the eastern side
of the gulf of Guayaquil, the Jambeli channel, the
northern shore of the gulf, and part of the Pacific
shore ; and the province includes the Island of Puná.
Agricultural and pastoral industries and sugar-
making are among the principal resources, together
with timber extraction and other forestal products,
fine straw-hat-making, fishing, navigation, and commerce. Guayas is the province of Ecuador possessing
the richest and most varied resources. There are
four cantons—those of Guayaquil, Yaguachi, Daule,
and Santa Elena, with chief towns of the same name.
The important seaport of Guayaquil is elsewhere
described. Excellent coffee, oranges, pineapples,
tobacco, etc., are produced in this province, and
the petroleum wells of Santa Elena afford some means
of industry. The province is partly traversed by the
Guayaquil-Quito Railway.

Los Rios has at the north the provinces of Leon
and Pichincha, on the east Bolivia, and on the south
and west Guayas. Its territory is flat, and crossed
by numerous rivers, from which it takes its name.
All these are tributaries of the Guayas or Bodegas
Rivers. The cultivation of *cacao* is the main agricultural industry, and cattle-breeding, timber extraction, and commerce with the interior are of
importance. The cantons of Babahoyo, Baba, Pueblo
Viejo, and Vinces have chief towns of the same
names.

Manabi is bounded on the north by the province
of Esmeraldas, on the south by Guayas, on the east
by Guayas and Pichincha, and on the west by the

Pacific Ocean. Its territory is fairly hilly, but without high mountains. There are no large rivers, the principal being the Portoviejo, the Chone, the Jama, and the Cuaque, and in the hilly interior part of the Daule and Quininde systems. The principal industries are the manufacture of "Panama" hats, timber extraction, *tagua* or ivory-nut gathering, rubber, and some agriculture and commerce. This sparsely populated province has six cantons—those of Portoviejo, Montecristi, Jipijapa, Santa Ana, Rocafuerte, and Sucre. All have chief towns of similar names, except Sucre, whose principal place is the bahia or port of Caráques, on the pleasing bay of that name. Jipijapa has given its name to a well-known variety of fine straw hats, an industry elsewhere described. The curious antiquities of the province are described in the chapter dealing with the antiquarian remains of the republic. Manabi covers a long stretch of territory on the sea-coast.

Esmeraldas lies north of Manabi, and has at its northern boundary the republic of Colombia, on the east Imbabura and Pichincha, and on the west the Pacific Ocean. It is hilly, without, however, any high mountains, and its principal rivers are the Esmeraldas and tributaries, and the Santiago and the Verde. The coastline is broken and diversified. The extraction of rubber, fine woods, and other forestal products, with some gold-washings and agriculture, form the principal resources of the province. There is one canton, of the same name, with the seaport of Esmeraldas as its chief town.

The remaining divisions of Ecuador are the Oriente, the region lying east of the Andes, and the Galápagos Islands, 500 to 600 miles off the coast. The boundaries of the Oriente, as elsewhere described, are undefined, pending the settlement of frontier question with the neighbouring republics. In the *Convencion Nacional* of 1884 the region is

described as "embodying the territories of Napo,
Canelos, and Zamora. The Napo territory embodies the *pueblos* of Napo, Archidona, Tena,
Aguano, Napotea, Santa Rosa, Suno, Coca, Paza-
mino, Avila, Loreto, Concepcion, Cotapino, San
Rafael, San Miguel de Aguarico, and the *tenencias*
of Sinchichicta, Asumy, Maran, and the other tribes
and territories that composed the old Gobierno de
Quijos as far as the Marañon. The territory of
Canelos includes the *pueblos* of Canelos, Zarayacu,
Pacayacu, Lliquino, Andoas, the tribes of Záparos
and Jibaros, and the others that composed the
missions of Canelos and the adjacent territories of
the kingdom of Quito, whose boundaries are to be
fixed in accordance with the respective treaties." The
wild regions of this part of Ecuador, including the
debatable territory claimed by adjoining republics,
is more fully described in another chapter.

The Galápagos Islands are also described in the
chapter devoted to that interesting archipelago.

As regards education in Ecuador, primary instruction is free and obligatory. But the schools are
insufficient in number, and a great part of the population is indifferent to education. The instruction
of hordes of low-class *mestizos* and Indians is a
difficult task, although it is to be recollected that the
aboriginal brown race of Latin America is intelligent and capable of being raised to a much higher
plane. The miserable salaries paid to school-teachers
prevents the best effort of these being put forward.
An official report has given 1,300 primary schools
throughout the republic, with a total of somewhat
more than 80,000 scholars in attendance ; of
secondary schools 40, with somewhat less than 400
teachers and 4,500 pupils. There are universities
at Quito, Guayaquil, and Cuenca, and six schools of
artes y oficios, or "trades and professions." The
University of Quito has a staff of thirty-three pro-

fessors, with five faculties, those of philosophy and *belles-lettres*, medicine, law, physical and natural science, and mathematics. There are also schools of agriculture and other technical and professional institutions. In general it cannot be said that the machinery of education in Ecuador is behind that of its Latin American neighbours, and in some respects it is in advance. Education may be expected to advance under a stable administration, as in theory the Latin American people strongly advocate the upkeep of schools and colleges.

The upper-class people of Ecuador, like all of their race, are in general too much addicted to following the more theoretical professions, neglecting those practical branches of work without which the life of the nation cannot flourish vigorously. The multiplication of professional men with the degree of " doctor," in law, medicine, and religion, is a marked and detrimental feature of Latin American civilization. In Brazil and Chile the doctorate has now been abolished as undemocratic, and with the hope of turning the attention of young men to more practical professions. The great need of such countries is for educated men who are not ashamed to work with their hands, or at least to take up professions concerned with trade and manufacture.

The standing of the Church has been the subject of much political strife in the history of the republic. According to the Constitution, the religion of the republic is the Roman Catholic Apostolic, and " all others are excluded." At times in its history the influence and power of the Church have been so strong that the Government became a theocracy rather than a republic. But in 1902 and 1904 the power of the clericals was greatly curtailed, as elsewhere described. Whilst the cult of religion is very strong in Latin American communities, especially among the female sex, the desertion of the Church and the reaction to materialism is becoming one of the most marked features of life in those countries.

The Ecuadorian army embodies some 6,000 men. The National Guard is composed of the three classes known as actives, auxiliaries, and passives. The first are all enrolled citizens of twenty to thirty-eight years of age, the second of thirty-eight to forty-four years, and the third of forty-four to fifty years. The total is estimated at somewhat under 100,000 men. The Military School is at Quito and the Naval School at Guayaquil. Ecuador does not pretend to enter into competition with her neighbours in naval armaments, and maintains only a few small vessels.

The usual postal, telegraphic, and telephonic services exist in the republic, but means of communication, as elsewhere described, are extremely backward, and social life and government suffer thereby. There are various excellent newspapers in Ecuador, notably those of Guayaquil and Quito. The Press of the Latin American countries is constantly growing in enterprise and independence, and taking a valuable part in civic progress.

CHAPTER XIV

THE ECUADORIAN PEOPLE AND RACES

THE people of Ecuador present in general appearance little difference from those of the neighbouring republics of Peru and Colombia, and, indeed, throughout the whole of Latin America, from Mexico and Central America to the republics of South America, the distinction between the different nationalities, as regards speech, bearing, physique, physiognomy, and customs and habits is remarkably slight, having in view the enormous extent of territory covered by the Latin American communities. The New World, from the United States frontier down to Patagonia, a Spanish-speaking territory 7,000 miles long, presents racially, perhaps the most homogeneous unit in the world. In comparison with the warring racial units existing over relatively small areas in Europe this characteristic of Latin America stands as a noteworthy one. The most marked differences, of course, are in Argentina, where the Indian race forms a minimum part of the nation.

Notwithstanding this homogeneity, however, the sense of nationality or *patria* among the Latin American republics is strongly marked and jealously guarded. To the foreigner who arrives in South America, the difference at first sight between a person of Ecuadorian, Peruvian, Colombian, Bolivian, or Chilean origin might be indistinguishable, but among these nations themselves jealousy of nomenclature and nationality is strong. Naturally the people of Brazil and Argentina differ most from the general stock, the first by reason of its Portuguese race and considerable negro admixture, and the second from the vast influx of Italian and other foreigners, such as also affects Brazil.

The Ecuadorian people are divided into the three classes or races common to the Latin Americans—that is, the whites, the *mestizos* or people of mixed race, and the Indians. To these must be added the few descendants of the Africans or negroes. Some further subdivisions, moreover, must be made, and are common to all the Andean peoples, who, therefore, may be more minutely divided into the whites, or people of pure European—mainly Spanish—descent ; the pure brown, aboriginal race or Indians ; the *mestizos*, formed of the cross between white and Indian ; the Cholos, formed by the union of *mestizo* and white ; the pure negroes ; the mulattoes, formed by the miscegenation of white and negro ; and the zambos, or cross between Indian and negro.

The number of the population of Ecuador cannot be stated with any approach to exactitude. A complete general census has never been taken. Political disturbances and governmental inefficiency account in part for this state of affairs, and added thereto is the aversion the population display from enumeration, a common circumstance in nearly all the Latin American republics, due partly to the fear of enforced military service and taxation. However, a careful calculation was made in 1889 by Dr. Cevallos, who took as his basis the various returns made to the Ecuadorian Congress from 1830 to 1887, and he arrived at a total population for the republic of 1,272,000 inhabitants. A later official estimate was made in 1900, which assumed the total population at 1,500,00. There is, however, a tendency to exaggerate the size of the population, among the Andean republics especially, due to a desire to augment their importance wherever possible.

The division of the various races or classes above enumerated, in their proper proportion, can only be performed approximately. Great exaggeration is made generally in assigning the number of white people in these republics, due to a desire to be considered white on the part of those who are only partly so. To have a high percentage of people of pure European descent, to be a person of such descent, is to augment national and individual prestige, and the wish is often father to the thought. There is something pathetic in the condition. The idealistic temperament of the Latin American, his pretension to a high civilization and to the status of the *caballero*, creates a natural yearning for the white skin. The pure white proportion of the Ecuadorians has been estimated between great extremes from above 600,000 (Villavicencio), which is manifestly wrong, to 300,000. Even this lower figure must include numbers of people who in reality fall into the *mestizo* class, and probably 100,000 would be nearer the truth. In none of the Andine countries can the proportion be as much as 10 per cent. of the population, except possibly in Chile. It is, of course, impossible to draw a hard-and-fast line, and intermarriage between white and *mestizo* is always proceeding, whilst the white immigration from Europe is practically nil. The people of mixed race, the *mestizos*, probably number more than a third of the population, possibly 400,000 to 500,000, leaving the large balance pertaining to the Indian or pure aboriginal race. The negroes, as a pure race, tend to disappear. They were but the product of slavery, which was abolished in 1854, and they form but a very small percentage, although they have left their mark upon the population in some cases.

The white race naturally forms the governing class. It holds, and in Ecuador strives to monopolize, the seats of authority, the making and enforcement of the laws. In Ecuador, as in Chile, the whites, and some of the *mestizos* of the nearly white class, form an exclusive governing caste or oligarchy. Furthermore, as in Chile, the land of the republic is divided among them, and consequently is largely monopolized in a very few hands, and this circumstance to a considerable extent is responsible for the backward sociological condition of the great bulk of the population. The *mestizo* class, where it has not acquired much wealth or position (and the two things are synonymous in the Latin American communities) forms the artisan element and the small traders and shopkeepers. As, however, some strain of *mestizo* blood enters into almost the whole " white " race, people of some slight shade of colour are found occupying high positions. There is no " colour line " in Latin America as understood in the United States and elsewhere, and consequently no real barrier to the elevation of the *mestizo* class, and through it of the brown race or Indian class. / The *mestizos* who live among the whites and intermarry therewith come to class themselves as " *blancos* " or white whenever their worldly goods are sufficient to enable them to maintain a position of economic stability. On the other hand, the *mestizos* whose lines are cast among the Indians in the more remote regions and small *pueblos* or villages, tend to revert to the Indian type. The *mestizos* of Ecuador have been described as being generally " ignorant, indolent, and non-progressive." [1] This, however, must be regarded as a harsh characterization. They have in large measure the defects of their surroundings and history. But behind them are also the traditions of earlier times, of the Inca rule before the Spanish Conquest, to which has been added the spice of desire for progress which the strain of Iberian blood has given. They cannot be said to be

[1] Article on Ecuador, *Encyc. Brit.*

INDIANS OF THE ENVIRONS OF QUITO.

[To face p. 222.

inferior to their neighbours of Peru or Colombia or to the mixed race generally of Latin America. They are not without the excellent traits of hospitality among their more enlightened members which marks out the Spanish character from the often sulky and distrustful Indian—distrustful, however, by reason of the oppression of his conquerors rather than by nature.

The people of the Andine republics (as of Latin America generally) have been subject abroad to considerable misapprehension. The traveller who studies them from an unbiassed point of view will find that his previous notions concerning them undergo some change. The cultured society of Ecuador, which includes the whites and an extensive upper part of the *mestizos*, have many of the habits and customs of all cultured peoples. The most marked difference between the upper class in Latin America and that of European or North American communities is not a lack of culture and ideals on the part of the former but an excess thereof. The desire to be considered as " highly civilized " displays itself quixotically at times. Almost an excess of courtesy is displayed, and an amiability towards the foreigner is shown such as is not encountered probably in any other part of the world. This is perhaps the most marked characteristic that the foreigner encounters. From the fact of being a foreign person of education, the traveller from Europe or the United States is received and entertained in a manner to which he would be a stranger elsewhere. Isolated in his more or less remote towns and cities, the educated Latin American looks eagerly towards the more advanced nations of the world, devours his newspaper, criticizes or absorbs what is new, and turns with feelings of friendship towards the traveller from Britain, France, Germany, the United States, or elsewhere. The women of the Ecuadorian upper class possess those pleasing traits which characterize their sex in Spanish America. They are often handsome, in their own special type, eminently *simpatica,* and as wives and mothers are a worthy and assiduous people. Whenever a more liberal social spirit shall invade these communities, as undoubtedly must be the case, the intellectuality of the Latin American women will expand. At present social custom is repressive. But of their devoutness in religion and their native refinement there is no question. Many of the best families of the Latin American communities—and the condition holds good in Quito and Guayaquil—send their sons to high-class schools and colleges abroad, and often the parents themselves have received a foreign education. For the foreigner, however, the most objectionable condition in Latin America—and it is very marked in Ecuador—is the lack of hygiene and sanitary appliances and methods, even in the large towns, and this counts as a reproach greatly against the civilization of these communities.

A serious drawback in the Latin American character is that quality which tends to substitute words for facts. The truth becomes distorted, exaggeration takes its place, and expediency or opportunism tends to colour social dealings, and chicanery to influence commercial and political matters. Often an agreement is an instrument which may be broken if circumstances so dictate. Yet there is a pretension to a very high plane of personal honour, which at least is a valuable ideal. But the strong individualistic character of the man of Spanish race constantly leads him into revolution. The laws he has made to govern the community are not necessarily to be followed by himself. The Latin American has the born instincts of the lawyer, but lacks those of the economist or engineer. That is to say, he is eloquent and argumentative rather than constructive. He cannot build a railway or successfully control a joint-stock company or readily develop the natural resources around him. The terrible political murders constantly taking place in the Latin American communities reveal an unsettled and ruthless mode in which the savage protrudes through the veneer of civilization. When these defects disappear much may be expected of the Latin American people.

The pure Indians or aborigines of Ecuador may be divided into three classes—those of the coast, those of the Andine region and uplands, and those of the Amazon forest region. Herein lies a difference from their classification in Peru. In the latter country there are but two divisions—the Indians of the Andine regions or sierras, and those of the Amazon forests, corresponding to the same two regions in Ecuador. But in Peru there is no special division of coast Indians, which are of the same character, in general terms, as the upland Indians. In Ecuador, due to the different climatic environment, the race of Indians inhabiting the northern littoral, especially in Esmeraldas, approximates to the character of the Amazon forest Indians, both having a tropic forested environment.

In order fully to understand the character and condition of the Indians it is necessary to recollect the history of the country. The Incas displaced the earlier governance of the Shiris, and substituted the Quechua language. Under the Spaniards the upland Indians became Christianized. This influence extended—as the Inca influence had done—to the Indians of the whole of the Andes and of the Pacific littoral of Peru, but it did not reach the Indians of the Amazon forests, although it affected those of the equatorial coastal forest districts of Ecuador somewhat. In fact, wherever the forest extended, there both the Inca and the Spanish influence was to a large degree absent, and the condition remains in great part to this day. The upland peoples of the Andine

15

regions, and of the Pacific coast in general, are under the civil and religious control of the various republics, whilst the forest people are styled *salvajes* or savages, and are outside the control or even the protection of the law. This latter circumstance was strongly exemplified in the case of the Indians of the Putumayo rubber forests.

The main division of the Ecuadorian Indians who inhabit the uplands, as in Peru, Colombia, Venezuela, and Bolivia, have formed the *mestizo* class, from the intermarriage and cohabitation of the whites with their women. From Spain very few women came to western South America, and the Spanish conquerors and colonists perforce mated with the native women of Quechua, Aymará, and other races. Similarly the upland Indians also form the basis of the Cholos, and these three divisions—*mestizos*, Cholos, and Indians—shade off into each other indefinably. There are certain distinctions between these people as regards colour, and a *mestizo* is offended by being called a Cholo, whilst the Cholo is angry if called a mulatto.[1] This last is natural, as the brown race is eminently superior to the black, which is altogether alien and exotic.

These Indians of the interior, the *sierra* or upland region, are of a copperish hue, at times of darker shades, at times of lighter. They are, in fact, the brown race of " Amerinds," as some writers have termed the American Indians. The " Red Indian " is a misnomer in America. The aboriginal people are brown rather than red. The *sierra* Indians are straight-haired, the hair generally long and smooth. It is worn sometimes in Peru and Bolivia and parts of Ecuador in a *trensa* or queue, both by women and men. There is no beard, or this is at best very scarce, the eyes are black and generally small (in the *mestizo* women the eyes are generally large and expressive,

[1] According to Cevallos.

INDIAN WATER-CARRIER, QUITO

INDIANS OF QUITO.

[To face p. 256.

a result of the Spanish strain), the face is broad, with well-formed nose, large mouth, and teeth generally white and even. They are near or below a middle stature, with broad chests and shoulders, and generally small feet. Their temperament is phlegmatic, and their character inclining to melancholy. They are generally of a lazy disposition, or at least disinclined to work more than is necessary to ensure a bare livelihood, and they are taciturn and full of distrust towards the foreigner, under which term all people of white race, even the Ecuadorians themselves, are included. Although lazy as to long-sustained work in wage-earning, these people are nevertheless strong and vigorous, and of peculiar aptitude in matters within their special province. They can carry enormous loads for great distances, and journey on foot, even in the most inaccessible territory, without fatigue, and often on the most meagre diet. They are humble even to the point of cowardice, before the white man or *mestizo*, and even allow themselves at times to be dominated by the few specimens of negroes or Asiatics, people who are inferior to them in most respects, but more alert and usurious. Under the influence of drink their ordinary cast of mind changes, and they become temporarily talkative and quarrelsome, developing an extraordinary obstinacy, during which frame of mind they will suffer death rather than give way. However, their habitual timidity is largely due to the sufferings and oppression they have undergone at the hands of the white man. They have naturally a keen woodcraft instinct and mountaineering aptitude, although they fear to ascend the untrodden snows of the great volcanoes. One of the characteristics of the Andine Indians and Cholos is their extreme care in small matters such as in the transport of articles. An Indian will carry a fragile object over the roughest country without breaking it.[1]

[1] The Author has fully described the Cholos in his *Republics of Central and South America, op. cit.*

The ordinary dress of the upland Indian has
naturally been determined by his inclement surroundings—the cold climate, winds, and fog. The
aboriginal of the lowlands and forests goes naked
or with a mere loincloth or loose shirt, but the
Indian of the *sierra* goes thickly clothed. The dress
of the men consists in loose, short drawers or
trousers of linen or cotton, coming below the calf
of the leg, a shirt, and, most important of all
aboriginal apparel, a *poncho* of woven wool. Upon
his head—and the women similarly wear it—is a
round, white felt hat, with a brim of medium width.
The feet are either bare or sandals are worn.
These sandals or *alpargatas*, as they are termed, are
generally made of *maguey* fibre, sometimes of raw
hide. Both the *poncho* and the sandal seem common
to Latin America, from Mexico to Peru and Chile,
and are aboriginal. The women wear a cloth that
covers the body from the waist to below the knees,
and another cloth covering the breast and back,
leaving the arms free. Covering the upper part of
the body over the under-garment is a *manta* or shawl,
which also serves to carry an infant slung therein,
or, indeed, any object. This shawl, like the men's
poncho, is formed of thick woollen cloth, generally
manufactured by themselves as home industry. The
upland Indians have always been good weavers, as
elsewhere described.

The dwellings of the Indian or Cholo, in the
country, are small *chosas* or huts of the most primitive character, built of earth in some cases and merely
of *paja* or upland grass or straw in others. Both
by reason of lack of material and for warmth the
chosas are of one room only, of small dimensions,
and they are absolutely bare of any articles of
furniture or means of comfort. The bed is formed
of sheepskins laid directly upon the floor, and here
the whole family, often of many children, sleep

together, with four or five dog's of the small currish
breed common to the region. A few of the most
rudimentary cooking utensils complete the domestic
equipment, the fire being made outside the hut, with
a few stones for backing. Food consists mainly
of maize ,and potatoe,s, and in the lowlands of
bananas, etc.

It is thus seen that the condition of the upland
Indians is of the most humble and often poverty-
stricken kind. This condition is not confined to
Ecuador, but obtains throughout the Andes and
through South America generally, whilst the description applies almost equally to the many million of
Mexican *peones*. The condition of poverty, privation, and ignorance in which the great bulk of the
people of Latin America live—for the *peon,* Cholo,
and Indian class vastly outweighs the small upper
classes which live in comparative comfort—is one
which indicates the slow civic advance of the Latin
American communities. The sociological conditions
of these vast regions reflect seriously upon the selfish
upper and governing class, in whose few hands the
wealth and education of the so-called republics is
monopolized. The lapse of four centuries of Spanish
(and Portuguese) civilization finds the Indians of
Latin America in a state inferior to that of the time
when the conquest of their territories was entered
upon, it is scarcely an exaggeration to say,. For the
student of native sociology it is impossible to regard
the excellent South American Indian race without
lamenting their unfortunate lot and condemning the
exploitation of which they are made the objects.
Whilst their position has improved somewhat since
the establishing of the various republics of Ecuador,
Peru, and others, the state of subjection and poverty
in which they live, the insanitary conditions of their
lives, and the lack of governmental effort to remedy
these, prevent any substantial advance. Exposed

to the burning sun of the tropics, which alter-
nates with the glacial cold of the *páramos* and
uplands, insufficiently clothed and fed, and a prey to
the inroads caused by fiery alcohol, upon whose sale
the large landowners and manufacturers make a
profit, the valuable Andine Indian race is rapidly
deteriorating. Once destroyed, this hardy mountain
race can scarcely be replaced, as the inclement
conditions of the atmosphere, the rarefied air, and
elevation are such as no immigrating people could
support, or not until they had become inured to the
environment by the lapse of various generations. It
is not that the Governments of these republics oppress
the Indians and Cholos of purposeful intent. There
are laws to protect them, but these humble people
are far below the position to which the laws of the
State entitle them. These laws cannot be enforced
in regions subject to political turmoil, in a state of
society so primitive, and among an upper class whose
tradition it is—tradition inherited from the Spaniards
—to regard the Indian as a born menial and use
him almost as a beast of burden.

It is not to be supposed, however, that these
Indians are altogether lacking in a spirit of protest
against the conditions of their lives. Before the
close of the Spanish regimen, and in some instances
since, there have been serious rebellions, in which
the Indians have attacked the whites and *mestizos*
and treated them revengefully, whole villages having
been wiped out at times. Such rebellions have been
overcome with considerable difficulty, and in some
cases could not have been suppressed but for the
lack of organization of the Indians among themselves. One of the main obstacles to a better understanding between the aboriginal race and the whites
and *mestizos* is the great barrier of distrust that has
been created by the double-dealing and oppression
visited upon the aboriginals, ever since the first

Spaniards landed, by these "foreigners." Forced
to work against their will, driven into the mines
when they often abhorred mining work, worked to
death therein, their wretched carcasses pitched aside
when life gave out under the meagre fare and onerous
toil, their small *chacaras* or holdings alienated, their
women outraged, their cattle confiscated—it is no
matter for surprise that a barrier of hatred and
distrust should have been built up between the *raza
conquistada* or conquered race, as it is generally
designated, and their overlords. Some of the worst
abuses have ceased since the growth of the republics,
but the same spirit prevails, and if the Indians are
subject to a less extent to forced work, peonage, and
practically slavery, they still suffer therefrom to a
considerable degree, whilst to it has been added
enforced military service, which they abhor. In
the name of the *patria,* by revolutionary generals
of this or that uprising party, the Indians have
become mere food for powder, dragged from their
simple industries, abused, and demoralized. The
Indian is far from being without defects himself.
His laziness, dishonesty, and untruthfulness, with
a love of strong drink, are grave defects. But it
is to be recollected that such defects as regards
primitive people have too often been acquired by
contact with the white race. "Laziness," as already
remarked, admits of qualifications. The Indian has
no idea of amassing wealth beyond his immediate
requirements ; and to work for the increment of
profits or dividends for others is a matter beyond
his comprehension. In his native state he is master
of his own actions, and to herd Indians into mines,
factories, and plantations breaks down the good
native qualities. The South American Indian has
nothing in common with the often brutal and bloodthirsty savage races of Africa or other black natives.
He is essentially peaceful and averse from blood-

shedding. His native weapons alone were indicative that his disposition was peaceful, for they were not adapted for warfare or attack so much as for hunting. It is noteworthy that the Indians throughout the Andine regions and coasts of all the western and northern republics of South America (with the exception of Chile, where the fierce Araucarnians predominated) do not settle personal disputes with knives. The dagger is not used in quarrels, but sticks and stones are employed. To shed blood appears to be abhorrent to all the people who came under the Inca influence. The forest Indians use the deadly blowpipes and often poisoned arrows, but these are not blood-shedding weapons.

The Indians of South America, as of Central America and Mexico, stand in a somewhat remarkable position, differing from that of the people of any other continent. They were not mere small tribes, living on suffrance and earning the gratitude of the conqueror by their earliest possible disappearance from the soil, as was the case in the United States, Canada, or Australia, but they form the actual population themselves ; they have formed the base of every Latin American nation (except Argentina), and it is by drawing upon them that the population is increased. Their colour, to a greater or lesser degree, tinges the face of the South American man and woman of whatever class, from President and Cabinet Ministers downwards. The form of their features has been transplanted into the faces of lawyers, generals, doctors, statesmen, and all others throughout the whole range of the score of Latin American republics. It is more persistent than the white man's face. To despise and maltreat the Indian is to abuse the stock from which the governing class largely springs. The native blood is inextricably mingled with all classes. It was the brown Indian women who formed the mothers of

CLOTHED INDIANS OF THE ORIENTE, OR EASTERN FOREST REGION.

[To face p. 264.

the Peruvians, Mexicans, Ecuadorians, Brazilians, Colombians, Venezuelans, Bolivians, Guatemalans, and others. The adventurous Spanish *conquistador* and colonist ran riot among the soft, pleasing, and unprotesting Indian girls, surrounded themselves with harems (and the custom still obtains largely), and with their great fecundity the Indian women have brought to being new nations ; and there is certainly nothing to be ashamed of in the origin. Notwithstanding this the *mestizo,* or man of mixed white and brown blood, pretends to regard the Indian as an inferior being, jealously oppresses him, sets him apart, regards him almost as an animal, and excludes him from civic rights and, whenever possible, from the enjoyment of property.

It is necessary that a due idea of proportion regarding the Indians of Latin America should be created. In the United States " a good Indian was a dead Indian," according to early frontier notions. The Indian was for long a being to be " wiped out " by the Anglo-Saxon colonists, and in this connexion it would be pharisaical to condemn the attitude of the Spanish colonist towards the particular division of the brown or red race which fell beneath his control. On the other hand, the number of aborigines in what is now the United States and Canada was very much smaller than in Latin America. It has been calculated as only about half a million, made up of numerous tribes, who lived by hunting and in tents. But in Mexico and Peru, and Latin America generally, the aboriginal population numbered many millions. Mexico was thickly populated in certain districts, under the Aztecs and other partly civilized people, and the Andine slopes and uplands and Pacific littoral sheltered possibly still greater numbers—people who lived a settled, ordered life. Such people might well form the basis of nations when the wandering tribes of

Northern America could not. The Spanish chroniclers have taken credit to themselves that Spaniards formed new nations in America by mixing with the old, whilst the Anglo-Saxon only repudiated or destroyed such. But it was the sheer force of numbers and necessity that brought about this condition in Latin America rather than any desire of the Spanish colonists to conserve the native races. However, to the Spanish monarchs, who from vast distances launched their decrees and *cedulas*, full credit must be given for their endeavour to preserve and Christianize the native people, a matter which the critic of early Spanish brutality in America too frequently overlooks.

The Indians of the Ecuadorian coast regions, as before remarked, differ essentially from those of the uplands. Before the Spanish conquest the population of the Pacific littoral between the Cordillera and the sea was, it is held, much more numerous than at the present time. This has been deduced both from written history and from the numerous ancient habitations and the articles recovered from the *huacas* or burial-places from Tumbez, south of Ecuador, to Tumaco, in Colombia. These Indians belonged to numerous tribes and families rather than forming part of one nation, and they were of different grades of culture and spoke different languages, as before described. Probably those tribes living nearest the coast were at first the most advanced. As time went on they lost their individuality largely by fusion with the whites and the Africans. Even the village Indians, which still remain in some number in the Morro and Santa Elena peninsula and in the province of Manabi, have lost their ancient languages and customs ; and the same circumstance has taken effect in the Loja province, except in the northernmost portion. The most typical and unchanged of the coast Indians are found in the province of Esmeraldas,

the northernmost of the republic. This region from
the first remained freest from the Spanish invasion,
and at the present time has the smallest white population. The Cayapas Indians have conserved their
customs and languages almost intact. They live
scattered along the margins of the River Cayapas,
the Onzole, the Rio Grande, and other tributaries
of the Cayapas, but their number scarcely passes
2,000.[1] They are of middle height, robust constitution, clear, copper-coloured complexion, inclining
to yellow, long hair, and pleasing physiognomy.
They paint their faces, arms, legs, breasts, etc., in
red, blue, and black stripes, showing a partiality for
vermilion, which they prepare from the fruit of the
achiote, and in some cases anoint the whole body
with the cosmetic thus prepared. Their mode of life
is similar to that of the Indians of the River Napo,
to the east of the Andes ; they support themselves
by hunting and fishing and form plantations of
bananas and yuccas. The only domestic animals bred
by them are swine, dogs, and fowls. They use the
blowpipe and arrows, at times poisoned, although
some are acquainted with firearms, and their domestic
utensils are of the most primitive character. Their
dress consists in a short drawers for the men and a
broad cloth for the women, which covers the body
from the navel to the knees. These garments are
made of native material, or else are procured at La
Tola or San Lorenzo, the natives exchanging there
for fruits, baskets, rubber, and other matters of their
own produce. Their houses are generally spacious
and clean, but, being anti-social, like many of the
American native tribes, they do not dwell in villages
and collect together only once or twice a year to
celebrate certain feasts. Their dwellings are thus
much scattered in the forest. They shrink from
contact with the whites, and even more so from the

[1] According to Wolf, *op. cit.*, and other observers.

blacks, and only from sheer necessity enter the coast villages. This exclusiveness has tended to preserve their customs, and they recognize the authority only of their own cacique, whom they call *gobernador*, who is recognized by the Governor of Esmeraldas. Apart from their taciturnity and reserve these Indians are docile and hospitable and affable with travellers who do not molest them. They have some reputation for native honesty, thieving being unknown among them. These Cayapas are Christianized, the *cura* or Roman Catholic priest of the locality visiting them once a year to baptize children and bless marriages. These Indians learn to speak Spanish with difficulty, but understand it somewhat, and they forbid their women to learn the language of the whites. Their own language is distinct from the Quechua of the *sierra* or Andine region, and is of some special interest as being the last remaining native language of western Ecuador. The language also differs from that of the Esmeralda Indians.

The relatively considerable black population of the Esmeraldas province, and the mulattoes and Zambas associated therewith have come about from a curious circumstance. In 1623, according to Cevallos, at the time when Esmeraldas was almost entirely inhabited by the Cayapas, a vessel arrived at the small port of Atacames with several hundreds of negro slaves on board, bound for Peru. The Africans broke out, overpowered and killed all the whites on the ship, landed and took possession of the town, killed every man, whether white or Indian, within their reach, and made themselves masters of the country for many miles around. The women were spared and taken as wives by the black men, who remained undisturbed in possession of the port and the lands they had taken. As a result, the numerous mixed progeny of coloured people grew up and formed the existing settlements.

The Indians of the eastern or forested Amazon region of Ecuador differ greatly from the upland Indians. Probably the difference is such as has been brought about by varying environments—the forest and hot climate on the one hand and the bare, mountainous uplands and cold climate on the other : and there is not, in all probability, any fundamental difference of race between the highland and the lowland Indians in South America. As elsewhere remarked, it has been affirmed by ethnologists that American Indians are of original Mongoloid descent, America having been overrun by Mongols in very early times. The Indians of this region are divided into a large number of tribes, which it would be difficult to enumerate, even if they were all known. Those which live nearest to the Cordillera are best known. Many of the tribes came under the influence of the missionaries in the seventeenth and eighteenth centuries, but with the destruction or decadence of the missions, especially after the expulsion of the Jesuits towards the close of the eighteenth century, the Indians reverted to savagery. In certain districts the missions have been retained, however.

About forty-six tribes of Indians have been enumerated north of the Marañon, some of them very small in number. Among them are the Orejones of the Napo. The name " Orejon " signifies " large ears," and has been applied to them on account of their custom of augmenting the size of the ear by hanging weights as earrings thereto. This custom has been traced to the Incas. It is also found among some African tribes. The people number about 1,500 or 2,000.[1] The Jíbaros are the most numerous, as well as the most feared. They destroyed the early Spanish colonies on the Amazon affluents in Ecuador

[1] Von Hassell, *Documentos Oficiales del Departamento de Loreto.* Lima, 1905.

in early times. They are described as well-formed, fierce, and revengeful. Another tribe, between the Napo and the Pastaza, are the Zaparos, and on the headwaters of the Aguarico are the Cofanes. Of sub-tribes there are many designations. Some of these savage inhabitants off the forests and rivers possess very curious customs and methods concerning religion, marriage, childbirth, etc., and in their dwellings. The blowpipe and bows and arrows are the principal weapons. The peculiar art of making the reduced human heads (specimens of which are found in some museums) was practised by certain of the tribes of this region. The singular *tunday*, or native signalling instrument, consisting of a notched hollow log suspended by a cord and similarly fastened to the ground, is used among them, an instrument by means of which messages or signals can be projected for considerable distances through the forest by blows producing different notes. The deadly blow-pipe poison, and the weapons themselves, form articles of commerce among these tribes. Some tribes dwell in community houses ; some are clothed, others naked ; and among some there is a primitive idea of a Supreme Being.

The Huambisa Indians inhabit the country between the upper reaches of the Santiago and Morona Rivers. They are descended, like the Jíbaros, from the pure Indian and the Spanish race—from the Spanish women who were captured by the Indians in 1599 at the sack of Sevilla de Oro—and in some cases are fair-skinned and bearded, due to the admixture, so differing from the usual copper-coloured and beardless natives of the Amazon basin. They have a reputation for cruelty and treachery, and before the middle of last century almost exterminated the civilized Indians of the missions in that region. In February, 1913, the Huambisas rose and massacred the soldiers of the outpost which was established by Peru in the

NAKED INDIANS OF THE NAPO, EASTERN FOREST REGION.

[To face p. 238.

district disputed by that country with Ecuador.   The captain of the troop was shot with his own gun by the Indian chief, whom he had just shown how to use the weapon.   The whole settlement was massacred, all those present at the time being killed. News of the occurrence was received in Lima by wireless telegraphy from Iquitos.   The outpost was, however, re-established, with a troop of soldiers and a steam-launch for river service.

The Indians of the Oriente tend to decrease rapidly, due to the methods of exploitation practised by the whites, and the acquisition of the white man's vices and diseases, to which they were originally, strangers as a rule.   It would seem at present that under the existing methods of commerce in the Amazon valley, this aboriginal race is doomed to disappear, but there are signs of protest against this selfish and ruthless destruction of a useful race.[1] Attention is also being drawn to the evils in the peonage system, on the Guayas plantations and in the uplands.   The " truck-system," even if it have some uses in such communities, lends itself to grave abuses.

[1] In large part due to the activities of the Anti-Slavery Society and Aborigines' Protection League, of London.   In his book *The Andes and the Amazon*, published in 1907, the Author drew attention to these matters.

CHAPTER XV

THE CHIEF TOWNS OF ECUADOR

THE republic of Ecuador is best known to the out-side world by its seaport of Guayaquil and by the Equator city of Quito, thle capital of the country, now connected with each other by railway. The two cities represent the extremes of climatic and topo-graphical environment—the one lying upon the hot, humid coast, the other in the cold uplands surrounded by mountains.

Guayaquil is the commercial capital of the republic, and its principal seaport. It occupies an advantageous position near the confluence of many navigable rivers, which give access to the various important districts of the littoral, and is at the same time accessible for ocean steamers and vessels which traffic upon the Pacific coast. The site of Guayaquil was well chosen by those who founded it. Had it been farther up the river, the depth of water would have been insufficient for a first-class port, whilst lower down it would have been approached with difficulty by the numerous small craft which bring its most important articles of commerce from the districts traversed by the navigable streams. The port is thirty-three miles above the junction of the Guayas River with the Gulf of Guayaquil, on the right bank, and lies in latitude 2° 12' south and longi-tude 79° 51' west. The town, with the exception of a small part of the *Ciudad Vieja*, or old town, lies on comparatively flat land, about thirty feet above

PART OF GUAYAQUIL.

[To face p. 246.

sea-level, and the tide rises and falls some thirteen feet or more in the harbour. The *savanna* or plain extends southwards from the base of three low hills known as Los Cerros de la Cruz, between the river and the Estero Salado, the sea-arm which reaches to the back of the town. The first view of Guayaquil is picturesque, with clusters of houses along the front, backed by verdure-clad hills, and the broad surface of the river beneath. The long lines of white buildings, with curtained balconies looking down upon the gaily clad Indians in the curious craft upon the water, give what may be described as a Venice-like aspect to the port. At night the impression is not dispelled, and observing the town from the steamer's deck it appears of great extent, the numerous gas lights extending far along the water front, reflected in the river, and disposed in terraces up the sloping ground at the back. The considerable shipping, flying the flags of various nations, adds interest and importance to the scene.

The town stretches for about two miles along the low banks, and the harbour, two and a half miles in length and bordered with one and a half miles of quays, exhibits considerable commercial activity. Quaint-looking, narrow gondolas, or canoes, and broad rafts, bringing down produce from the rivers, mix among the steam-launches and sea-going steamers. The landing from the steamer is by shore boats, after the fashion of South American ports generally, a method of much inconvenience to the traveller, the only redeeming feature of which is that a means of livelihood is afforded thereby to the strange-looking but generally good-natured and willing watermen who swarm over the vessel when she drops anchor. Produce from the wharves is carried out in lighters, and tram-lines traverse the quays, laden with the tropic articles of commerce. Steamboat connection is regularly maintained with

16

the rich agricultural districts of the Guayas fluvial system, ₁as described elsewhere, the boats running as far as Bodegas or Babahoyo, eighty miles up the river of that name, and forty miles on the Daule River. For smaller boats upon the Guayas system, the aggregate length of navigable water is about 200 miles. The Guayas River is navigable up to Guayaquil for steamers drawing twenty-two feet of water. Vessels of larger size anchor at Puná, forty miles below the port, and cargoes and passengers are there transferred to or from the vessel by lighters. Puná lies on the island of that name ; its deep-water port is six and a half miles outside the Guayas bar on the eastern end of the island. Here, also, is the quarantine station. Among the industries of Guayaquil is a shipyard, where vessels are built or repaired. The river off Guayaquil has been likened to the Mississippi at New Orleans.

Santiago de Guayaquil was founded on July 25, 1535, St. James's Day (Santiago), by Sebastian de Benalcazar. It was abandoned on two occasions before being permanently developed by Francisco de Orellana in 1537. During the seventeenth and eighteenth centuries the place was captured and sacked several times by buccaneers, among them Jacob Clark, in 1624, and by French pirates in 1686, and English freebooters, under David, in 1687. In 1707 William Dampier attacked it, and Clapperton in 1709. Later on, when the town was made a Governor's residence, a castle and other defensive works were erected. Conflagration has been rife at various periods, and the town was burnt in 1707, 1764, 1865, 1896, and 1899, the flimsy wooden construction lending itself easily to the flames. Severe earthquake shocks have visited it, but, due to the wooden construction of the houses, much loss of life has not occurred. The valley of the Guayas is so named from the word meaning " Valley of Lamentations," from a defeat which befell the Spanish arms in the early years of colonization.

Santiago de Guayaquil, which is the full name of the city, embodies a new and an old town. The latter, the upper or northern part, is inhabited by the poorer classes. The streets in this section are tortuous, badly paved and undrained, pestilential and dirty, and in large part responsible for the evil reputation of Guayaquil as a centre of fever and plague from which the port suffers. In 1896 a great fire destroyed a large part of the old town, the buildings of which were mainly of wood and cane, and the insanitary condition underwent some improvement in its reconstruction. The southern part of the city, the new town, forms the business and residential quarters of the better classes, but even here the houses are mainly of wood, and the streets are provided only with surface drainage. Part of the town becomes flooded in the rainy season. In general terms, however, Guayaquil must be regarded as a pleasing and, in some respects, attractive place, far superior in modern comforts and convenience to any of the upland towns of the country.

The population of Guayaquil, according to the census of 1890, was 44,800 inhabitants, of which about 4,400 were foreigners. In 1897 the estimate was of 51,000 inhabitants, which has increased at the present time probably to 60,000. This population has doubled since the middle of last century, the area of the city has increased considerably, and its appearance tends to improve. The principal streets are wide and straight. The buildings are of two and three stories, but of little or no architectural pretensions. The traveller who observes the façades of the churches and public buildings and of many private houses, with their considerable adornments, scarcely realizes at first sight that these structures are of wood ; and the *gremio*, or fraternity of carpenters of Guayaquil is worthy of credit for the effect of its work. One of the notable architectural features is that of the balconies to the houses and the projecting upper stories of the business buildings, which thus form covered ways or arcades for the footpaths of the streets. There are many first-class shops in Guayaquil, where almost everything familiar to the foreigner can be purchased. In addition to the cathedral, whose towers and façade are noteworthy, there are seven churches in the city, and a governor's and a bishop's palace, town hall, national college, episcopal seminary, the San Vicente schools of law and medicine, a theatre, hospitals, customhouse, and various asylums and charitable institutions. Guayaquil is also the seat of a university corporation, having faculties of law and medicine. There is a gas manufacturing plant and factories for ice-making, for chocolate, a brewery, iron foundry, machine-shops, etc. The water supply is brought through iron mains from the Cordillera, some fifty-three miles distant, and the mains pass under the Guayas River and discharge into a large distributing reservoir on the hills north of the city. The streets of Guayaquil are provided with electric and horse trams, and are lighted by gas and electricity, and there is a telephone system. Telegraph communication with the outside world is maintained by the West Coast Cable, controlled by an English company. The cable lands at Santa Elena, on the Pacific coast. There are several pleasing *plazas*, or squares, in the city, one of which contains a statue to Bolivar.

From the fortress-crowned hills at the eastern end of the city, especially that of Santa Anna, a fine panorama of Guayaquil, its river, bay, and general environs is obtained. The roads leading out to the suburbs are rough and dusty, after the usual fashion of Latin American towns, and to traverse them on foot is unpleasant. A drive in the environs reveals the tropical capabilities of the soil, which are scarcely in evidence in approaching the city by water. Groves of coconut-palms and plantations of sugar-cane, forests blazing with flowers of such vivid scarlet hue that the trees almost appear to be on fire, and pineapple fields and banana plantations, loaded with fruit, are passed. The tropical vegetation is of exceeding beauty, with a profusion of mingled colours, crowned by the slender, graceful palms. A journey up the Guayas River by steamer reveals to the full the richness of the tropic lowlands and the commercial wealth yielded thereby.

As regards its climate, Guayaquil has been greatly abused, but the plagues and fevers generally associated therewith are due less to the climatic condition than the backward and insanitary condition of life among the people, especially those of the poorer classes. As described in the chapter dealing with the climate of the republic, the year is divided into a wet and a dry season, the former from January to June, when the hot days are followed by floods of rain at night. The mean annual temperature is about 82° to 83° F. The summer, or dry season, is pleasant and healthy. Malarial and bilious disorders are common at certain seasons, and " Guayaquil fever " is a scourge. Epidemics of yellow fever are not infrequent ; but, on the other hand, there are years when no case of such exists in the city. It has been asserted that if yellow fever were not constantly imported into Guayaquil the disease would not reappear of itself. Further, it cannot be said that the effects of yellow fever in Guayaquil are as severe as regards mortality as the epidemics of cholera, etc., in other parts of the world which enjoy a temperate climate as contrasted with a tropical one. It has been stated that yellow fever is not endemic in Ecuador, that it is confined to Guayaquil, and has been imported from Panama. It cannot be said that the inhabitants of Guayaquil are of a sickly appearance, or languid disposition, or that they are naturally indolent, and the supposed enervating effect of a tropical climate is not apparent in that seaport. In comparison with the *serranos*, or people of the mountainous interior, it is held that the inhabitants of Guayaquil, whether of the upper or lower classes, are hard-working. The death-rate of the town is not necessarily high, and is increased by the advent of people suffering from infirmities who come in to seek medical advice.

The insalubrity of the climate of Ecuador has been subject to some exaggeration by travellers. Guayaquil has been condemned as a pest-house of plague and yellow fever, and is often avoided by the steamers of the coast which ply between Panama and Peruvian and Chilean ports, under fear of quarantine, which might be incurred after calling at the port. Unfortunately, there is considerable ground for the unenviable reputation, but conditions have improved of late years, due in part to the advent of the Americans in the work of the railway. The descriptions of travellers have been perhaps too pointed. It was recorded by Whymper, the Andine traveller, that he " made a collection of fifty different specimens of vermin which infested the bedroom he occupied at Guayaquil," including cockroaches, mosquitoes, bed-bugs, fleas, etc. But the insanitary conditions cannot be palliated or denied, and are very offensive.

The insanitary conditions are not due to climate but to the mode of life of the inhabitants of such places. The natural swamps or inundations of themselves are not insanitary, but in Guayaquil and elsewhere the formation of stagnant pools and foul spots, full of rotting animal and vegetable matter, gives rise to disease. It is less remarkable that so many

THE GUAYAQUIL HARBOUR FROM DURAN

[To face p. 46.

persons are attacked by disease in such surroundings than that so many escape, and this must be attributed to the benignity of the climate. After the streets have been washed by the torrential rains diseases are minimized or disappear, showing that it is not to the humidity that they are due, but to the accumulated filth. In the houses and *patios*, or courtyards, especially those of the poorer classes, the greatest negligence of ordinary sanitary conditions exists, and those most common precautions demanded by a tropical situation are unregarded. If the streets of Guayaquil were well paved and properly drained, accompanied by extermination of mosquitoes as carried out scientifically elsewhere, there is little doubt that this ill-reputed seaport would become one of the healthiest of tropical towns.

As regards yellow fever in Ecuador, this does not arise spontaneously in the outlying villages, or even in the immediate neighbourhood of Guayaquil. During some years there has been no single case of yellow fever in the city. On the other hand, there have been very severe epidemics, and between the years 1909 and 1912 more than 1,000 persons were attacked by yellow fever, and twice as many by plague, whilst smallpox and other epidemics had to their account many more victims. Huigra, at 4,000 feet elevation, on the Guayaquil-Quito Railway, is described as being above the yellow-fever zone.

The opening of the Panama Canal will doubtless be of great economic value to Guayaquil, and to the republic generally, as affording a means of transport for its products without transhipment at Panama, avoiding the long route to Europe or the United States which the journey round South America involves. Guayaquil, which lies so vast a distance from New York by the Cape Horn route, is only 2,800 miles via Panama. From Liverpool via Cape Horn the distance to Guayaquil is 11,321 miles, and from New Orleans 11,683 miles, which distances will be correspondingly shortened.

The principal articles of export from Guayaquil are the *cacao*, or chocolate beans, followed by rubber, coffee, tobacco, hides, cotton, " Panama " hats, cinchona bark, and ivory nuts. The total value of this export amounts to more than three-quarters of that of the whole republic.

Quito, the capital of Ecuador, is not without an atmosphere of interest and even romance. Remote and inaccessible as it has been until, in the last few decades, the railway united it with the outer world, Quito still conserves its character of a mountain capital, surrounded by lofty snowclad volcanoes, whose names are bywords in geography. There are many large towns in the Andes, throughout Peru, Colombia, Bolivia, and Venezuela, but both by reason of its history and its topography the capital of Ecuador is among the most interesting. The Quito valley lies at an elevation of 9,500 feet above sea-level. Around the upland valley are twenty noble volcanic summits, whose variety of form is remarkable, from the truncated to the perfect cone, from jagged and sunken crests to smooth, snow-covered, gleaming domes, among them the beautiful, if dreaded, Cotopaxi. These mountains are fully described in dealing with the peaks and volcanoes.

The historical interest of Quito lies in the fact that it was the ancient centre of the Shiri empire, formed by the mysterious Caras and the Quitus, as described in the historical section of this work, whose dynasty fell before the Incas under Huayna Capac, who in their turn gave way to the Spaniards. The famous Inca road, traversing the Cordilleras and tablelands, joined Quito with Cuzco, passing through the various centres of Inca civilization, with their stone-built temples and palaces, flanked by hill

THE PLAZA, QUITO.

[To face p. 248.

fortresses which guarded the heads of the valleys to the east or the west against the attacks of savage tribes. The remains of this road still exist.

As regards the character of the climate and surroundings of Quito, opinions differ considerably. It is difficult to comprehend why the Shiris and the Incas should have built or maintained their capital city upon such a spot, a small, broken *meseta*, or plain, as is that of Quito, or why the Spaniards perpetuated it upon a site of so little advantage and utility, when near at hand are the flat lands of Turubamba and Añaquito, and not very far off the spacious and delightful valleys of Chillo and Tumbaco. Of all the towns on the inter-Andine *hoyas* Quito is the highest and coldest. The surrounding vegetation is poor and of melancholy aspect, and corresponds with the inclement situation. The position is healthy and even agreeable for those who are acclimatized thereto, but the descriptions lavished by some writers thereon of " delicious " and of " eternal spring " are exaggerations, says one observer.[1] Another authority says that " the traveller is charmed in looking at the carpet of perpetual verdancy on which Quito stands. The climate is delightful. It is neither summer nor spring nor winter, but each day of the year offers a singular combination of the three seasons. Neither cholera nor yellow fever nor consumption is known there. The mild and healthy temperature which prevails is something admirable. In short, it may be said that the great plateau of Quito is a kind of paradise."[2] Thus extremes of opinion are seen to exist.

The annual death-rate of Quito is given as about 36 per 1,000,[3] but this might undoubtedly be reduced under better sanitary measures. It is a well-known circumstance that the high upland regions

[1] Wolf, *op. cit.*   [2] Professor Orton of New York.
[3] *Bulletin* of the Bureau of American Republics, Washington.

and towns of the Andes are generally free from pulmonary consumption, and tubercular disease of the lungs, which on the coastal lowlands of tropical America is very frequent, is unknown above 8,000 feet.

The aspect of Quito is picturesque. The first impression is that of a white city, relieved by roofs of red tiles, the streets thronged with interesting people. As seen from the slopes of Pichincha, which descend to the city on its western side, or from the summit of the Panecillo, a small hill standing within the borders of the city, or from other high points near at hand, the city unfolds pleasingly to the view. It may be likened to a city of the third order in Europe. In spite of the broken character of the land upon which it is built, the streets are nearly all straight, the principal thoroughfares being wide and paved. It is traversed from west to east by two deep *quebradas*, or ravines, which descend from Pichincha and other hills, and one of these is arched over in order to preserve the alignment of the streets. The city follows the general Latin American system of town-planning, being laid out mainly in great rectangular squares, the streets at right angles to each other. The architectural type of the houses is that embodying the old Spanish or Moorish style, well known to the traveller in Latin America, from Mexico to Peru or Argentina : the picturesque and often chaste character of façade (although some may term it monotonous), with iron grilles before the windows and high, wide entrance doorway, or *saguan*, admitting a mounted horseman. The main feature of the house of this type is the interior *patio*, or courtyard, upon which the rooms open, often followed by a second *patio*. The material of which the houses are constructed is *adobe*, or sun-dried earthen brick, which in the dwellings of more pretension are generally covered with stucco or plaster, whitened, and at times painted with vivid colours. Stone is also used. The use of colour on the walls of houses in Latin American towns gives a picturesque appearance at times even to the meanest *pueblo*, and relieves what might often be an extreme poverty of appearance. The roofs of the Quito houses often project over the footpaths, affording protection from rain, and balconies overhang from every window.

The public buildings of Quito are of the heavy, square, colonial Spanish type. Looking upon the great square, or *plaza mayor*, occupying the whole of its southern side, is the cathedral, and on the western side the Government palace, with a handsome façade, whose main feature is its long row of columns. On the north side of the *plaza* is the palace of the Archbishop, and on the east the municipal hall. This arrangement, with some modification, is one encountered in nearly all Latin American capitals, wherein are grouped upon the *plaza* the principal edifices of Church and State, the former taking the place of honour. The arrangement is generally a pleasing and useful one. The *plaza* is the pulse of the community, and during those times when the band plays in its garden it forms a meeting-ground for the people and the sexes. There are other smaller *plazas* and subsidiary squares in the city, including those of San Francisco and Santo Domingo. The many ecclesiastical buildings are an indication of the part which the Church has played. The finest building in the city is the Jesuits' church, with a façade elaborately carved, and the university occupies part of what formerly was the Jesuit college. There are eleven monastic institutions, six of which are nunneries. One of the convents, that of San Francisco, covers a whole *cuadra* or block, and takes its place as one of the largest institutions of this nature in the world. A part of this great building is in ruins, and another part has been used for the purpose of a military barracks by the Government. The university has faculties of law, medicine, and theology—those three professions which appeal so strongly to the Latin American character ; but the institution is regarded as backward, and it has been but poorly supported.

Of the population of Quito various estimates have been made, often with considerable exaggeration. Villavicencio calculated it, in the middle of last century, as 80,000—an impossible figure—and Ulloa, in 1735, gave 50,000 to 60,000. Stübel calculated it at 25,000 to 30,000, and Wolf considered that 40,000, in 1890, was a proper estimate. In 1906 an official estimate gave 50,840, of which 1,370 were foreigners, mostly Colombians, and at the present time the figure is generally given as 80,000.

The commerce of Quito is small : there is little produced in so high a region for export. Superior hand-made carpets are woven, and much skill shown in wood-carving and in gold and silver work. These industries were often characteristic of the ancient people of America, and weaving was essentially a widely practised craft among the Andine races. The beautiful textile fabrics of the Incas and pre-Incas, some of them probably thousands of years old, which have been preserved attest the taste and skill of these people. The native manufactures of Quito include *ponchos*, blankets, mattings, and coarse woollen carpets, also tanned leather, saddles, and shoes. There is a tendency among all the Andine people to preserve their interesting home-crafts and cottage industries, which a wise, economic spirit would endeavour to assist. But cheap imports menace them.

The streets of Quito are thronged from morning to evening with horses, mules, donkeys, and oxen, also llamas, with loads of all kinds, and ladies in victorias drive about, or to the shops, which are replete with merchandise from London, Paris, New

CLOISTERS OF THE CONVENT OF LA MERCED.

[To face p. 294.

York, Vienna, or Berlin. Officers in regimentals and gentlemen in top-hats and frock-coats, are numerous, and Indians with red and yellow *ponchos* and white cotton trousers and hats. But as regards modern conveniences Quito is backward, and the lack of hotels and public hygiene is very serious, and the general conditions surrounding public health call for urgent improvement.[1]

The town next in importance in point of population to Guayaquil and Quito is Cuenca, head of the Azuay province. Its population is calculated at 30,000, mostly of the Indian race. The surroundings of Cuenca are more cultivated and agreeable than those of Quito. Its elevation above sea-level is about 8,640 feet, or 700 feet less than Quito; and the temperature is consequently higher. The city creates a pleasing impression upon the observer, although it does not possess public or private buildings of any particular architectural merit. It is the seat of a bishopric, and possesses a college, university faculty, a cathedral and several churches, and various other public institutions. The manufactures include sugar-making from the lowlands plantations, woollen goods, and pottery, and *cinchona* or quinine bark is brought in from the Amazon forests, and hats, cheese, cereals, and hides. The city stands in the *hoya* or basin of Cuenca, at the head of the Paute River, which, breaking through the eastern Cordillera, forms the upper part of the important Santiago River, a large affluent of the Amazon, as elsewhere described. Lying far to the south of the railway system of Ecuador, between the transverse ridges of Azuay and Loja, communication with the outside world is difficult, being maintained only by the pack-mule roads which descend the Andes to the west.

[1] A recent London traveller summed up his impressions of Quito as " a city of seventy churches and one bath." But there has been some improvement since.

Nevertheless, the commerce of Cuenca is of some importance. Cuenca is about 190 miles south of Quito, and seventy miles south-east of Guayaquil, but communication with both points is arduous. A railway line is to be built. The pre-Hispanic town of Tomebamba, near by, was of considerable importance, as shown by its ruins. Cuenca was the birthplace of various distinguished Ecuadorians, among them Lamar, a President of Peru, and the artist Zangurima.

The towns of Latacunga and that of Riobamba both appear as having populations of 12,000, and both are fortunate in being served by the Guayaquil-Quito railway. Ambato lies between them, also upon the railway. The elevations of these three towns above sea-level are respectively 9,055 feet, 9,020 feet, and 8,435 feet. The houses of Latacunga are constructed of pumice-stone, which gives a grey character to the streets. There are fine churches, colleges, and the usual public buildings. The town lies in a situation exposed to the outbursts of Cotopaxi, which overlooks it, and it has been destroyed in part on various occasions in its history, the floods of mud from the volcano having been specially destructive. There are interesting quarries of pumice-stone in the neighbourhood, and broad, fertile lands. The stream flowing past the town is that which forms the headwaters of the great Pastaza River, descending to the Amazon. Latacunga ranked among the first native towns in pre-Hispanic times. It had a royal palace and a temple of the sun.

Riobamba lies in the midst of a sandy plain, with straight, wide streets and low houses, and possesses a cathedral, six churches, and the customary public buildings, and is the residence of a bishop. Upon market days Riobamba presents an animated spectacle, the Indians flocking in from the country, around in their picturesque dress, after the fashion

WATER-CARRIERS, QUITO

[To face p. 298]

of life in the Andine market towns.   In 1799 Riobamba was destroyed by an earthquake.   From this
town it is, moreover, that much of the revolutionary
element which figures so largely in Ecuadorian
politics proceeds, and it has played an important
part in the history of the republic.   In Riobamba
were born various prominent persons—Velasco the
historian, Maldonado the scientist, Orosa the poet,
and others.

Ambato lies beneath the shadow of Carihuairaza,
or " Chimborazo's wife," the snowy mountain of the
western Cordillera.   The stream which flows past it
is also a tributary of the great Pastaza, descending
to the Amazon.   The local modification of climate
at Ambato gives rise to a warm, equable temperature, and to the pleasing fruit-gardens with which
the town is surrounded, notwithstanding that the plain
is edged by barren, dust-covered ridges exposed to
a cold wind.   The population of Ambato is given
as over 8,000.   There are various churches and the
usual public buildings.   The " fair " at Ambato is
described as the most renowned and best attended
of any town of Ecuador.   Near at hand lies Mocha,
famed in ancient Indian times, and an important
pueblo for muleteers.

The remaining Ecuadorian towns all have populations of under 10,000 except Loja, which has that
number.   Loja lies in the south of the republic,
over the ridges from Zaruma, of gold-mining fame,
and enjoys a healthy climate, its elevation being
7,300 feet above sea-level.   It is the residence of a
bishop, and is of the usual type of large upland
town.   Esmeraldas, with a population of 6,000, is
the seaport in the north of the republic, lying in a
pleasing situation at the mouth of the river.
Guaranda, with 6,000, lies at the head of the River
Chimbo, below Chimborazo, a town of pleasing
aspect which in the past had considerable import-

ance. It stands on the main road uniting the littoral with the Sierra, at an elevation of 8,800 feet, but lies some miles from the railway. Its climate is colder than that of Ambato at a similar elevation, due to the proximity of the Chimborazo *páramos*. Below it lies great forest wealth. Tulcan, in the extreme north, and Ibarra are both mountain towns of some 5,000 inhabitants, the first at 9,830 feet and the second at 7,340 feet above sea-level. Ibarra possesses the good Moncayo library, and was the birthplace of Viescas, the poet. Portoviejo, with 5,000 population, lies near the coast, north-west of Guayaquil, and is now reached by railway from the port. Azogues, with a population of 4,000, lies in the high Cuenca basin, and takes its name from the old quicksilver mines. Babahoyo is the important river-port of the Guayas, with a population of 3,000, and a busy commerce, giving the aspect to the town of a " perpetual fair." Machala, with a slightly larger population, lies on the coast south of Guayaquil, upon the shore of the Gulf. The two last-named are famous for their cocoa-producing districts, as elsewhere described.

The foregoing, except the last two, are capitals of provinces. The remaining towns of any note are principally in the uplands, and are generally described as *pueblos*. Many of them are of special interest, many extremely remote and backward. The names of the principal of these are given as the chief towns of the cantons elsewhere. Otavalo should be mentioned for its handsome women, and Caranqui as the birthplace of Atahualpa.

CHAPTER XVI

MEANS OF COMMUNICATION—RIVERS, ROADS, RAILWAYS

THE most important, as amongst the most neglected, features of economic and civic life in the Latin American republics are the means of communication. The traveller who is acquainted with the execrable trails that, under the name of *caminos* or roads, traverse the broken and mountainous regions which form so large a part of the territory of South and Central America, needs little reminder that matters of travel and freight thereover call for special attention. The Latin Americans are not a road-building people. In the Andine and other districts there are no roads for wheeled vehicles, the mule-train being the only means of transport, except in those few places where the railway has appeared. This lack of roads is in some cases due to the negligent character of the people. Roads could often be built of material upon the spot, employing native engineering and constructive talent and the exceedingly low-priced Indian labour which is available. Throughout Peru, Bolivia, Chile, Ecuador, Colombia, and indeed all the Spanish-speaking countries of America, the unenterprising native, even when of an educated class and engaged in commerce, is content to dwell in his isolated interior towns, paying enormous prices for the carriage of material from the seaports, and often looking upon a journey to the capital of his country as an incident of a lifetime.

17

His one hope is in some foreign company which may build a railway.

Yet perhaps a word of exoneration must be given to the inhabitants of these backward countries in the matter of road-building.   In certain districts the effects of climate and topography renders the upkeep of roads almost impossible.   Furthermore, mule-carriage as an art has been marvellously developed by the native *arriero* of Latin America, and he would be an ungrateful traveller who, having known this fraternity, had no word of praise for their ingenuity and patience.   Let it not be forgotten, moreover, that the carriage of goods by mule competes, in some instances, with that by rail, in point of cost.   The mule trains of Ecuador actually compete with the Guayaquil-Quito railway, and in some cases the same is true in Peru on the Oroya line.

The means of interior communication in Ecuador are, first, the rivers, especially those of the littoral, in the Guayas and other provinces, and, as elsewhere described, the Napo and other streams in the Oriente should prove a valuable asset of transport in the future ; , second, the few railways ; and third, the ordinary mule-trails.

The navigable rivers of Ecuador are very important. They are to be classed as belonging t'o the two hydrographic systems of the country, that of the Pacific littoral, and that of the Oriente or Amazon system beyond the Andes.   These systems have been fully described in their respective places.   The navig-able rivers of the littoral include the system of the Guayas, most important of all, those of the Esme-raldas and Mira, and the smaller rivers and *esteros* or tide-water channels, along the coast.   The total navig-able length of river on the Ecuador littoral is cal-culated as 600 miles.   Thus it is apparent that the littoral waterways of Ecuador are of much import-ance.   The Guayas system forms a veritable network of natural canals, navigable by steamers, boats, and canoes, traversing what may be regarded as a rich garden. The other systems are of less value and much less developed, but have their uses for the future. The navigable waterways of the Amazon, the Napo, Pastaza, Tigre, and others, afford means of communication for the wild regions of the Ecuadorian Oriente. They are but little used at present, and their development must depend upon the future use made of that neglected part of South America, the Amazon basin.

In the littoral river systems the steamboat, the *chata* or flat boat, the raft and the canoe, of all sizes, replace the horse and the mule-train of the mountain districts. The steamboats on the Guayas vary from twenty-five to 125 tons capacity. The *chatas* are of a lighter draught, boats without sails, carrying from four to fifty tons. The rafts are also an important type of craft in river transport. They are constructed both of bamboo and of *balsa* wood. This last-named is a species of timber of very light weight, its floating capacity being almost equal to that of cork, and a log of this wood, fifteen inches in diameter and forty feet long, will carry as much as two tons weight. Rafts consisting of twenty or thirty such logs, lashed together, carry a considerable load in addition to the families of the raftsmen. These rafts are covered with roofs, looking like low, thatched houses ; they float down on the current and return on the flood-tide. The bamboo rafts also carry considerable loads, and their material is sold at Guayaquil for the construction of buildings. This *caña de Guayaquil*, as the great bamboo is termed, is a valuable product of the region. The canoes will carry from 500 lb. to 5,000 lb. of freight, and are by no means an element to be neglected in river transport. They descend the rivers fully laden, many coming from remote backwaters and *esteros*, with valuable freights of *cacao* and other produce, and return laden with supplies for the up-river places. The ease with which these primitive craft of boats and rafts are enabled to traffic on the Guayas fluvial system is due to the rapid ebb and flow of the tide, the current running often at five miles per hour up and down the river, and a raft or boat, without any means of propulsion whatever, by taking advantage of the tide will cover a distance of forty-eight miles per day. The steamboats also take advantage of the tides. By this system of river transport most of the interior products of Ecuador have their outlet, and the imports are largely distributed by the same method.

There are few roads or trails in these well-watered districts. The *trocha* or forest trail, cut out with the *machete*, in the tropics disappears after a few weeks' disuse, and becomes covered by the forest. But a good canoe, managed by one or more rowers, takes the place of a whole mule-train. The network of navigable streams could be vastly improved and extended with hydraulic works of comparative simplicity in many cases. But the Ecuadorians are poor and without much spirit of enterprise, and are content to make use of the waterways in the state in which Nature has provided them, even where these traverse their richest territory. Waterways are as much neglected as mountain trails. The flotilla of regular steamboats from Guayaquil that serve the Guayas fluvial system throughout its principal arteries—the Santa Rosa, Machala, Balao, Naranjal, Yaguachi, Bodegas, Baba, Vinces, and Daule Rivers, etc.—and which in winter penetrate up to the very foot of the Cordillera, might enjoy a still larger field of operations if the Government were in a position to give attention to the conservation and development of these natural waterways, the canalization of others, and the opening of artificial canals. An example of such lies in the Vinces River. Another is in the Estero Salado

behind Guayaquil. In 1884 the city was alarmed
by the danger that the Guayas River might break
through the thin barrier which separates the two
waterways, and open a course to the Estero. Some
works have been contemplated recently to improve
this important waterway. Given means of communication between the river and the Estero, as of a canal
with tide gates, the fine Estero Salado waterway,
which at present is practically unused, would form a
quiet and commodious approach to Guayaquil more
useful possibly than the river itself. This old estuary,
it is observed, forms an arm of the Gulf of Guayaquil.
Such a work, it is stated, would present little engineering difficulty.

The roads or trails of the littoral are generally
good in the dry season, but in the wet season are
almost intransitable, due to inundations. In summer
it is sufficient to open a *trocha* or cleared path
through the jungle to secure a good trail in any
direction, as for six months there is no rain and there
are no ridges to be crossed. But in winter and in
those districts where rain falls throughout the year,
as at the foot of the Cordilleras, the trails are perhaps
worse than in the *sierra* as the waters stand upon the
land. In some cases the construction of a solidly
built road for vehicles in the coastal districts would be
almost as difficult and costly as that of a light railway.
In the well-populated provinces, such as Guayas, Los
Rios, and the southern part of Manabi, the *pueblos*
and *haciendas* are joined by mule-roads, which in
summer are good, but in the unpopulated districts,
such as the *montañas* of the interior of Manabi and
Esmeraldas, etc., there are no such trails. The only
" road " north of the Bay of Caraques is that which
follows the sea-coast between the small ports and
villages, and this is good where it follows the sandy
beach at low tide, but execrable where it runs above
high-water level over the promontories. This class of

" road " is common to the Pacific coast, all along its vast extension through Peru. The coast-dwellers of Ecuador, accustomed to trafficking in *chatas*, boats, and canoes, by sea and among the rivers and *esteros*, use the coastal trail but little. The sea is usually calm and lends itself to navigation by small craft. The whole coastal interior, or jungle-covered plains, lack even such trails, although the rubber-gatherers and others from time to time make *trochas* which, after a few weeks, become overgrown again. The traveller who journeys with beasts of burden is obliged to make his way by dint of axe and *machete*, and the employment of considerable work and patience. The word *trocha* is important in the vocabulary of the tropical woodsman or inhabitant.

As regards the Andine interior, there is but one good road, a cart-road from Quito southwards, 115 miles long on the Guayaquil route. This was begun by President Garcia Moreno ; it traverses several of the mountain provinces, but has suffered from neglect. The trails which lead into the eastern regions are more like goat-paths, upon which only journeying on foot is possible, and the traveller often finds his passage stopped for days by swollen rivers. There are five trails or routes leading to the Oriente region—first, that of the province of Pichincha through Papallacta, for the Napo *pueblos*, the most travelled of all ; second, that of the province of Tunguragua, through Baños for Canelos, which, as it does not pass the high *páramos*, is capable of improvement ; third, that of the province of Chimborazo, to Macas ; fourth, that of Azuaz, through Sigsig to Gualaquiza ; and fifth, that of Loja, which leads through Vilcabamba and the Sabanilla " knot," and descends the River Chinchipe to Zumba and Chito, and thence goes to Jaen. There is also a little-used trail in the Imbabura province, to the Cófanes and Aguarico Rivers, and another in Latacunga, over the slopes of Cotopaxi to the Napo.

Communication from the great *callejon* or inter-Andine valley with the littoral provinces scarcely exists—that is, from Imbabura and Pichincha to Esmeraldas and Manabi, although there are some mule and foot trails, which have fallen into disuse here and there. There are also bad and neglected bridle-paths in the interior, between various places, which do not reach the coast. The want of roads in the northern part of the republic is partly explained by the lack of population. Traffic between the coast in that region and the almost inaccessible uplands of the Andes would scarcely yield any commercial returns. In the more populated littoral provinces, where commerce has made its way, there are many bridle-paths and mule-roads from the coast upwards. The first is that by the Quevado valley to Latacunga, to which the Vinces River gives access, and from the Zapotal valley, above Bodegas, to Angamarca, Latacunga, Ambato, and Guaranda. From Babahoyo in the Guayas valley there are a number of roads to various places in the *sierra*. The San Antonio road ascends the Pozuelos River to Pacana, San Antonio, Pucará, and Guaranda, another goes to Balsabamba, Guaranda, and Chapacoto ; there is also the old road up the Chima valley, and thence to Chimborazo. From Chimbo, which earlier was the terminus of the Guayaquil railway, various roads branch out to the uplands. Up the Ricay valley from the Boliche River, whose mouth lies opposite Guayaquil, a road ascends to Cañar and adjacent places, and another more frequented from Cañar to Naranjal, with a branch to Cuenca. The *camino real*, or high-road, leaves the Naranjal valley and ascends the Chacayacu. Up the valley of the Tenguel a road runs for Pucará in the Jubones basin and to Machala ; and to the south is the road to Santa Rosa, Zaruma, and Loja. Lastly, two roads go to Tumbez and Catacocha and places adjacent and beyond. It is to be recollected that all these roads, even when termed high-roads, are only trails for horsemen and mule-trains, such as in Latin America are known as *caminos de herradura*—that is, bridle roads.

These roads are much alike, and the traveller who is acquainted with one or two in the tropical and mountainous districts of South America or Mexico knows what he has to encounter in any given district. From the plains of the coast the trail enters upon a valley between the lateral branches of the lower *sierras*. At first the valley is fairly wide, and the slope upward is gentle, and the accompanying river, born far away in the Cordillera, more or less placid. But by degrees the sandy nature of the trail changes, the hills approach nearer to the stream, and—in Ecuador—the humid jungle is entered. Here the difficulties and trials of the road begin. The valley narrows, the gradient becomes steep, the torrent leaps over cascades, and the trail ascends by a series of terraces and often of rough boulder-steps, alternating with ponds, sloughs, and slippery rocks, at times with danger of a fall into the ravine below. At such points where the rock escarpments reach the edge of the river the trail has perforce to wind around these, on the face of the precipice, or as an alternative the river must be followed, with the water perhaps up to the saddle-bags, a situation not without discomfort or danger. The latter method, however, is often preferable to the execrable ascents and descents of the trail over the rocky spurs and promontories. Added to these trials, in the districts where vegetation is thick, are the arms of thorny shrubs, which tear the traveller's clothing or flesh, and enormous entangling roots, among which the mule leaps wildly, whilst the continuous rain falls day and night. Or otherwise, in the dry season, or in an arid region, the sun beats down throughout the day in tropical fury. In the primeval jungle a

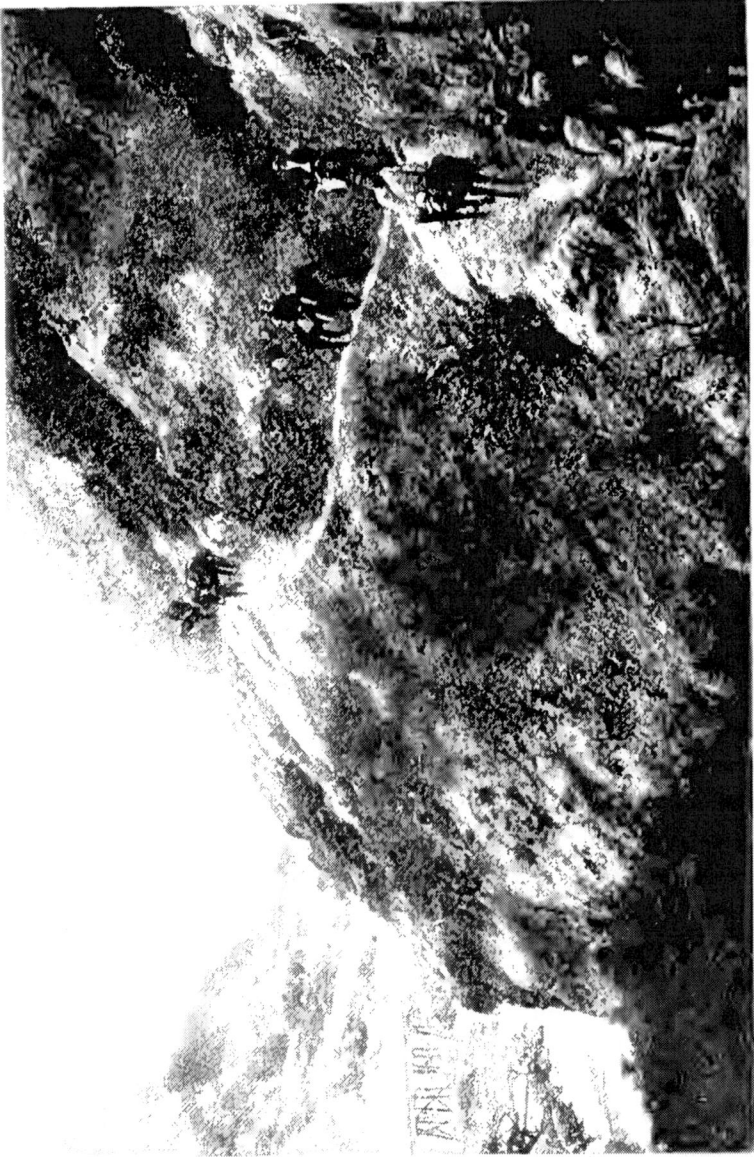

A MOUNTAIN ROAD

[To face p. 264

profound silence reigns, only interrupted by the chatter of monkeys or the shriek of parrots, varied by the cry of some approaching *arriero*, or mule-train driver. The mule train, in passing, may leave but little of the narrow trail available, and if the passage occur upon a precipitous stretch, with a rocky wall rising on the one hand and a sheer chasm descending on the other, the horseman is well advised to keep the wall, and let the mule train take the outer side. Even thus the bulky articles carried by the mules may cause the horseman considerable discomfort as they pass him. At times, oppressed by the circumstances and surroundings, the traveller is almost disposed heartily to curse the road and the negligent inhabitants whose territory it traverses, and to quicken his pace in order to escape from such surroundings. But, bathed in perspiration, both animal and man are obliged to journey slowly. At the elevation of 2,000 feet or more, the trail perhaps leaves the valley and follows the side of the mountain-spur, leaving the steep, **V**-shaped ravine to the torrent which occupies its bed. The trail then zigzags up the slope, doubling constantly upon itself until the crest or summit which forms the dividing line between that and a neighbouring valley is reached. The crests of ridges and hills in Latin American countries are generally marked by rude wooden crosses, set in a pile of stones, a circumstance which evinces the curiously devout character of the primitive *arriero*, whose occupation calls upon him to pass that way with frequency. This piety, however, covers a multitude of other qualities. Still ascending, the traveller at length emerges from the region of the woods or jungle, above the line of tree life, which marks the higher region of the Andes. But not by reason of this change does the execrable road improve. On the contrary, it becomes steeper and worse. Its angle approaches often the natural one of the hill slopes, and the traveller is constantly in anxiety as to whether his saddle will slip backward bodily off the tail of the animal he is riding, or, on the descent, whether he is likely to be precipitated over the animal's head. It is necessary when starting out upon such a journey, to look well to the saddle and its appointments, and a crupper should always be used, as well as a breast-strap, thus preventing movement of the saddle. In the humid regions the decomposition of the rock on the trail causes a slippery and muddy surface. The porphyries and diorites, or other rocks, of which the mountains are composed, become reduced to a yellow or brown clay, forming at times an impassable bog. Often it is necessary for the traveller's attendants to place stones in such a position that passage may be effected over such points. Huge ruts become worn in this clayey matter, so deep that the beasts at times rest their bellies upon the ridges and refuse to go on. Cross-ruts known as *camellones* are another obstacle. The *arrieros* strip themselves almost naked in the heat, and work with fury to adjust burdens and to extricate their charges from the impassable mud, and by dint of shouts and oaths—in which the Spanish language is picturesquely profuse—and with the aid of ropes, sticks, and blows the *mal pasaje*, or bad spot, is passed. At times cargo remains in the mud, abandoned, or falls over precipices, and not infrequently the beast shares the same luck. The traveller, looking over the verge, may discern the carcass of some beast which has thus perished lying below.

But there are compensations for the traveller in these difficult and thorny paths. In their respective elevations the rare and beautiful flowers and shrubs of the forest unfold to the view. The great, sombre forest lies below, and a fresh breeze refreshes man and beast, descending from the uplands. Sweet

odours float upon the air, changing shapes of plant
and palm delight the eye, and the gracious forms
which Nature has hidden there seem brought forth
as a reward for the hardships of the way. Beyond
are the glorious stretches of the Andine moors, sterile
it may be, but bathed in the beauty of illimitable
distance and the peculiar atmosphere of the mountain, which act as a tonic upon the traveller's being.
The unfolding landscape becomes a source of delight,
at least to the traveller whose scientific knowledge
or love of Nature enables him to appreciate such
matters. If, moreover, he be well mounted, the
difficulties and dangers of the road are minimized.
The traveller who neither possesses the spirit which
can extract enjoyment from such journeys, nor is
enabled to secure a good beast to carry him, with
proper attendance, is well advised not to enter upon
such an expedition at all, and to avoid the Andine
countries entirely.

An idea of the heights attained and crossed by
the roads of Ecuador in the mountainous interior may
be gathered from observing those of the *camino real*,
which traverses the republic from south to north
longitudinally along the *callejon interandino*, or great
Andine valley. This road runs from Macara, a town
on the river of that name (which runs into the Chira
or Achira on the Peruvian border), in the province
of Loja, on the Pacific slope, to Carachi, near Tulcan,
in the extreme north, on the river of that name,
the frontier with Colombia. The elevations given
are from barometric observations (mercurial) made
by Reiss and Stübel, Wolf and others. At Macara
the elevation is 430 metres above sea-level, at Gon-
zama it rises to 2,243 metres, near Ramos-urcu
3,259 metres, at Puente de Udushapa it descends to
2,312 metres, near Tinajillas it rises to 3,424 metres,
and in the *plaza* of the city of Cuenca descends to
2,581 metres, at the town of Cañar it rises to 3,176

metres, and at Puca-loma it attains the highest point
on the old (Inca) road of 4,445 metres (or about
14,660 feet), with 4,347 metres at Quimsa Cruz,
on the newer road at Azuay. Thence it reaches the
Zula and Chanchan Rivers at 1,857 metres and
ascends to the Incapampa ruins at 3,201 metres.
At Riobamba (old) it has a similar elevation, which
rises at Sanacajas to 3,607 metres ; at the city of
Ambato, the *plaza*, the elevation is 2,608 metres,
and at Latacunga it reaches 2,801 metres, in the
plaza of that city ; it rises to 3,604 metres at Huinzha,
and with ascents and descents reaches Quito at 2,850
metres, descending to the Guallabamba bridge at
1,881 metres ; thence it rises to the Alto de Cajas
at 3,099 metres, and at the town of Ibarra is at
2,225 metres, descending to the Chota bridge at
1,532 metres ; at the Pucara Alto it reaches 3,122
metres, descends to 2,874 metres near Tuza, and
rises to 3,405 metres on the *páramo* of Boliche,
descending to 2,977 metres in the *plaza* of the town
of Tulcan.

Several of the mountain roads pass in elevation
4,000 metres at certain points, such as that from
Quito to Papallacta, 4,173 metres ; Quito to Anti-
sano, 4,115 metres ; Latacunga to Angamarca, 4,496
metres ; Ambato to Angamarca, 4,381 metres ; and
Naranjal to Cuenca, 4,135 metres. These examples
serve to show the great altitudes attained by the
" roads " of Ecuador, giving communication between
the towns of the various Andine valleys and uplands.

Across these primitive roads equally primitive
means of crossing streams and rivers exist—fords
when the water is low and rude suspension bridges
across deep chasms and torrents. The primitive
suspension bridge of Latin America is well known.
The Incas in Peru erected such of considerable
stability and of great length. In Ecuador these
suspension bridges are generally constructed of

maguey fibre, and consist of one or more cables. In the case of a bridge formed by a single cable this is known as a *taravita*, and the passenger and his luggage are hauled across in a kind of basket, suspended therefrom, running on a loop or ring, attached to a cord on either bank. When two or more cables form the bridge, these are joined by a kind of platform of bamboos or branches, laid on and lashed thereto, a frail and hazardous structure for the unaccustomed traveller. A bridge of this kind is a *chimbo-chaca*, and is in reality a rude prototype of the suspension bridge of the modern engineer. Such bridges were found in early South America, as in India and China. When of considerable length these sometimes sway and oscillate greatly. The Spaniards when they first appeared in South America feared to cross them, but the Indians would even gallop a horse across the structure.

The topographical description of Ecuador shows the difficulties attending railway construction in the country. Not only have great elevations to be passed, but the character of the ground traversed, the friable nature of the soil under the effect of tropical moisture, is an element equally costly to overcome, and the cause of expense in maintenance. The traveller who is acquainted with the mountain railways which ascend the Andes, such as the Transandine of Chile, the Arequipa, and the Oroya railways and others of Peru and Bolivia, is well enabled to understand the conditions in Ecuador, rendered still more onerous by reason of the humid climate of the Pacific slope. In Peru and Chile the Andine slopes are often dry and stable ; in Ecuador the reverse is often the case.

The principal railway in Ecuador is the Guayaquil-Quito line. Its construction was conceived by President Garcia Moreno during the latter half of last century, and the work was first carried out as far as the Chimbo bridge, at the foot of the western Cordillera. The whole line to Quito, 290 miles in length, was completed in 1908, when the last section was formally opened at Quito on the 25th of June of that year.

The starting-point of the railway is at Duran, the small town on the bank of the river opposite Guayaquil, and passengers are ferried across by the boats of the railway company. The Guayas at this point is almost three-quarters of a mile wide, and the tide is exceedingly swift, with a total rise and fall of twelve or thirteen feet and a current velocity at times of eight miles an hour. At Duran are situated the locomotive and car-repairing shops of the railway, with the warehouse and offices belonging to the company, and the dwellings of the employees, which are constructed somewhat after the manner of the buildings of the Panama Canal enterprise, screened against the invasion of the mosquito. The total length of the line, from Duran to Quito, is 288 miles, and the gauge is 3 feet 6 inches. The highest point on the line is Urbina, between Riobama and Ambato, where the elevation above sea-level of 11,841 feet is reached. This height, although considerable, is much exceeded by the Andine railways of Peru, where the Oroya line reaches 15,645 feet and the Arequina line 14,660 feet above sea-level.

At the town of Yaguachi the river of the same name is crossed by a steel bridge of three spans, with stone piers and abutments. For some thirty miles from Yaguachi the railway traverses a fine country, cultivated with sugar-cane, coffee, cocoa, bananas, and plantains, which latter are the principal food of the working population of the region, and the district wears a prosperous appearance. Bucay Junction lies at the foot of the Cordillera beyond Naranjito, fifty-seven miles from Duran, and

THE RAILWAY WHARF AT GUAYAQUIL.

[To face p. 279.

at 975 feet above sea-level. At this point the mountain section of the railway begins, necessitating shorter trains and more powerful locomotives. These latter are of American type, from the Baldwin Locomotive Works, eighty-five tons in weight. Such an engine, however, so steep is the gradient, draws but five cars. At Bucay, which is only a division terminus, are coaling-sheds and repair-shops. From this point the line enters the Chan-Chan valley, and the heavy constructural work of the railway becomes evident. This valley is rarely more than 300 yards wide, with steep mountain walls, and the river runs torrentially through it, necessitating a number of steel bridges. The curves on the section are of twenty-nine degrees, and the gradient in places reaches 4½ per cent. At Huigra, which stands at 4,000 feet, the valley widens somewhat, and an attractive little town has grown up, with quarters for the railway employees, and a hospital. The spot was chosen for settlement for railway requirements on account of its good climate, and from the fact that it is above the yellow-fever zone. At this elevation the appearance of the native inhabitants changes also, from the Europeanized coast-dweller to the pure Indian of the uplands, clad in his *poncho*. Beyond Huigra the steep mountain section entered is subject to landslides and washouts, with corresponding difficulties of maintenance. An upland and broken country, almost terrific in character, is passed ; yet in the small valleys away from the line land is cultivated under the singular terraced farm system of the Andes, and fruit, vegetables, and cattle are brought for shipment to the railway. In this section occurs the famous " zigzag " or switchback, upon the mountain-spur known as *El Nariz del Diabolo,* or the " Devil's Nose." Here the line passes through a narrow ravine between the mountains, and then, reversing its direction, the train backs up the face

of the precipice on a ledge cut out of the rock.
A rise of 1,000 feet in the line brings into view
the Chan-Chan valley below. The Alausi " loop "
is then reached, at 8,553 feet elevation, a noteworthy
piece of railway construction. The town of Alausi
lies on the eastern slope of the valley, and a magnificent view is obtained from the train, with the deep
gorge of the river below and the mountains unfolding
to the horizon. Here the system of terrace cultivation is well seen ; the hill slopes up to an elevation
of 12,000 feet, being cultivated in this way, every
available foot of land, even upon the steepest hillside,
being made use of in this primitive system of farming. From Alausi barren country is traversed for
a distance of twenty-five miles, upon the great central
plateau, the Palmira pass lying at 10,600 feet above
sea-level. Heavy rains occur at times in this section,
softening the ground, which acts against the stability
of the line, a condition which is augmented by the
use of the permanent way as a bridle-path in wet
weather ; the hoofs of horses and mules undermine
the ties, or sleepers. The native *arriero* insists on
thus making use of the line, against regulations.

In this upland region typhoid fever is a serious
scourge at times, and the traveller avoids both the
milk of the district and the water, and preferably
uses mineral or boiled waters. German beer is
plentifully obtained, of good quality.[1]

At Guamote, 10,000 feet elevation, the river is
crossed by a fine steel bridge, and a fertile country
covered with deep soil is traversed. On every side
are cattle, sheep, and goats, with fields of grain,
alfalfa, beans, and potatoes. The potatoes of the
region are exceptionally fine and plentiful, and the
zone of their cultivation extends from Siambe to
Quito. The line passes Lake Colta and enters Caya-
bamba. The lack of sanitary methods of the upland

[1] 2s. to 3s. per quart bottle.

PISTISHI MOUNTAIN : THE "DEVIL'S NOSE."

[To face p. 322.

towns is generally evident, even from the line. Riobamba is reached at 9,020 feet. The town is lighted from a hydro-electric station in the mountain stream. Beyond this point Chimborazo bursts upon the view. The great mountain displays a double peak, the snowclad crests of which are outlined against the upland sky, at those times when the firmament is free from clouds. The plateau of Riobamba has a healthy climate, described, on the authority of Humboldt, as one of the best in the world. In this region a considerable increase in the production of wheat has followed upon the building of the railway.

Between Riobamba and Ambato the Chimborazo pass is crossed, at Urbina, the highest point reached, and thence a rapid descent is made to Ambato, 8,435 feet, in the midst of a district producing fruits and foodstuffs abundantly. Along the Latacunga valley, comparatively flat and some ten miles wide, rich pastures, intersected by irrigation ditches, abound, with numerous bands of cattle and horses. Grain, corn, potatoes, alfalfa, apples, peaches, strawberries, etc., are products of this high fertile district, and good cheese and butter are made. Beyond the town of Latacunga, 9,055 feet elevation, the line crosses the base of Cotopaxi, whose snowy cone is surmounted by the thin, unceasing smokewreath from its crater, the cloud hanging in the atmosphere. This point of the line is 11,653 feet above sea-level, only slightly less than that of the Chimborazo pass. Beyond Cotopaxi lies the fertile valley of Machachi, one of the most pleasing districts in Ecuador. On either hand is the row of famous volcanoes, a mighty avenue of great peaks, often clothed in green up to the line of perpetual snow. A view is obtained from the railway of the Chillo valley, with various cotton and woollen mills, actuated by water power. In these establishments, hydrau-

18

lically worked from the river, cloths of cheap
character for native clothing are made. Still
descending, the railway approaches and enters the
city of Quito at 9,375 feet elevation.

The construction of this remarkable railway from
Guayaquil to Quito was mainly due to the activity
and enterprise of an American financier and railway
builder, Mr. Archer Harman, whose work in connection with which began in 1897. The line remains
as a worthy monument to this man, whose grave
lies at the pretty town of Huigra. A strong impulse
was given to the progress of Ecuador by the building
of this railway and by the influence of its builder,
and the republic has cause to remember his name with
gratitude, as indeed has the traveller.

The Guayaquil-Quito Railway has had a troubled
history, but its earnings have increased. The following table shows the gross traffic receipts and
operating expenses of the railway company for the
years 1908-9 to 1911-12. (The *sucre* is equal
to 2s.) :—

June 1st to June 30th.					Gross Receipts. Sucres.	Expenses. Sucres.
1908–9...	...	...	...	...	1,518,986	1,611,874
1909–10	...	...	...	...	1,684,269	1,557,209
1910–11	...	...	...	...	1,766,725	1,560,800
1911–12	...	...	...	...	2,401,688	—

The difficulties of maintenance due to washouts are
considerable, and the line suffers in consequence.
Of American design and construction, the line has,
besides its office in New York, an English Bondholders Committee. The Ecuador Government has
guaranteed the payment of interest on certain issues
of the railway bonds, and at the present time has
been meeting its payments. The heavy expenses
leave little margin for interest or dividends, and the
present problem is to enable the line to continue
covering its working costs. The heavy price of fuel

WEED-KILLING ON THE RAILWAY.

(coal costs at times 40s. per ton) is a serious item in its operations.

The other lines of Ecuador are short. From Manta, the Pacific coast port in the north, a line runs towards the town of Santa Anna, in the province of Manabi. This is a British enterprise, a company with a capital of £100,000, and twenty-five miles of line are built and in operation to Portoviejo. American rolling stock has been imported. The track is of three-quarters of a metre gauge, and there are no special engineering difficulties. The district produces large quantities of *tagua*, or vegetable ivory-nuts, also coffee. From Bahia de Caraquez, the port somewhat farther to the north, a line has been built to Chone, also in Manabi, a length of about fifty miles, the centre of the cocoa district of northern Ecuador. The line is designed ultimately to reach Quito by ascending the western Cordillera. In the south of the republic a short line runs inland from Puerto Bolivar to Machala, the important cocoa-growing district. This line is intended ultimately to ascend and cross the Andes, and thence to descend to a point on the navigable arm of the Santiago river, giving access to the Amazon. Other railways are projected, including one to Santa Elena and one to Cuenca, and these doubtless will be built as economic conditions improve.

CHAPTER XVII

NATURAL HISTORY

THE indigenous plant (and animal) life of any American country, and especially of those which lie within the tropics, covers a large variety of species. It is, however, true to say that the most useful varieties are exotics — those plants and animals brought in from Europe or Asia after the discovery of America. The plants of economic value as food-producers were of comparatively limited range. There was no wheat, barley, oats, sugar-cane, grape-vine, coffee, or olives. There was maize, however— the Indian corn, which even at the present time furnishes the staple food of the people in many Latin American countries. Chocolate was a valuable gift of the New World to the Old, being indigenous to the woodlands of the torrid zone of Latin America, as were tobacco and the potato. Rubber was first made known to the world from its use by South American and Mexican natives, as was quinine ; and cocaine and other valuable drugs and medicinal herbs are original products of the Latin American tropics. The well-known *yerba máte* or Paraguayan tea, largely consumed in southern South America, is a peculiar product of that continent, although it is not found in Ecuador or elsewhere in the Andine countries. The coconut-palm is indigenous to tropical America, which may, indeed, have been its original home. The economic products of Ecuador are more fully described in treating of the agricultural industries of the country.

The flora of Ecuador varies widely, in accordance with the variation of temperature due to the topography of the land. Five principal zones are marked : First is the arid region of the coast, in which the greater parts of the trees lose their leaves in the *verano* or summer dry season ; second, the humid coast region and low, hilly section of the littoral, in which the greater part of the trees retain their leaves the whole year ; third, the region of the woods—always humid and green—on the outer slopes of the high Cordilleras, from their base to the line of tree life. This zone, in the lower part, embodies a tropical flora, and in the higher a subtropical, passing by degrees to the Andine zone ; fourth is the inter-Andine zone of the cereals, occupying the *hoyas* or plains, whose flora (primitive sub-Andine and subtropical) has been modified by the presence of man ; fifth is the Andine region, or that of the *páramos,* extending from the line of tree-life to the perpetual snowline, whose flora is mainly of Andine forms. These various zones are not, of course, very sharply defined, but merge one into the other.

In the chapter dealing with the coastal region the dry and humid parts of the littoral have been marked out. The coast from Puná to Santa Elena and Manta is under the influence of the Peruvian current, the dry zone extending from Tumbez to Caráques, interrupted only by the humid belt between Machala and Naranjal and Azangue and Salango, interruptions resulting upon the approach of hills to the sea. In the Guayas basin the humid belt extends far inland upon the *sabanas* or plains and *lomas* or hills.

The most persistent trees on the tropical seashores are the *manglares* or mangroves. This may be re-

garded as "constructive" vegetation, as it plays
an important part in retaining the soil washed down
by rivers to the sea, helping thus to form fluvial-
marine plains. Banks and shoals in rivers, and
mud-deposited promontories in these, when uncovered
with vegetation, constantly change ; but once the
mangrove obtains a foothold there they tend to
become permanent and are augmented in size. Such
mangrove-covered banks are encountered freely in
the Guayas gulf and elsewhere on the Ecuadorian
coast, as before described. Fluvial-marine lands are
well developed on the deltas of the Mira and Santiago
Rivers. The formation of the great alluvial plains
of the Guayas are a gift of that river, as Egypt was
of the Nile, and doubtless commenced in the
Quaternary epoch. At the end of that period the
gulf of Guayaquil extended much farther inland,
and the silting-up process continues around Guayaquil
at the present time. The mangroves are "amphi-
bious" trees. The roots advance through the fine
mud deposited at the edge of the banks, and the land
thus captured breeds grasses and other low vegetation, which further serve to retain the capping of
soil, which slowly increases in height. The mangrove
is then seen to be out of its element ; its back part
dies and the front roots press forward towards the
water. This constructive process is of considerable
interest.[1] Behind the mangrove thickets open *sabanas*
are formed, which are known as *tembladeras* when
inundated. The vegetation on these, as they become
drier, offers abundant herbage for cattle when the
surrounding plains are rendered arid by the sun's
heat, especially in winter (*invierno*). The ordinary
mangrove (*Rhizophora mangle*) predominates in
Ecuador, but there are other species. The trunk
reaches a height of sixteen or seventeen feet and gives
a hard and durable timber, useful in works of con-

[1] This process is well described by Wolf, *op. cit.*

MANGROVE THICKETS.

[To face p. 332

struction, and it forms a considerable article of export.

The coco-palm (*Cocos nucifera*) prefers the proximity of the sea and a salty soil. Inland, indeed, where it grows up to the base of the Cordillera, it is fertilized with salt. It has been thought by some naturalists that this valuable tree had its origin in the Central and South American coasts, from Mexico to Ecuador, but it is found distributed all over the tropical world. In Ecuador, where it flourishes, it is but little cultivated, although its propagation might yield excellent results commercially. In Central America, Africa, and elsewhere attention is being drawn largely to coconut cultivation, due to the great demand for copra and the vegetable fats and food products which it contains. In the Guayas, Manabi, and Esmeraldas coastal plains there are large areas available for the plantation of the nut.

The principal plants of the dry coast pampas, where of a desert character, are great espinas and tunas (*Cactus opuntia*), familiar to the traveller in western America and elsewhere. Armed with thorns and conserving moisture in their succulent leaves and stems, these plants are always an interesting example of the operation of Nature in the adaptation of organic life to its environment. They flourish in the desert, by reason of their peculiar structure and powers, where nothing else will live. The algarrobo and its relatives (prosopis and mimosa) are also found. These yield a wood of almost imperishable character, greatly valued in the construction of foundations for buildings. It is also an excellent combustible, and its leaves and fruit are useful as fodder for cattle. The *palo santo* also grows here, and is a useful timber.

The orchilla (*Rocella sp.*) grows freely in this dry zone. It is a lichen, white or ash-coloured, propagating on the stones and on the trunks and branches of trees, and is common in many parts of western America. It was formerly gathered and exported in considerable quantity for the fabrication of dyes, but the aniline dyes of commerce displaced it.

The woods of Puná, Chongon, and those between Guayaquil and Santa Elena, and along the Daule and the Bodegas Rivers are naked in winter, and do not present a tropical aspect, but they produce good timber. The corpulent ceibos (*Bombax ceiba* and *Eriodendrum*) of these forests produce a vegetable wool which is collected for industrial purposes. The opening of the great yellow flowers of this tree announces the approach of the wet season. The fine timbers of the Guayaquil—the ebony, the roble laurel, and others—develop best in these districts, but also flourish in the humid districts. The Peruvian balsam (*Myrospermum peruiferuno*) also grows. The tamarind is found cultivated on the littoral, and is one of the largest and finest trees of the dry region. Among other large trees is a variety of euforbias, and the *gossypium* or wild cotton, also various species of cerezo and anil (*Indigofera*). The ciruelo is one of the best trees of the dry region, and the jaboncillo (*Sapindus saponaria*) produces fruit which is used as a soap. As before remarked, the dry zone is distinguished by the deciduous character of the trees, reminiscent of the change of seasons of extra-tropical lands. A period like spring supervenes, and after the first *aguaceros* or rain-showers have fallen the aspect of the land is changed by the sudden growth of leaf and flower, and the singing of birds and movements of animals, and the agreeable temperature. This period lasts, with a very rapid growth of vegetation, for four or five months, to the end of May, when the leaves begin to fall again, and in September the desert aspect once more covers the region.

The humid region of the coast has a truly tropical

COCOA PLANTATIONS: LOS RIOS.

CABUYA, OR MAGUEY.

[To face p. 336.

aspect, differing from the foregoing. The winter begins earlier and ends later, and during the summer months frequent *garuas* or mist-drizzles and heavy dews counteract the diurnal evaporation. The trees preserve their leaves and the woods are green. The *cacao* or chocolate, the palm, the *tagua*, the vanilla, and other trees and shrubs flourish. This zone is extensive, north of Cape Pasados covering the littoral ; in the south it verges upon the dry belt and extends inland towards the Cordillera. Nearly all this region is covered with woods, natural *sabanas* or open plains being rarer. A good forage, however, is encountered upon them. The giant grasses on these *sabanas*, reaching at times six or nine feet in height, form almost impenetrable barriers. Sensitive mimosas are characteristic, and the edges of the woods in many cases form impenetrable walls of foliage sixteen to twenty feet high, composed of cane, cactus, and other thorny shrubs bound together with lianas, and only by cutting a way with *machetes* is it possible to traverse the jungle. Such walls follow the banks of the rivers and *esteros*. The great palm (*Cocos butyracea*) is the queen of the forest ; it reaches the height of the coco-palm, but its trunk is straighter and thicker and its crown fuller and wider. It is not found everywhere, but it is " social " in character, forming colonies. It abounds in the interior of the province of Esmeraldas. Another variety of the palm is the pambil, whose timber is useful for building purposes and is prized by the Indians for their houses. The chonta-palm yields an agreeable fruit of a nature similar to apricots. Two useful plants, characteristic of the humid zone, are the cadi and the toquilla—of a palm-like appearance, but belonging to another family (*Cyclanthaceas*). The first (*Phytelephas macrocaspa*) has gigantic leaves, which are used for roofing houses in the villages ; but it also yields the *tagua*, known as vegetable ivory, which forms so important an article of export. This tree grows up to an elevation, on the Andine slopes, of 2,500 feet. The toquilla (*Carludovica palmata*) has the appearance of a small palm without a trunk, with fan-shaped leaves rising directly from the soil. It yields the fine straw for the so-called Panama hats, and is found in great abundance in the low and humid regions. The method of employing this plant is elsewhere described, in dealing with the industries of the country. There are many kinds of valuable timber in these woods, but not generally so durable as those of the dry zone. The Guayacan and the Roble lose some of their good quality in this respect. Cedar is found, and the *palo de balsa*, whose wood, lighter than cork, is extremely useful in the construction of rafts. The great matapalos (*Ficus dendrocida*) gives good shade to the *cacotales* or cocoa plantations, and there are various " milk "-producing trees, although poor in *caucho* or rubber.

The caucho or *jebe*, the rubber-producing tree of western Ecuador, is the *castilloa*, not the *siphonia*, which is found in the Amazon region only. The *castilloa* is the Central American and Mexican rubber-tree. Due to the irrational system followed in the past in its exploitation, the tree is rare in this zone, well-developed examples being found only in remote spots in the forests—the same fate that has befallen it in other lands.

The tamajagua is a well-developed tree, whose inside bark the Indian makes use of for a species of bread, and also in their clothing. Well-known fruits cultivated in this zone are the succulent *mamey*, the *aguacate*, the *sapote*, all common also to Central America and Mexico, and the *mango*, introduced from eastern India, also the bread-fruit-tree, from Polynesia. Oranges and lemons, although they grow up to an elevation of 8,250 feet above sea-level on the Andine slopes, are more natural to the hot zone, and are found apparently wild in the forests. It has been surmised that the orange, and perhaps more especially the lemon, may have existed before the Spanish Conquest. The *mate* (*Crescentia cujete*) yields a large fruit, whose exterior portion, cleared of the pulp, is largely used by the country people to make vases and cups. There are other useful and curious fruits in this zone.

Western Ecuador is the home of the *cacao*, or cocoa. It is doubtful if the true *cacao* (*Theobroma cacao*), which in Ecuador is cultivated on so large a scale, is indigenous, or if it was introduced from Central America. The wild *cacao* encountered in the forests, which presents no difference from the cultivated kind, may have been disseminated by animal agencies, such as monkeys or squirrels.

A characteristic and valuable plant of Western Ecuador is the *caña de Guayaquil,* or Guayaquil cane (*Guadua latifolia*). It propagates in extensive areas, known as *cañaverales,* and from its social or exclusive character prevents the growth of other plants in its midst. These gigantic grasses are noteworthy both for their great thickness and height, reaching at times 100 feet, and for their graceful and elegant foliage. They are of the utmost value in tropical countries, and form a considerable article of export from Guayaquil to the arid coast of Peru and Chile, where they are used in the construction of houses. Besides growing wild, the *caña* is cultivated around the *haciendas.* The isolated groups of these great canes along the banks of the rivers or in the midst of plains, add much to the beauty of the landscape.

The *Plátano* and the *Guineo* (*Musa paradisiaca* and *M. sapientum*), known abroad popularly as the banana, is largely grown in Western Ecuador. Plantations are found in the middle of the forests, moreover, where there is no vestige of ancient habitations, nor traditions of such, as, for example, in the interior of the province of Esmeraldas. There are not wanting authorities who assert that this plant, if it is not indigenous to tropical America, was at least introduced before the time of the European Conquest. Others, however, doubt this. Much discussion has centred around the subject. It has been thought that the plant may have been carried by ocean currents from the Old World, where it is found throughout the tropics, to the New, and also by man in that period of earlier intercourse before the Colombian discovery of America. The evidence of its existence in America before Columbus, however, is not conclusive. It is the sub-species, *sapientium*, which is generally eaten raw, whilst the plantain, the *paradisiaca*, requires cooking. This gigantic herbaceous perennial plant sends up a stem to twenty feet in height. The leaves of this and a smaller *plátano* are useful for roof coverings, and for fibre in rope-making. The fruit is one of the most valuable native articles of diet. The characteristic and elegant form of the banana plants are well known to the traveller in all tropical regions.

The aerial flora of western Ecuador is a rich one, embodying many varieties of beautiful orchids which cover the trunks and branches of the trees to their summit. Among the valuable orchids are the *Stanhopes*, the *Cafasetum*, the *Cynoches*, the magnificent *Sobralea rosea*, the *Gongoras*, the splendid *Maxilarias*, and the odorous *Pescatoria Roezlii*, also the *Aspasia ephdendroides* common upon the *cacao*-trees. This region is also the home of the Vainilla, in two species. There are many *enredederas*, as the bejucos and lianas or climbers are termed, some of which are useful as rope in the construction of rafts and houses. The sarsaparilla (*Smilax officinalis*) is also a bejuco, and flourishes in abundance in the sub-tropical Andine zone. There are also various medicinal plants, some but little known.

The humid wooded region of the Andine slopes may be taken as extending from an elevation of 700 or 1,000 feet above sea-level to 10,000 feet. This includes the tropical and sub-tropical belt, the common feature being the humidity. The palms reach somewhat over 5,000 feet. The seasons are but little divided, and *verano* and *invierno* are scarcely distinguishable. Virgin forests cover the zone, whose economic values are small by reason of the distance from means of transport. In these dense forests the orchids seek the very treetops in search of light and air. The timber is of less durable quality than lower down.

It is in the middle belt of this forest region, from 6,600 to 8,600 feet elevation, in which the sub-tropical flora reaches its most typical development, that the quinine-yielding shrub, the *Cinchona* or *Cascarilla*, is found. It has been encountered as high as 9,570 feet and as low as 2,000 feet. The *Cinchonas* are proper to the Andes, and are found on both sides of the Cordillera from Colombia to Bolivia, except that they do not appear on the littoral south of the Ecuadorian forested belt. Ecuador possesses many species, but the most valuable is the *Cinchona succiruba*, or red *cascarilla*. Cinchona is the generic name of a number of trees belonging to the natural order *Rubiaceæ*. Some varieties of these trees reach a height of eighty feet, with ever-green leaves, and their geographical range is that of western South America, from 10° north to 22° south latitude at the elevation above described. The use of the trees is in their bark, which contains the most valuable febrifuge and antipyretic medicine, quinine, known to medical science. Its properties were first made known in the year 1638, when the wife of a Peruvian viceroy, the Countess of Cinchon, was cured of an attack of *tercianas*, or malarial fever, by means of doses of the bark, and from that lady the medicine took its generic name. It was recommended for her by the *corregidor* of Loja, in Ecuador, who himself, it was said, had been cured of a fever, eighteen years before, by the drug. It became known as " Jesuits' Bark " in Europe, through its dissemination by members of the Jesuit brotherhood. Another account states that the discovery first followed on the treatment of a Jesuit missionary, who was ill with fever, by an Indian. In 1738 La Condamine discovered the Ecuadorian red quinine, which was named after him by Humboldt. The industry of quinine-gathering has been important for Ecuador.

From 7,000 to 10,000 feet the forest is much richer in flowers, with a multitude of small trees and shrubs, whose elegant foliage or beautiful blossoms attract the eye. Fuchsias, micomas, buddleias, solanums, gloxinias, lobelias, and others are encountered. The palms disappear, and the sub-tropical flora mingle with the sub-Andine, and tree life is scarcer as the 10,000 feet line is approached.

Leaving out for the moment the inter-Andine region between the Cordilleras, the flora at the foregoing elevation on the eastern slope may be lightly considered. This also embodies the tropical and the sub-tropical, and the vegetation is essentially the same as on the corresponding western slope. But there are some additions—among them the *canella* or cinnamon-tree, the Brazilian mahogany, which grows upon the Napo, and the cedar (*Cedrela odorata*). The *caucho* or rubber-tree is the *Siphonia elastica* in this belt.

A poisonous plant is the *Strychnos toxifera*, from which the Indians prepare the poison for their arrows, the urari. A narcotic plant is the aya-huasa (*Banisteria caapi*), an infusion of which, taken by the Indians, produces a curious state of inebriety in which visions are seen, after the manner of opium. There are some delicious but little known varieties of fruits in this region.

The inter-Andine region extends from 6,600 to 11,250 feet above sea-level, and is mainly distinguished for the cultivation of cereals. On the interior versants, in the lower portions, the subtropical element enters through the transverse valleys of the Rivers Catamayo, Jubones, Chimbo, Chanchan, Pastaza, Guallabamba, and Mira at about 6,000 feet. The upper limit of the inter-Andine region is at 11,000 feet, which coincides practically with that up to which barley may be cultivated. The climate is temperate, and even cold, and much drier than below. The aspect of the land is generally monotonous in comparison with the tropic vegetation lower down. Struggling trees are found in the ravines, but otherwise the woods have terminated. The human inhabitants which have settled in this region since very remote times have altered the aspect of the vegetation, especially since the Spanish Conquest, when the cultivation of cereals began. But far from enriching and beautifying the landscape, the work of man here, due to the backward system of agriculture, has often sterilized it. Typical of the region are the plains of Riobamba, Latacunga, and Quito, at an elevation of about 9,200 feet. Lower down, in certain valleys such as those of Catamayo, Yunguilla, Guallabamba, and Chota, the aspect differs little, except that there are some cane and coffee fields and a few fruit-trees. The dryness which reigns in these valleys is in great contrast with the humidity of the outside versants at the corresponding altitude.

The absence of forest trees in the inter-Andine zone brings into prominence the species of shrubs, fruit-trees, and small vegetation. The native prune is cultivated around the huts of the Indians,

and the *sauce* or willow lines the swamps and ravines.
Fruit-trees are cultivated in the *haciendas* of the
sheltered valleys, such as those of Chillo and Tumaco,
Guallabamba and Ibarra.   In these gardens the
orange, the lemon, myrtle, guava, and others are
found.   Wherever the land is most arid, the thorny
plants and cacti flourish, especially the well-known
nopal, or prickly pear, sometimes called the wild
fig by reason of its delicious fruit, known as *tunas.*
This plant is well known to the traveller in Latin
American countries, and indeed in other parts of the
world.

The cacti are the most grotesque form of plant
life in the Andine regions.   Crotons, mimosas, and a
raquitic algarrobo are found, from whose scanty
branches hang beard-like parasites, which, agitated
by the dry, hot winds, at times like the sirocco of the
Sahara, add their melancholy appearance to these arid
spots, whose aspect alone is sufficient to produce the
sensations of hunger and thirst in the traveller.
Higher up, however, above the *altiplanicies* or
plateaux, to where the *páramos* begin (for example,
on the slopes of Pichincha above Quito), the flora is
somewhat more attractive.   From 10,000 feet to
somewhat over 11,000 feet natural shubberies exist,
often in flower, and these perhaps represent more truly
the primitive Andine flora, which have disappeared on
the plain, due to cultivation.   The elegant calceolaria
is found here, as in Peru and Colombia, and there are
curious and useful wild shrubs and plants.   The
granadillo is found both wild and cultivated, yielding,
its agreeable fruit, and the *Taxonia manicata*, with
its beautiful scarlet flowers, enlivens the landscape in
places, tangled among the shrubs on the edges of the
trails.   All the garden vegetables of Europe grow,
well in this zone, as do also the well-known European
flowers, the violets, pansies, and pinks.   These, on
the other hand, do not flourish on the coast.   There

CACTUS AND OTHER VEGETATION AT 4,000 FEET ELEVATION.

[To face p. 346.

are many kinds of grasses in this upland zone. The monotonous appearance of the zone is in part the fault of its human inhabitants, who have despoiled it, little by little, of its vegetation and tree life, without endeavouring to replace these by artificial fertilizers and planting. It is largely from this cause that the sterile pampas originated, such as those between Ambato and Latacunga, whose scanty grasses are scarcely sufficient to maintain the herds of sheep which browse upon them.

The fifth division, the Andine region proper, known as that of the *páramos*, has a wide range in vegetation. It occupies the broad Cordilleras, the inter-Andine *nudos* or knots, and other intermediate or isolated mountainous sections which exceed the elevation of 10,000 or 11,000 feet. The singular climatic conditions are elsewhere described. Its highest limit is at about 15,000 feet, and the flora develops or degenerates, little by little, as ascent is gained on these bleak uplands to where organic life is finally lost in the perpetual snows. The *páramo* region is marked on its lower side by very characteristic shrubs and plants. There are calceolarias, valerias, potentillas, and others. The well-known and useful *ichu* grass (*Stipa ichu*), so characteristic of the inclement uplands of the Andes everywhere, begins in the sub-Andine zone last described, but its indisputable domain is in the higher *páramos*. With other kinds of grasses it forms the *pajonales*, the open, treeless plateaux, with their sterile rock outcrops, whose dreary expanses cover so many thousands of square miles of the Andes. The ichu grass disputes space with the " Alpine " plants, choked by its straw, and only towards the snowline, where the grass thins out, can these other inhabitants of the heights develop. The grasses of the *pajonales* are peculiar. The bunches are generally two-thirds dry and of a yellowish-brown colour, the new blades being greenish

19

or olive in tint. The tufts present, in the highest
areas, the peculiarity of being charred on one side
at certain seasons, as if they had intentionally been
burnt. This is the result of the alternative action of
sun and snow. In the Alps the flora has some
advantage over that of the Andes. Nature awakens
from its winter sleep to a new life, and suddenly
changes the aspect of the landscape with the bright
colours and flowers of May and June, but in the
dreary *pajonales* of the Andes the unchanging season
does not serve to relieve the monotony of a poor but
imperishable vegetation, which struggles on almost
unrenovated. On the *páramos* of Ecuador, or the
punas and uplands of Peru and Bolivia, there is
neither spring nor summer, autumn nor winter, only a
continuous sameness as regards plant life. There
are, perhaps, few regions of so melancholy an aspect
anywhere. Yet to do justice to the Andes, the vast
open spaces, the boundless horizons, the curious rock-
forms, the splendid cloud effects, the colour of the
landscape on the grasses and the rocks under the
rising or setting sun, have their own peculiar beauty,
redeeming what otherwise would appear to be a
vacant, unfinished, and forgotten world.

The upland vegetation is not without interest for the
botanist, with peculiar forms of plant life, and the
páramo region is valuable for its pasture. The
stunted shrubs of the ravines ascend above the general
arboreal line of 11,500 feet. On the slopes of
Antisana dense *matorrales* or thickets and bush
growths of six feet in height are found of the
Chusquea aristata, up to more than 13,250 feet, and
the twisted Quenua trees (*Polylepis sp.*) form small
woods on Chimborazo and other mountains in certain
spots up to almost 13,900 feet, but these are isolated
phenomena. Some woody and fruit-bearing plants are
found close to the perpetual snowline, but they
scarcely raise themselves above the lowly herbs around

them, and so do not present the appearance of shrubs. At 14,900 feet the hardy grasses grow only in isolated bunches, and then disappear completely. Here some Andine plants, some with large, handsome flowers, are able to survive, and the flora at this point is gayer than the Alpine flora. Almost as in a botanical garden, and separated by patches of sandy material, are found handsome groups of gentians, valerians, and other flowers, with a grotesque lupinus. The *Wernerias* and a small *Umbellifera* form a thick "turf" or mattress, in places of a spring-like verdure, among which are the red cylinders of the singular *Jamesonia cinnamomea*. Above 16,000 feet forty-two species of the flora of the highest Andes were found by Whymper, mainly from Chimborazo and Antisana. Of mosses twelve genera were found above 15,000 feet, and fifty-nine species of flowering plants above 14,000 feet, of which thirty-five species were from above 15,000 feet, and twenty from above 16,000 feet. Mosses were found on Chimborazo at 16,600 feet, and the Polypodium fern at 14,900 feet, the *Culcitium nivale* and others living among patches of snow above the perpetual snowline at 16,300 feet, geranium at 16,000 feet, ranunculus at 16,500 feet, currant-bushes at 14,000 feet—all on Chimborazo, with fuchsias on Sara Urcu at 12,780 feet. Thus these flowers struggle to maintain themselves in the frigid temperature on the equator. The sandy patches are covered in places with great areas of ash-coloured or white lichens, the highest specimen obtained being the lichen *Lecanora subfusca* on the south side of Chimborazo, at 18,400 feet above sea-level.

Here the organic world has made its last effort, and the equatorial sun shines through the thin, cold air upon a world void of life, where the only contrast is that afforded by the jagged rock strata, protruding here and there from the gleaming snow mantle of the Andine crests, and the only living thing is the occasional condor hovering above the edge of some snowy volcano.

The zoology of Ecuador has not been fully studied, but, as before remarked, it has a wide range, following naturally upon the range of the climatic zones. The country, like all those of the Andes, is comparatively poor in mammals. The *Quadrumana*, the monkeys, are represented by a large number of species, and Ecuador, in its Amazon district, contains the species common to Brazil and Peru. The monkey inhabits only the tropical regions. The commonest kind are the *Micos*, of several species, and these cause at times considerable damage to the maize and cocoa plantations, and for this reason are hunted by the husbandmen. The black monkeys are much larger. At dawn and sunset they congregate in the highest tops of the trees, at times near the *haciendas*, singing in chorus, in stentorian tone, causing the woods to resound with their cries. The long-armed monkey is another denizen of the Ecuadorian eastern forests ; its extremities are very large, and it has only four fingers. Its flesh is good eating, and travellers on the rivers frequently fall back upon it for their food supplies. From the region of the Napo some very graceful little monkeys are brought, which are easily tamed, although they soon die in a climate which differs from their own hot, humid forests. There are about forty species of monkeys in Ecuador altogether. Unlike Peru, there are monkeys on the Ecuadorian coast.

The carnivora are largely represented in Ecuador. There are five or six feline species, including the puma or American lion (*Felis concolor*), found from the littoral to the upper *páramo* zone. It is not dangerous to hunt, and the Indians of Papallacta catch it with the lasso.[1] It is smaller than the jaguar and less ferocious. This, the American tiger (*Felis onca*) is found in all tropical America, in the hot regions, and

---

[1] The Author has seen the same operation performed in Mexico.

is the largest and most-feared wild beast on the continent. It rarely attacks man, unless wounded or provocated, but often destroys the young cattle in the *haciendas*. It is not rare in the forest regions, and its spoor is frequently seen and its roar heard, although the traveller very rarely sees it.[1] There are other smaller feline and carnivorous animals.

The canine family is represented by a beautiful fox, which is known as a *lobo* or " wolf " by the Indians ; it inhabits the high regions and *páramos*. At the time of the conquest America possessed its own species of dog, but none is found wild in Ecuador now, the domestic dog of the Indians being the result of a cross between the indigenous animal and the imported European dog.

A regular-sized bear lives up as far as the *páramos*, and in the lower regions the *cuchuche* bear is esteemed for its meat, and is also easily domesticated. *Tejon* or " skunk " are also encountered, and there is a small marsupial, of rat-like form. Rodents are numerous of all kinds, among them the *cui* or guinea-pig, whether on the hot coast or the frigid *páramos*, serving as an article of diet for the Indians. This useful little animal is found throughout the Andine countries. Roast *cui* with potatoes is one of the best dishes of the *sierras*. Squirrels and porcupines are found, and armadilloes and ant-bears. The *multungulos*, whose principal representative in the Quaternary period was the mastodon of the Andes, are now represented by the species of tapir. This, the danta or *Gran-Bestia*, is a singular animal. In appearance it may be said to partake of the donkey, the elephant, and the pig, about the size of the first-named. It is the largest indigenous mammal of the South American continent. The commonest specimen is the *Tapirus Americanus*, elephant-skinned, living in the Amazon rivers and

[1] The Author heard but did not see it, in the Amazon forest of Peru.

swamps, and never found on the western slope of the Andes. The smaller kind, with a woolly skin, is found on the *páramos*. The flesh of the tapir is eatable. There is also the *jábali* or peccary, found in bands and occasioning damage to plantations on the littoral. It is also eatable.

The class of the *Solidungulos* became extinct in South America in the Quaternary epoch, and their two representatives, the horse and the ass, were introduced from Europe. The Ruminants are not numerous. The llama (*Auchenia lama*) is not found wild now, nor is it bred and used to the same extent as in Peru and Bolivia, in which countries it forms so marked a feature of the upland landscape, and so valuable a possession of the Indians. Only in the provinces of Tunguragua and Leon are considerable bands maintained. In the high regions certain kinds of deer (*Cervus chilensis*) are common, and others on the coast.

Seals occasionally visit the coast, and are found on the coast of the Galápagos Islands, where there are also whales, whose fishing forms a lucrative occupation. The Reptilia include countless numbers of alligators in the Guayas River and its tributaries, and in the tide-water channels of the smaller coastal rivers. In some cases these reach nineteen feet in length. The alligators of the Guayas and Tumbez Rivers are shown to be true crocodiles. These are at times seen floating down the Guayas River on natural rafts of driftwood. On the coast two kinds of large turtles are hunted for their flesh and shell, and the great Galápago, found only in the islands of that name, are elsewhere described. In the Marañon tributaries—the Napo, Pastaza, etc.—myriads of small turtles are encountered, known as charapas, and these form a valuable food resource for the riverine dwellers by reason of their excellent meat and for the oil from their eggs, which is used as lard. There are also small land tortoises in abundance, also iguanas and graceful black lizards, marked with blue and yellow. Serpents and snakes are plentiful, from the great Anaconda of the Amazon tributaries to the beautifully marked coral snake. The great boa-constrictor reaches sixteen feet in length, and the anaconda, or *Mama-yacu*, of the Indians, twenty-three feet. Many fables are told of these last, but neither attacks man, unless irritated. On the western side there are smaller boas. There are also various venemous snakes. As for the frogs and toads, their voice is heard at all elevations, from the inundated streets of Guayaquil to the *páramos* of Chimborazo. A small frog is found even at 13,500 feet. A single species of fish, the Preña-dilla, is found in the Andine lakes up to 10,000 feet. This is famous as being the subject of the tradition published by Humboldt, elsewhere mentioned. Probably the true explanation is that the lava-flows caused the lakes and rivers to overflow, so scattering the fish about the plains. On the coast the *sardinas,* especially at Ancon, are plentiful, and the shark and swordfish ascend the rivers to the mountain base. The latter was encountered by Wolf twenty leagues from the sea. Fish on the coast is one of the principal articles of food. As regards the Amazon, there are more kinds of fish in the river, according to Agassez, than in any other fluvial system in the world. The camarones, the excellent large fresh-water prawns, are consumed through all the western littoral of South America, and lobsters and oysters—the latter the basis of the great fishing industry—are plentiful.

The birds, of bright-coloured plumage, are denizens of the tropical zones ; those of the Andine regions are generally of sad-coloured plumage, conforming with the melancholy *pajonales* and *páramos*. An exception, however, is in the picaflores, small birds which, like coloured electric sparks, dart tirelessly through the thin air among the fuchsias and other flowers of the uplands, feeding on insects ; and near the perpetual snowline beautiful humming-birds hover among the flowers on Chimborazo and Pichincha. There are but few songsters in the tropical regions, a fact noted by all travellers from temperate lands, where the song of birds is so pleasing a feature of the woodlands ; for the tropical forests are silent as regards these winged beings, as if Nature, having dowered them with brilliant plumage, had deprived them of sweet voices. The tropic birds are plumed in pure scarlet, green, or blue, or in black velvet with yellow markings, or with harlequin colours ; some with luxuriant crests, others with resplendent tails, and small ones like sapphire, topaz, or ruby. The hotter the temperature the more showy is the plumage, and Ecuador is probably the richest of all South American countries in the variety of its birds. Chief of the feathered tribe is the great condor of the Andes. It is very common in Ecuador, from Azuay to Colombia, in the neighbourhood of the great volcanoes. The male bird measures nearly ten feet from tip to tip of its wings. In Chile this great bird descends frequently to the sea-coast, it is said, but in Ecuador it never leaves the cold uplands, where it is seen rising and circling around the snowy summits of the volcanoes, 20,000 feet above sea-level. The condor of Ecuador is well described by Whymper.[1] Another bird of the Raptores, or predatory species, is the vulture, or *buitre*, whose commonest variety, known as the galli-nazo, is of great use as a scavenger. This bird devours offal and carrion in the neighbourhood of human dwellings, and it has been described as a, more efficient dustman in Latin America than the human variety employed by the authorities. From

[1] *The High Andes of Ecuador.*

this habit it is protected.[1] There are falcons and kites, and various kinds of owls. Of the latter the largest is the Buho, known by the Indians as *cuscungo*, living solitarily in the forests of the littoral or the caverns of the rocky *páramos*. The weird cry of the owl, heard at night, the Indians take as an evil augury. A small owl on the dry coasts of Manabi and Santa Elena has the curious custom of living in holes, which it excavates in the earth, in company with a rabbit, or *armadillo*, and its life is a daily instead of a nocturnal one, the day being spent mainly in sitting in front of its cave, like a sentinel, or in hunting smaller birds. This bird is found throughout South America, even in the Argentine pampas. There are many kinds of wild doves, whose soft cry resounds in the neighbourhood of the villages, and numerous partridges, both on the littoral and on the uplands. Among the song-birds should be mentioned the " flautero," so called from its flute-like mellow note, proceeding from a bird magnificent in appearance inhabiting the eastern forests. Among the palmipeds and swimmers are the alcatraz, frigate-bird, gulls, and graceful sea-nightingales. The albatross and the penguin are found on the Galápagos Islands. Ducks also, both wild and tame, abound. In the Amazon region live the macaw, the parrot, the toucan, the curassow ; and there are herons, ibises, cranes, storks, and eagles. The avifauna of the republic is thus marked by its great variety of genera and species.

A large, venomous spider exists, which is said to catch even small birds, and the *alacran*, or scorpion, in the dry region, those of Puná being the most venomous. Insects generally in Ecuador are extremely numerous, embodying those orders the largest

[1] The traveller in Vera Cruz, in Mexico, will have observed the remarkable activity of this bird in the streets of the town as a scavenger.

and most brilliant, as well as the most noxious, and the hotter the region the more plentiful and beautiful are they.   Clouds of butterflies are encountered at times in the tropical regions, of varied and brilliant hue, and a large moth caught by Whymper reached $7\frac{1}{4}$ inches from tip to tip of its wings.[1]   Dragon-flies and fire-flies abound, the latter lighting up the woods at night, and armies of voracious ants eat up garden vegetation, and at the same time clear the houses of noxious vermin.   In the low, hot, swampy lands the mosquitoes are a terrible plague, but they disappear at an elevation of 1,000 or 1,200 feet above sea-level, and are scarce on the cooler coast districts.

[1] In the Mexican highlands the Author caught a butterfly measuring $7\frac{1}{2}$ inches.

CHAPTER XVIII

THE GALÁPAGOS ISLANDS

THE archipelago of the Galápagos, or Galápagos Island, is a territory of considerable interest, although relatively little known and unfrequented. It is possible that these islands may play a more important part in the future, due to the circumstance that they lie almost in the direct path of vessels on the route across the Pacific from Australia and New Zealand to the Panama Canal.

These islands, which belong to the republic of Ecuador, lie in part exactly under the Equator, 580 miles west of the mainland. The archipelago consists of five larger and two smaller islands, with a total area estimated at about 2,870 square miles. The name is derived from the *galápago*, the giant tortoise, which abounds in the islands. The archipelago was discovered by the Spaniards in the sixteenth century, but as they were uninhabited little importance was attached to them. They formed at times a convenient stopping-place for whalers and pirates, but until the year 1832 no attempt at colonization was made. All the principal islands bear English names, which were probably given to them by buccaneers—viz., Albemarle, Indefatigable, Narborough, James, and Chatham, the largest extending from the Equator to one degree south ; three small ones, of Abingdon, Bindloe, and Tower, lying north of the Equator, and of Charles, or Floreana, and Hood, south of the first degree. There are

generally enumerated thirteen islands, including those
of Barrington, Duncan, and Jervis. In addition,
there are numerous islets surrounding the larger,
two of which, Wenman and Culpepper, lie twenty-
seven leagues north-west of Abingdon. The total
length of the archipelago, from Chatham to Narborough, is fifty-three leagues, and the breadth, from
Floreana to Abingdon, forty-one leagues, so that
the islands are distributed over an ocean area of

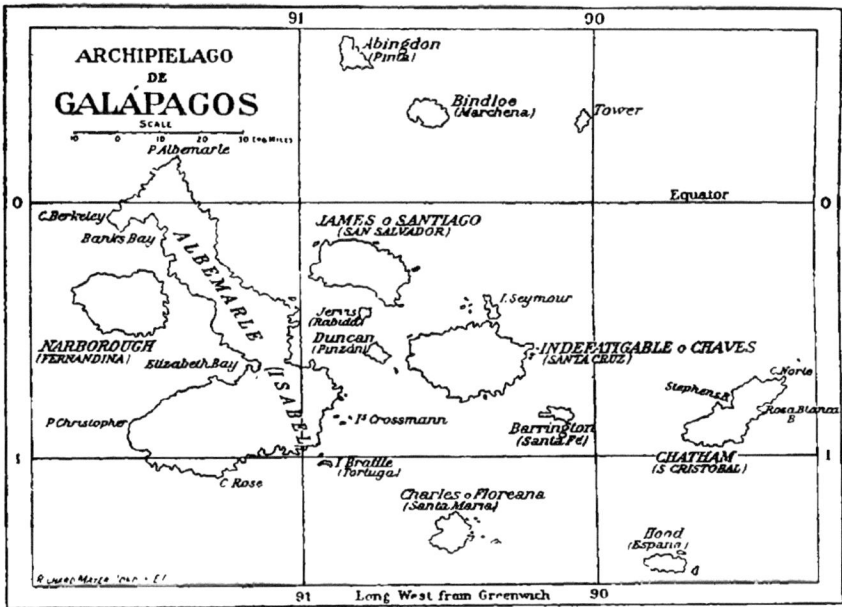

more than 2,000 square leagues. Albemarle has
an area of 138 square leagues, Indefatigable
33, Narborough 21, James, or Santiago, 18½,
Chatham 14, and Floreana 4½. The archipelago was annexed by Ecuador in 1832, and
Floreana, or Charles Island, was founded by the
Ecuadorian general Villamil, who named it in honour
of Juan José Flores, President of the republic. Later,
in the nineteenth century, the Congress of Ecuador
changed the names of the islands, renewing in part

the designations given thereto by the Spanish discoverers.

The formation of the islands is, geologically, recent, since the Tertiary period. More than 2,000 volcanic craters, according to Darwin, are found therein, a few of which are stated to be active, which argues a volcanic formation for the territory. The central cones reach only 100 to 170 feet elevation above sea-level. In some places the ground is covered with small craters, presenting a fantastic appearance. Between those and the enormous blocks of lava which are strewn about the trunks of weirdly formed cacti arise, and crawling among them or resting stolidly are the monstrous *galápagos*, or land tortoises, and groups of the ugly sea-lizards, sunning themselves on the burnt rocks. The whole presents what might be characterized as a kind of nightmare aspect, the weird specimens, both of the organic and the inorganic world, being in harmony with each other, and bringing to mind the imaginary antediluvian landscapes reconstructed by geologists.

The rock is generally basalt, but the formation reveals an older and a newer formation. In the middle of black lava-fields, which extend around the coast, arise horseshoe-shaped hillocks, which are seen to be fragments of volcanoes, in many cases filled with secondary lava-flows. The decomposition of the basaltic lava forms a clayey red soil, which, mixed with the rotted vegetation, is fertile. The absence of fresh water on the islands is due to the porosity of the lava, which rapidly absorbs moisture, and there are scarcely any streams or lagoons to be found. Water is obtained from wells. There is little guano or phosphates on the islands, and no metalliferous minerals, as far as is known. A certain amount of lime is exported to Guayaquil.

The climate of the Galápagos is described as one of the healthiest and most agreeable in the world.

Lying directly under the Equator, the temperature is nevertheless low, due to the effect of the Antarctic or Peruvian current, which, deflected from the South American coast, in part bathes the coasts of these islands. The average temperature of the lower parts of the archipelago is between 70° and 72° F., and of the higher part, 660 feet to 3,300 feet above sea-level, 63° to 68° F. The lower part is a dry zone, the upper a more humid. The winter falls in the same period as on the Ecuadorian coast, but at times rain is lacking throughout the year. In the *verano*, or summer, the *garua*, or mist-drizzle, occurs, as on the Peruvian and Ecuadorian coast, and this is sufficient to form deep mud on the trails. The winds are almost always from the south-east. The lunar rainbow is observed at times, during the *garua* period.

The vegetation of the lower zone consists mainly of a few stunted shrubs. Among this poor flora are a *Lautana*, a *Croton*, *Euphorbias*, etc., and the *Algarrobo* and *Palo Santo* occasionally reach twenty to thirty feet in height, as do also the cacti, the latter often growing on the margins of the craters. There is some dry grass, but many large areas are entirely without vegetation. The *Orchilla*, a lichen of the genus *Roccella*, which for many years formed an article of export, is found only in the lower parts, where it derives its sustenance almost from the ocean. Higher up the cacti disappear, and the algarrobos are taller. Still higher the damper soil is covered with green turf, and the woods, of varied trees and shrubs, are equally green, and there are some scanty wild fruits. Otherwise the vegetation is similar to that of the Andine uplands, with pampas of grass like the *páramos* of the mainland. But none of the luxuriant species of the Amazon tropics are present. In some places on the coast there are dense mangrove thickets.

The *fauna* is poorer than the *flora*. In some of the islands the giant galápago has disappeared, due to the presence of man and of the domestic animals introduced, which latter thrive well. Human agency is causing changes in the biological conditions generally. The sea life, however, is very rich, with abundance of fishes, crabs, etc., and whale-fishing has been profitable. Whale-vessels are generally found in the vicinity. The giant sea-tortoises abound generally, and seals are plentiful. The birds are numerous, and their nests in some of the small islets literally cover the ground, in the case of the aquatic birds. But *guano* is not freely formed, as on the Peruvian coast and islands, due to the rain. In Hood Island albatrosses are found, having followed the Antarctic current, and their eggs form a diet for transitory orchilla-gatherers. There are no brilliant land birds. Darwin's collection contained twenty-six species of land birds, which, with the exception of one, were entirely unknown in other parts of the world. The land birds are so tame that they may be caught by hand, or with a butterfly-net, but the aquatic birds are as shy as usual. Notwithstanding that the land birds have now been persecuted for centuries, they do not yet distrust man. They seem slowly to learn to fear him, but once the instinct is acquired it is hereditary.

The reptiles are all endemic—the tortoises and galápagos, the iguanas, lizards, and snakes. The galápago (*Testudo elephantopus*), at first found in great abundance, is becoming scarcer, due to hunting for the excellent oils it yields and for its flesh and eggs, which are agreeable articles of food. These reptiles devour the branches of the cactus in the small islands and in the larger ones gather in bands on the grassy pampas, where they herd together like cattle. They have formed wide-rutted trails in various directions, " like high-roads made by

man." [1]   These " roads " lead generally to the
drinking-places, and as the latter are scarce upon
the islands it follows that many of the tortoise-roads
converge upon these points from considerable distances.   The drinking-places are generally besieged
by fifteen or twenty of the galápagos.   The tortoise
drinks only once in every three or four months, but
then with excess, putting its head in the water.   A
journey from the high pampas to the water-holes
takes the tortoise three or four weeks, and some
are only able to waddle sixty or seventy yards in
a day.   They cannot run or defend themselves, and
when a human being approaches they retire into their
shells, remaining immovable although wounded to
death.   In the remote highlands of the islands—
where, it is said, they live for 100 years—the
galápagos are at times enormous, weighing as much
as 610 pounds.   But, due to the difficulty of carriage,
only smaller ones are exported to Guayaquil.   With
the colonization of the islands these interesting but
defenceless creatures tend rapidly to disappear, and
means for their protection and conservation should be
taken.   No living species or remains of these tortoises
are found on the American mainland, and only in
one other part of the world, the Mascarene Islands,
in the Indian Ocean, east of Madagascar, do they
exist.   It has been stated that the presence of these
giant reptiles on the island group is the chief fact
on which a former land connexion with the continent
of   America   may   be   sustained.   " Nearly   all
authorities   agree   that   it   is   not   probable   they
have crossed the wide sea between the islands and
the American continent, although, while they are
helpless, and quite unable to swim, they can float
on   water." [2]   If   their   ancestors   had   been   drifted
out to the islands by a flood they must at one time

---

[1] Wolf, *op. cit.*   [2] Wallace.

have been numerous on the continent, but no remains are found. Some writers think it is more natural to assume the disappearance of a great stock of animals than to assume the disappearance in recent geological times — the Eocene period or later — of enormous land masses. That great elevations of land in South America have taken place since the Eocene, and possibly great subsidences, is known. Such subsidences in the Indian Ocean have been argued from the similar distribution of the Mascarene giant tortoises. In the Galápagos Islands, of the seven species of these creatures, each is confined to its own islet.

There are two species of large iguanas on the island of a genus unknown on the mainland. One of these, which lives in the sea, is interesting as being the only living representative of the marine saurian. This sea lizard is of repugnant aspect, more like a salamander than a lizard, sometimes four feet long, yellow and red underneath and dark grey above. It is not eatable, as is the land lizard. The latter is also of ugly appearance but smaller, and lives in the arid part of the islands, in caves and holes, at times digging such with its claws. Its oil is of some value and its flesh is consumed. Scorpions and centipedes are found on the islands— the latter very large, at times more than a foot in length. These horrible giant centipedes are very venomous, but beyond them are no noxious creatures in the islands and mosquitoes are few.

On Charles Island, the most important of the group, there is a small colony and the soil is cultivated. Cattle and horses live in considerable numbers on the uplands, and other domestic animals, in many cases in wild bands. On Chatham Island there is a convict settlement with about 300 inhabitants, under the supervision of the Ecuadorian authorities. It is considered that, under good conditions of management, a much more numerous population could be sustained on the islands.

Since the Galápagos were visited by Darwin, in the voyage of the *Beagle* in 1835, various scientific expeditions have visited the archipelago, and complete collections of its *flora* and *fauna* have been made. Among these were Dr. Habel, in 1868 ; Wolf, in 1875 and 1878 ; the naturalists of the *Albatross*, between 1888 and 1891, Messrs. Baur and Adams ; and in 1897-8 the journey of Mr. Harris, at the instance of Walter Rothschild.

From its isolated position the Galápagos Archipelago possesses a peculiar advantage from the fact that its natural history has never been interfered with by any aborigines of the human race. In its future colonization by Ecuador, if such takes place, it may be hoped that the peculiar animal inhabitants, especially the giant tortoises, will not be exterminated.

Of recent years the prospective strategic value, due to the building of the Panama Canal, of the islands has motived various negotiations by foreign Powers for their acquisition. In 1909 some sensation was caused in Ecuador by the publication of ex-President García's private papers, showing that there had been proposals for sale of the Archipelago, first to France and then (that in view of the Monroe Doctrine having been found inadvisable) to the United States. In 1911 there were dealings between President Estrada and the United States for a proposed lease of the islands for a term of ninety-nine years, under a payment of £3,000,000 to Ecuador ; but the American offer was refused, as its acceptance would have affronted Ecuadorian patriotism.

CHAPTER XIX

THE ANTIQUITIES OF ECUADOR

ALTHOUGH there are not found in Ecuador the massive prehistoric monuments such as, in Peru and Bolivia or in Mexico and Guatemala, bear witness to the culture and constructive powers of the early inhabitants of the land,[1] nevertheless, the ancient objects of stone, metal, pottery, etc., which exist are of much interest, and certain of them are unique in the archæology of America.

The remains of stone buildings are those of structures belonging to the Inca regimen, which followed on the invasion of Quito by the early Peruvians. The ruins of Incapirca are situated upon the end of a mountain spur, which extends westwards from the high Azuay *nudo*, forming the southern part of the Cañar *hoya* separating the small Huairapungo and Silante Rivers, which form the headwaters of the Cañar or Naranjal River, whose outlet is to the gulf below Guayaquil. This ancient Inca fortress stands upon a high promontory at 10,430 feet above sea-level, one of the most interesting monuments in the country. The ruins embody a circular wall of finely hewn stone, enclosing an area with a well-preserved building in the centre, roofless, after the manner of all the ruins of the Incas, whose buildings were probably covered with poles and thatch. Inca-Chungana, near at hand, is a smaller enclosure. In the same neighbourhood

[1] Described in the Author's *Secret of the Pacific*. Unwin : London (2nd edition).

the image of the sun and other devices are sculptured upon the face of a rock, known as Inti-huaica —" Inti " being the Quechua term for the sun. At Paltabamba, on one of the hills between Pichincha and Esmeraldas, are the remains of a conical tower and temple and the buttresses of a bridge. There are also numerous tombs, from which mummies and plates of silver have been recovered. Near Cotopaxi the buildings of the old Inca palace of Pachusala is used by the *hacienda* at the present time, and there are other relics in the district. Among the pre-Hispanic objects recovered are five and six-rayed stars, which are numerous.

The Paredones are other ruins of the Inca period near the Culebrillas, a tributary of the Cañar-Naranjal River, on the border of a beautiful lake fed thereby. These ruins are of a great Inca *tambo* or halting-place on the Inca road. According to Reiss and to Wolf the structure was not a fortress or palace but a building for ordinary purposes, and rudely built although of considerable extent. The river and lake of Culebrillas, on whose banks the ruins stand, have been described by some observers as artificial hydraulic works of the Incas. But it has been argued by the writers above mentioned that this is an error, and that the stream and lakes are natural, that lakes are constantly found in the valleys of the *sierra*, and that the winding course of the waterway is naturally due to the flatness of the plain traversed, and that it would be inconceivable for the Incas to have constructed a place for pleasure and for bathing in a situation nearly 13,200 feet above sea-level, where snow frequently falls and windstorms rage. The Inca road, which passes thereby—of which marvels have been related—is, it is further stated, simply formed with the old lava blocks, and there are no vestiges of a pavement made of cement or of lime and bituminous substances. The

Azuay knot is not a place to linger upon, but no doubt the *tambo* was of value in bad weather. The Indian tribes that inhabited Cañar, with their considerable culture, has been made the subject of an interesting monologue by Dr. Suarez.[1] The comparison of the Inca roads with those of the Romans —such as was made by the Spanish chroniclers— is an exaggeration.[2]

Of equal, or perhaps greater, interest among the antiquities of Ecuador are those of the coastal region, whose origin is unknown. The province of Manabi has furnished the archæological objects of greatest interest, followed by Esmeraldas.

As has been seen in the historical section of this book, Huayna Capac, the great Inca, subjugated the territory as far along the coast as Cojimes, where he ordered a fortress to be built. But the Inca dominion over the people of the Ecuadorian coast region was short and influenced them but little. The Incas came late there, only a brief time before they themselves fell before the Spaniards. It may be assumed, therefore, that the antiquities of Manabi are of an indigenous nature, free from Inca contact or influence. Whether the comparatively high culture which is evidenced by the sculptures is autochthonous, or whether it was imported by some immigrating people, cannot be decided. The most recent observers seem to think that the culture was a native development of the soil. The best account, the only full and modern one, of the Manabi antiquities is that published by the Saville expedition [3] in 1906 to

---

[1] *Estudio historico de los antiguos Cañaris, por* Dr. D. F. Gonzalez Suarez.

[2] Described in the Author's *Republics of Central and South America.* Dent & Co., 1913.

[3] Marshall H. Saville, Loubat Professor of American Archæology of Colombia University, undertaken with the financial support and co-operation of Mr. George G. Heye, of New York City. Two volumes, fully illustrated : New York, 1907.

North-West Ecuador. Apart from this excellent account there is but little information concerning the archæology of the district, and previously its real history had never been written, notwithstanding the extreme historical importance of that part of South America in having been that in which the Spaniards first received any definite information about the Inca empire. The provinces were visited and described both by Wiener and Gonzalez Suarez, who gave some description of the famous prehistoric stone seats ; and in 1892 Dorsey spent sixteen days on the island of La Plata. Some of these singular seats found their way to various European museums.

It is believed that the people whose remains are found in Manabi were not connected with the Incas or Quechuas of Peru, or with any Andine culture. " Possibly they came along the coast from the north, perhaps from Central America." [1] Suarez thought that they were related to the Mayas of Yucatan and the Quiches of Guatemala. According to this authority, the Quiches reached the gulf of Jambeli, and gaining the coast of Machala, they entered the province of Azuay, and looking for a place well fitted for life, established themselves in its sheltered valleys. The Mayas did not cross the western Cordilleras, but remained on the island of Puná and the coast of Manabi.[2] Reference is made to a Maya colony which, among the emigrations to the Ecuadorian coast, was established between Monta and Santa Elena and on the island of Puná, with orthographic Maya derivation of names. The great emerald, before described as in possession of the Manta people, called " Umiña," is also traced to Maya origin, as regards its name. The name of the site of the artesian wells found near Jipijapa, still called Choconcha, is said by this authority also to be derived

---

[1] Saville, *op. cit.*
[2] *Atlas Arqueologica Ecuatoriano.* Suarez.

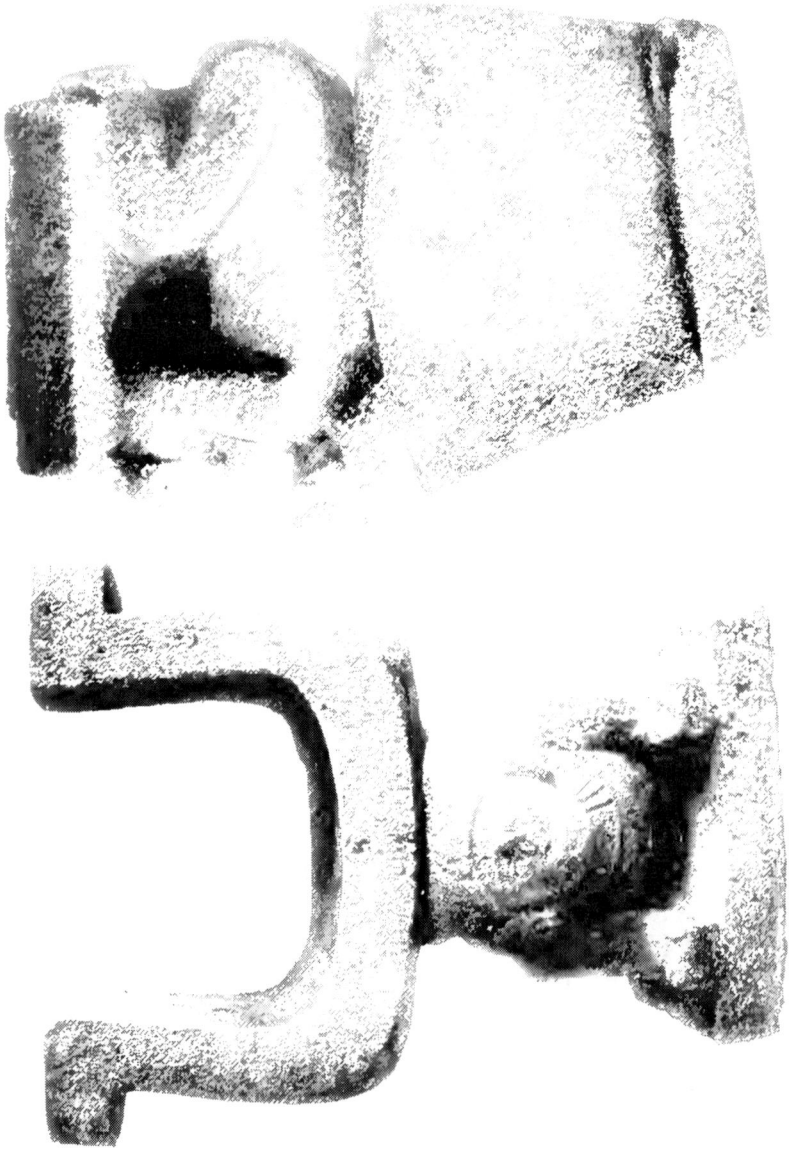

ANCIENT STONE SEATS, MANABI

from Maya terms, and it is added that the physical formation of the ground is similar to that of Yucatan, which was the home of the Mayas.   The student of Central America and Mexican archæology is familiar with the curious sacred well of Chichen-Itza in Yucatan, around which the remarkable sculptured temples of the Mayas are found.[1]

The deep wells found in considerable number in the arid Ecuadorian coast region early attracted the attention of the Spanish discoverers of Manabi. According to Cieza de Leon they were ascribed by the natives to the " giants," who, wanting water, dug wells in the living rock and lined them with masonry.   They are also obscurely referred to by Zarate, and were known as *jagueyes* by the natives. The " wells of the giants " are referred to by other writers, among them Villavicencio.   The giants, according to tradition, come from other parts. Suarez[2] describes the most notable of the artesian wells, " mistakenly attributed to giants," near Jipi-japa, eight in number, some of which were filled up, but which might be easily cleared out.   At Gaudil and at Monte Cristi there are others, the latter still used for drinking purposes by the people of that place and of Manta.   The coast of Ecuador here is arid, and these deep wells were cleverly made as a water supply.   Between Jipijapa and Santa Anna is a well with the name of Chade.   The makers were doubtless guided in their search for well sites, it is averred, by the small green patches of verdure which exist when all other vegetation in the summer is parched, indicating the place of concealed springs. At Toalla there are also ancient wells.   In the ruins behind the town of Manta, which extend from near the beach to several miles inland, there is a circular

[1] See the Author's *Mexico* in this series ; also his *The Secret of the Pacific*.   T. Fisher Unwin.
[2] *Historia del Ecuador.*

well cut through the solid rock, which was discovered
a few years ago.   It was covered with a stone and
filled with earth and small stones.   This was cleared
out to about 42 feet deep.   The well is cut in a
sort of special fashion through the rock, and is but
2 feet 3 inches in diameter at the top.   In the Cerro
de Hojas is a well, now cleared out to 25 feet deep,
8 feet in diameter, but not in the solid rock.   The
sides are walled up with rough stones.   Near the
base of the same *cerro*, or hill, is another old walled
well, with an abundance of water, used by the people
of the neighbouring ranches.

Throughout the province of Manabi exist many
remains of ancient houses of the pre-Hispanic people,
and some of the sites of these ruins near Santa Elena
are connected with the myths of the giants, according
to Cieza de Leon, and are believed by the natives
to be the ruins of the first giant settlements.   Near
the town of Manta are found the ruins of a large,
early settlement, formerly known as Jocay, and it
is stated that the origin of the place was unknown
to the Indians.   The Spaniards, when they arrived,
tortured the Indians to secure their gold and
emeralds, and the population diminished—a process
which so frequently followed upon the work of the
conquistadores.   The ruins of Jocay lie south of
Manta, and extend thereto, and in former times
possibly reached to the seashore.   Hundreds of house
sites and mounds exist, and innumerable red pot-
sherds are scattered about.   These houses, as described by Saville, are often of one room, but some
have two or more, and some have seven ; but little
is left of the walls, which are of rough stone set
edgeways in the ground.   The average width of
the walls is from three feet to four feet.   The place
has served for generations to the people of Manta as
a quarry, which has led to destruction of the walls.
Some of the buildings have been of enormous size—

one is 190 feet long and 39 feet wide, inside. The thickness of the side walls is 4 feet 6 inches. A platform or graded way was built on the side facing the sea as an approach, 35 feet long. The orientation is generally from north to south, but the variation is much greater than in the Mexican and Central American structures. Another house is 150 feet long by 41 feet wide. The stones, set edgeways in the ground for walls, are 2 feet high. There is also a graded way at one end.

In this district, scattered here and there, are numerous mounds, probably burial-places, and in one group of rooms a number of much-weathered stone sculptures. One group of fine sculptures contains a human figure, the head broken off, 4 feet 9 inches high, with other stone pigmies, and a single stone 6 feet long with carving upon it. These are greatly weathered, and the character of the carving scarcely decipherable. The stone is in some cases calcareous, and also a gritty sandstone. Two very curious sculptured animal figures, taken from the Manta ruins, are preserved in the Casa Tagua, a business house at Manta, in a better state of preservation, four feet in height. Possibly these images represented conventionalized llamas. The famous Cerro de Hojas, and its neighbourhood contains many relics of large houses, and from these have come the peculiar stone seats which from time to time have been taken to musuems in Europe and America. Near the small village of La Secita thousands of spindle-whorls have been found, and many house sites. In Cerro de Hojas the remains of the houses are found on the level tops of the hills, and level terraces on the slopes were made, each of which had a house. On many slopes the terraces are one below the other, like an enormous flight of steps. One house here measured 161 feet long and 41 feet wide. Stone columns were also found therein and certain curious sculptures. In the houses on Cerro Jaboncillo numerous interesting stone low-reliefs have been excavated. In one house the walls are of squared stone, and this may represent a later type of building. In no case do the walls remain more than two feet in height, and they are of rough slabs placed edgeways in the ground.

The stone seats, of which mention has been made, are the most remarkable feature of the Manabi archæology, and a large number of these has been found on the summits of the hills not far from the sea. These objects are unique. They are found only on the hills, within a small area about twenty miles in diameter. No objects of a like character are known in any other part of America, whether South or North. These seats are not mentioned by any of the early writers or explorers, and doubtless the places were ruined and overgrown even when Pizarro and his followers passed through the province. The first notice about them is given by Villavicencio,[1] who stated that they existed in a circle on the Cerro de Hojas, thirty in number, of stone, well worked, and that they may have been seats for conference by the chiefs of the Cara nation, who lived there before entering upon the conquest of Quito. Two seats were taken for preservation in Guayaquil. Examination by Saville showed that the seats were not arranged in a circle. They existed in the rooms or house sites, some rooms containing one, others from two to five, or at least that was the condition on the Cerro de Hajas. Cerro Jupa and Cerro Agua Nuevo also contained seats. Some of the seats are of argillaceous shaly sandstone, but the majority are of andesite.

These Manabi seats may be divided into two types, broadly distinguished by the character of their

[1] *Geografia de la Republica del Ecuador,* published in New York in 1858.

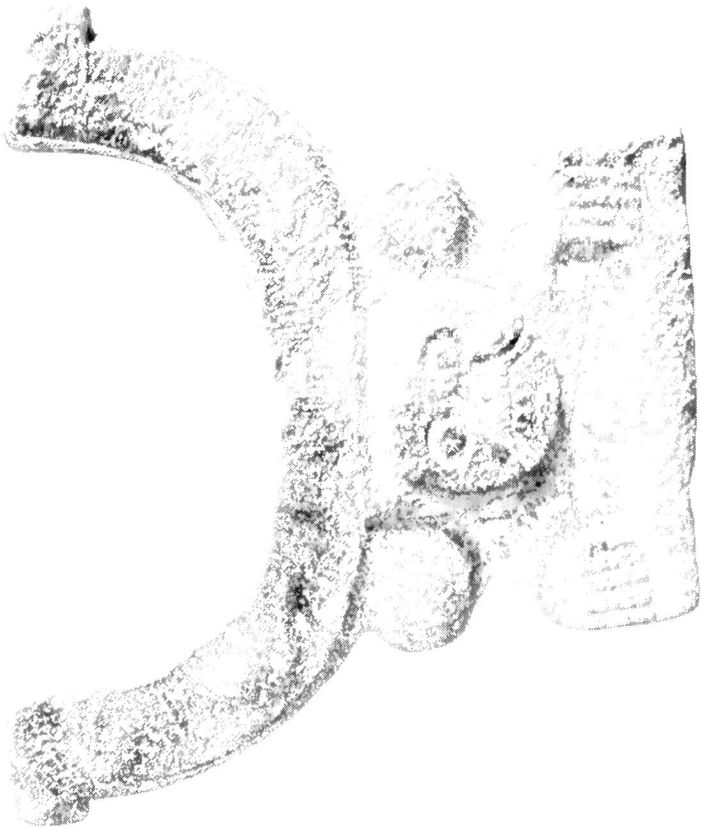

ANCIENT STONE SEAT, MANABI

(To face p. 376)

sculpture, namely, those whose supports are of carved human figures, and those which are of animal figures. The puma appears largely in the latter, but there are other animal and bird forms. Six different motives are traced in the support of the seats : first, the crouching human figure ; second, the crouching puma-like figure ; third, the bird or lizard ; fourth, the bat ; fifth, a monkey-like figure ; and sixth, the representation of a copper disc. There are some other types in addition. All the seats from the Cerro de Hojas and Cerro Jaboncillo are of andesite, except two specimens. Several hundreds of these seats are seen. Some of the seats have geometric designs carved on their borders. There is not a single human or animal figure in which the proportions of the body are accurately brought out in the supports of the seats. The general form is that in which the arms curve up from the seat above the pedestal, as shown in the accompanying illustration. The seats are beautifully formed, and of attractive appearance, and are described as being exceedingly comfortable to sit in. The largest seat in the collection [1] is also the second in size of any of the Manabi seats, the largest specimen being preserved in the town of Monte Cristi, the property of the municipality of that place. The size of this second largest seat is : extreme height, left side, 35 inches ; extreme breadth, $25\frac{1}{2}$ inches ; breadth inside of seat at upper part of front, $13\frac{1}{4}$ inches ; back, 13 inches ; extreme length of seat from front to back, inside, $18\frac{3}{4}$ inches ; extreme thickness of seat, $3\frac{1}{2}$ inches ; extreme height of human figure, $14\frac{1}{2}$ inches ; average height of pedestal, $3\frac{1}{2}$ inches. This seat is from Cerro Jaboncillo.

In Saville's book, from which the above description is taken, about sixty of these seats are fully described, and illustrated by excellent reproductions

[1] Made by Saville.

of photographs. The whole forms a remarkable collection of objects worthy to rank, in their way, as one of the archæological wonders of the world.

.What were the uses of these strange seats, and who were the people who made and used them? It is impossible to reply. Suarez says : " The Cerro de Hojas was a very important place in the province, and without any doubt was destined for reunion and religious assemblies by the towns of the district." Wiener has described the seats as the works of the Cañaris, but subsequent writers have well objected that such cannot be, as the Cañaris were an Andine people, of Azuay, and were very far from the coast. Saville says : " .We believe we have shown conclusively that there can be little doubt that the historical accounts of the settlement of the Caras in this region are correct " ; also that " points of resemblance between the people of the coast of Ecuador and Central America might be brought forward."

Whatever be the truth of the theories of origin of the early American peoples, it cannot escape the notice of the student that there are some well-marked common signs and patterns on ancient objects recovered from all parts of America, from Mexico (and even north of that country among the cliff-dwellers of Arizona and Utah), through Yucatan and Central America, Panama, Colombia, Ecuador, Peru, and Bolivia—in fact, wherever any form of geometrical ornament is found, whether on pottery, stonework, or textile fabrics. Two of the most noteworthy of these constant occurrences are what may be termed the step pattern, and the square involute or scroll, or " Greek fret." These are found, always in the same general form, though varying in size or arrangement, upon such objects as pottery of the cliff-dwellers, the pyramids of Zochicalco in Mexico,

LOW RELIEFS FROM MANABI

ornaments from Teotihuacan, the great sun-pyramid of Mexico, the façade of the beautiful ruins of Mitla in Mexico, the façades of the equally fine ruins of Chichen Itza, Copan, and others in Yucatan and Guatemala, the great stone stelæ of Guatemala, on the *ponchos* of the savage Indians of the remote Panama forests, the *metates* of Nicaragua and the Mosquito Indians, the stone seats and bas-reliefs of Manabi, in Ecuador, the textiles and exquisite pottery recovered from the old tombs of the Peruvian coast, the pottery of the Ucayali Indians of the Amazon valley, and on the *ponchos* of the Indians in the Amazon interior, and, perhaps most important of all, upon the famous monolithic doorway of Tiahuanako, on the Titicaco tableland of Peru-Bolivia, the oldest building in the New World.

Other articles of stone found in some profusion were columns, probably table supports, carved human figures, and carved stone slabs, like the headstones of graves. None of these was over two feet in height. Female figures predominate. The carving is often geometrically handsome, and in 'some cases shows the stepped pattern and square involute. Some had carved images of the sun and moon, which the Caras adored. Many *metates*, or corn-grinding mortars, of the Indians were found, also axes, pestles, mortars, hammers, and polishing-stones ; weights for looms, knives and scrapers of chalcedony and obsidian, discs of obsidian or mirrors, and " record stones " were other objects recovered. These latter, it has been concluded,[1] the small engraved and symbolic stones, are " graphic," and were used by the Caras for records in place of the *quipos* of the Incas. (The latter were the bunched and knotted cords of the Inca mnemonic system of records.) Velasco also writes of these stone records among the Caras

[1] By Señor de la Rosa, in *Revista Historica de Lima.*

and Scyris. The interesting method of historical count by means of these little coloured and vari-shaped stones was peculiar to the Caras, and the stones are found on the coast at La Plata, Cerro Jaboncillo, and La Tolita. Some are perforated for suspension, others are pointed. The large obsidian disc or mirror found at Cerro Jaboncillo is nearly circular, seven inches in diameter, and one inch thick at the centre. It is highly polished, with a surface like glass, and slightly convexed. This class of object is stated to be rare in South America, the only other examples from the Ecuadorian coast being three very small ones from La Tolita, and one from La Piedra, near the town of Esmeraldas. According to Ulloa, who was in Quito about the middle of the eighteenth century, obsidian mirrors must have been considerably used by the Caras in that region. Circular obsidian mirrors, it is to be noted, are found in Mexico, in the Nahua culture-area. The occurrence of these mirrors appears, says Saville, to lend colour to the Cara emigration along the Esmeraldas River. Obsidian is not found upon the coast, and no doubt it was brought down in the rough from the deposits in the mountains, as elsewhere remarked.

The province of Esmeraldas takes its name from the emerald gem, but few emeralds have been found. All early historians, however, relate that the Spaniards took large numbers of these stones from the natives, and, as has been described, the Indians of Manta worshipped a large emerald, the offerings to this deity being small emeralds which were regarded as its children. According to Acosta, the emeralds of the region were superior to those of New Granada. Although diligent search was made by the *conquistadores* for the mines where the Indians obtained these precious stones, they could not find such, and no emeralds are found to-day in

Manta and Atacames. According to Wolf, the emeralds come from the mines of Colombia, where they are still mined ; and he states that there is no geological formation in Ecuador which might contain emeralds. It has been stated, however, by other observers that the geological formation of Manibi does not necessarily preclude their existence in Nature. The geology of the region is largely unstudied. The tradition of the great emerald of Manta is still preserved among the Indians.

The gold and copper metallurgy of the Manabi and Esmeraldas ancients is of much interest. Copper objects were found overlaid with thin gold. Such gold-plated copper objects are found in Chiriqui (Panama), where the old native metallurgical art was perhaps more developed than anywhere else in the Americas. This similarity seems, again, to point to connection between the culture areas of Central America and the Ecuadorian coast, according to Saville. The overlay or plating of gold in the Manabi objects is either fused or hammered on to the copper matrix, and the lamina is of fine-grade gold. In the Cara region of the interior province of Pichincha, Saville found four copper discs with gold-plating on the obverse side, which much resemble those from Manabi and Esmeraldas. A pair of tweezers was found with a skeleton in one of the mounds excavated by Saville, $1\frac{1}{4}$ inches long, overlaid with gold inside and out. Tweezers for depilatory purposes are not uncommon in various parts of ancient America. Furthermore, what may be termed prehistoric dentistry was practised in north-western Ecuador, as shown by the discoveries of Saville in 1913, in a further expedition to the Esmeraldas province. A number of skulls were excavated, containing teeth " crowned with gold caps and filled and stopped with gold, equal to the best work of modern dentists, many of the teeth, especially the front ones, being ornamented with gold filagree work in the form of stars and half moons." Matters of this nature had been much earlier discovered, however. According to Cevallos, one of the great pottery urns used by the ancients to bury their dead was unearthed in digging a well near La Tola in 1836. One of the urns contained a skeleton of a man, and in the well-preserved skull it was found that the teeth had been fastened to each other by means of gold wire. Cevallos also describes the statuettes, pottery, utensils, jewellery, and weapons of this interesting district.

A copper axe was obtained by Saville in the village of Papagallo, said to have been found in Cerro Jaboncillo. It is $3\frac{3}{8}$ inches long, $2\frac{1}{8}$ inches wide, and $\frac{1}{4}$ inch at its thickest part. It is not of the usual South American type, but resembles the Mexican and Central American copper axes. Another copper axe, $3\frac{1}{2}$ inches long, was also found. Three small copper bells from Cerro Jaboncillo were recovered. Copper discs from the coast of Ecuador, now in some of the European museums, are of considerable size. There is one in the British Museum, and that at Berlin is $14\frac{1}{2}$ inches in diameter. They have puma heads in the centre. Probably these discs were used as gongs, and were worn on the breast, Saville considers. Gold and copper discs are found in the culture-area throughout Ecuador. The three from Manabi found by Saville are massive, the largest being nearly twelve inches in diameter, with the puma head raised $1\frac{3}{4}$ inches. A thin copper axe, $4\frac{1}{2}$ inches high, was found on the Island of Puná, and, Saville states, resembles some of the axes from Oaxaca, in Mexico. A massive copper axe with a semilunar plate from Manglas Alto is of much interest, but it was considered to be the work of the interior, known as the " Cuenca type." Axes of this shape are found in large numbers in the Cuenca section of Ecuador, though they are also found to the north, in the great interior plateaux. This massive axe is of pure copper, nearly five inches high, with the plate 5¼ inches long. The type is also found in Peru. A battle-axe of almost pure copper, of undoubted Peruvian origin (according to Saville), was found in Puná. It is a six-starred club-head, but with a semilunar knife or axe blade at right angles to the star-shaped head, 4¾ inches long, with the blade 2½ inches long. It is stated that this type of weapon, the six-pointed copper club-head, was in ancient times quite common along the western part of South America.

Of the ceramic art of the early Ecuadorians but little was known until recently. But the Saville expedition made a large collection of pottery in Esmeraldas, also moulds and casts and pottery figures. The pottery depicted from Ecuador has not the beauty of design and execution of the exquisite pottery of the Peruvian coast, especially that of the Chimus, unearthed a few years ago in the Chicama valley.[1]

A unique specimen of pottery from Manabi was a whistling-jar, the whistle being in each ear of the squirrel-like animal, seated on its haunches, of which the jar is moulded. It is about seven inches high, and is the only specimen obtained, although one was discovered from the department of Guayas which resembles the whistling-jars of Peru. But the exquisite moulding of the Peruvian jars is absent. This type of vessel is peculiar to the Peruvian coast, where large numbers have been recovered from the *huacas*, or burial-places. The principle of the Peruvian whistling-jar (which is made to emit the sound of various birds and animals with remarkable exactitude) is that, having been filled with

[1] Illustrated in *The Secret of the Pacific, op. cit.*

water, and the vessel reversed so that the water
will pour out, the air becomes compressed, and in
escaping through the whistles produces a shrill sound.
The same effect is produced by sucking in the air
through the orifice, and in some cases on pouring
in the water. The early Peruvians had a curious
knowledge of acoustics. Some of the objects from
Manta and elsewhere on the coast reminded Saville
of Maya ware, and of pottery at Copan, in Honduras.
Many *ollas* were found, the largest 2 feet 2 inches
in diameter.

Spindle-whorls in vast numbers were found in
Manabi, but few in Esmeraldas. Throughout
America, in pre-Hispanic times, cotton and woollen
thread was spun on wooden spindles, weighted with
baked clay, pottery, or stone. In the Peruvian Andes
at the present time the traveller will 'observe, even
in the most remote places, the native women and
girls incessantly twirling their little spindles whilst
minding their flocks or walking about, and men also
occupy themselves in the same way, spinning thread
to make the homespun cloths for their garments.
There is considerable variety in the Ecuadorian types
of whorls. The majority are of the conical type,
but some are head-shaped. The decorations are
all incised, and the patterns generally geometric.
More than a hundred of these are illustrated in
Saville's book. A large number of pottery whistles
are also shown, in human and animal forms. Many
human figures modelled in clay and pottery were
found, and they are described in some cases as reminiscent of Zapotecan culture in Mexico. Many
small figures from Esmeraldas are modelled playing
the pan pipes.

There is nothing in Manabi to reveal the age of
the remains on the hills. It has already been remarked that the Spanish invaders made no mention
of the stone seats, and probably the region was

abandoned even at that period.   They are shrouded in the same mystery that covers the relics of the Peruvian coast.   The student who desires more minute information about these curious objects from Ecuador should consult Saville's comprehensive book.

CHAPTER XX

AGRICULTURAL AND PASTORAL INDUSTRIES

THE conditions surrounding agriculture and the pastoral industries in Ecuador vary according to the topographical and climatic zones into which the country is broadly divided. In common with certain other republics of Latin America, the physical structure of the territory is such, as before observed, that the country might be regarded as a vast truncated pyramid, with its base set in the tropics, its middle in a temperate region, and its summit in a semi-arctic zone. This natural arrangement permits a very wide range of products, and the inhabitants, by going up and down the slopes of the national farm, can enjoy all those varieties of food products which in countries differently constituted have to be brought together from widely separated parts of the earth.

The staple economic plants and animals brought into South America by the Spaniards flourish, in general terms, well upon the soil of that continent, and in Ecuador all these are cultivated and propagated. In the chapter dealing with the natural history of the country the conditions surrounding plant and animal life have been set forth. From the Pacific coast upwards to an elevation of 3,000 to 4,000 feet, the vegetation is tropical, the principal economic products, cultivated or forestal, being *cacao* or chocolate, cotton, sugar, tobacco, rice, maize, yucca—known also as cassava and mandioca—bananas, peanuts, sweet potatoes, yams, arracacha, indigo, rubber

SUGAR-CANE PLANTATION: COASTAL LOWLANDS.

[To face p. 324

of the Castilloa variety, ivory nuts or *tagua*, cinchona or quinine, and bread-fruit. Most of these become rare at 3,000 feet, but the sugar-cane may be cultivated much higher, up to 8,000 feet.

It is interesting to note the far greater variety of products on this part of the Pacific littoral than on the corresponding region in Peru, to the south. The Peruvian coast produces neither chocolate, rubber, ivory nuts, quinine, coco-nuts, nor coffee. These products are only found in Peru on the Amazon slope, where they flourish in abundance. The reason for this variation in the vegetable world between Ecuador and Peru is the change of climate, as described elsewhere.

The alluvial valley of the Guayas and the coast generally produces *cacao*, coffee, coco-nuts, pine-apples, oranges, lemons, guavas, grape-fruit or shaddock, pomegranates, apricots, chirimoyas, granadillas (*Passiflora quadrangularis*), the delicate paltas (*Persea gratissima*), otherwise known as "alligator pears," *tunas*—the excellent wild fig, or fruit of the prickly pear, or *nopal*, mangoes, pacayas—and the *aji* or Chile pepper (capsicum), also the "toquilla" fibre used in the making of the "Panama" hats, as elsewhere described. There are cabbage palms, several species of cinchona, vanilla, and dyewoods. The large trees valuable for their timber include the redwood (*Humiria balsamifera*), Brazil wood, algarrobo, palo de Cruz, holy wood, rosewood, cedar, and walnut.

From the elevation of 6,000 feet to 10,000 feet above sea-level the products and flora are of a very different character. The indigenous species include the potato, maiz, oca (*Oxalis tuberosa*), the quinua (*Chenopodium quinou*). Of the exotics are wheat, barley, oats, alfalfa, and most of the fruits and vegetables of the northern temperate zone. Above 10,500 feet wheat does not ripen, whilst below 4,500 feet it does not form into the ear. Above 10,000 feet the

larger forest trees are rarely seen, except occasionally
on the outer slopes of the Cordillera. Certain shrubs,
however, reach an elevation of 13,000 feet, with some
kinds 500 feet higher. Very characteristic of the
plateau and upland valleys is the maguey (*Agave
Americana*) known as cabulla or cabaya (in England,
the " century plant "). This cactus is of great value
to the native, in the manufacture from its fibre of
cordage, sandals, and other useful articles. (In Mexico
this plant is even more valuable, yielding the national
drink of *pulque*, in addition to its other uses.)

On the eastern slope of the Andes, where the rainfall is heavy and continuous, the vegetation and forest
growth is profuse and varied, and resembles that of
the *montaña* of Peru and of Colombia. The species
are extremely numerous, and include rubber and cinchona ; and sugar-cane, coffee, cotton, the vine, and
other cultivated products grow excellently in that zone,
wherever they have been propagated.

On the arid portion of the coast zone it is scarcely
possible to speak of agriculture as such, cultivation
being limited to a few fruit trees, small gardens, and
vegetable patches, with small banana plantations, and
here and there meadows along the river banks. The
drought of the long summer renders difficult the cultivation of plants not indigenous to the region. In
the humid districts of the coast, however, the difference is very marked, and with comparatively little
work plantations of all the products of the tropics
flourish luxuriantly. Agriculture in tropical lands
differs greatly from that in temperate lands. The
plough is but little used ; the axe and the *machete* are,
in the primitive cultivation of the torrid zone, the principal implements. Thus, in Ecuador, for the making
of a plantation of cocoa, coffee, or other, or of a
potrero or pasture, the first operation is that of the
desmonte, or cutting down and burning of the thick
brushwood. In the virgin jungle this is a difficult

operation, due to the entangled network of trees, shrubs, and *enredaderas*, or climbers, the whole being bound together in a dense mass. The brushwood is cut, piled, and burnt, giving room for the felling of the larger trees. The roots of these remain in the soil, to rot by slow degrees. This accomplished, sowing is proceeded with by the method of making holes in the ground with the *machete* for the grass roots if a pasture is being formed, or for the seeds of cocoa, rice, maize, etc., or cuttings of banana, sugar-cane, yucca, or other plants, if plantations of these are to be made. The only work afterwards required is that of keeping the plantation free from weeds, as, if untended, a dense growth would cover the land, which soon tends to revert again to the jungle state. Manure is unknown in this form of agriculture. When the land begins to lose its fertility it is abandoned and a new area prepared, and the old patch soon becomes jungle again. It is worthy of note that the wild growth which takes possession of the abandoned spaces is not at first similar to that of the surrounding jungle from which the land was wrested, but is markedly different, and may be distinguished twenty or thirty years afterwards. Wild plants almost unknown to the immediate district grow up and cover the soil, a phenomenon which, however, is common to all countries.[1] It is remarkable how rapid is the growth of this new herbage and brushwood, which disputes the advance of the old jungle.

The sugar-cane, although cultivated in some of the inter-Andine valleys as high as 6,500 feet above sea-level, is more at home in the lower districts, where it develops enormously within a few months. The cane was formerly used only for the distillation of

---

[1] The observer, even in the English countryside, will have noted that great colonies of thistles, or other plants, often come to being spontaneously on land that has been turned over and left.

aguardiente, or native rum, until sugar factories were erected. The lands capable of growing sugar-cane in Ecuador are very extensive in all the littoral provinces, although its cultivation lies mainly in those of Guayas and Los Rios, the vast area of Manabi and Esmeraldas being much neglected. Much of the sugar-cane is still turned into rum, as is the case in other Andine countries. The over-consumption of this fiery product must be regarded as a great national evil, tending to the deterioration of the Indian and lower class *mestizo* population. Notwithstanding the considerable production of sugar, the supply does not meet the home demand. The production reaches some 8,000 metric tons annually. The railway now enables the interior to be supplied, thus ousting the Colombian product.

The most valuable product of Ecuadorian agriculture is cocoa, and its production tends largely to increase. The export of the cocoa-bean is the basis of the prosperity of Guayaquil to large extent, and it is upon this staple article that the foreign commerce of Ecuador mainly depends. A considerable area is devoted to the cultivation of the plant, but there is much more land available and suitable therefor. There are two methods of cocoa cultivation in Ecuador, of which the first is the simpler. In those tracts where the *Cacao silvestre*, or wild cocoa shrub, is found growing plentifully, all the surrounding brushwood and trees are cut down, leaving only such high full-crowned trees as may afford shade to the cocoa shrubs, such as they require. The cocoa " plantation " is then ready, only requiring periodical weeding and harvesting. These natural plantations, where the cocoa shrubs are irregularly dispersed, isolated, or in groups, are termed *almacigales*, as contrasted with the *huertas regulares* of the sown plantations. These last are prepared by clearing a suitable tract, leaving, if such exist, shade trees, as before. The cocoa seeds are then sown in holes, two to three yards apart, four or five *fresh* seeds being placed in each hole. These seeds rapidly sprout. At the same time the necessary shade plants are sown between the rows, and as they grow up, keep off the rays of the sun from the tender cocoa plants, which otherwise would perish from the heat. During the first two years, maize or yucca is used as a shade plant, but often the banana plant is set, forming *plátanales*, which remain until the cocoa shrub is six to nine feet high, or at times until it begins to yield. This is at its sixth or seventh year. The small shade trees, which have also been sown in addition at certain distances, have by then developed—the *Guabo* and *Portorillo*, or Palo prieto, and others are used—and yield the necessary shade, and the banana groves are then cut down. The cocoa plantation thus made remains indefinitely, because, although the cocoa shrub dies after sixty or eighty years of life, a new growth always appears from its roots, which growth is more than sufficient to replace the old trees, which fall or are cut down. The only care that the finished *cacotal* or plantation requires is that of weeding, at least once a year, with occasional pruning. The *cacao*, although it bears its flowers and fruits all the year, comes to its principal bloom at the beginning of the *invierno*, in December, and the principal harvest is in March and April. The partial harvests, which are yielded every month, especially in November and December, are also abundant. The felled fruit, in form not unlike an oblong melon, is opened in the plantation, and the mass of beans or grains, with the saccharine pulp adhering thereto, is carried away in leather sacks, known as *agollas*, to the *haciendas*, where it is spread out and dried. The product is then conveyed to the Guayaquil market for foreign export. In Ecuador it cannot be said that scientific cultivation of the cocoa plantation is carried out, and much remains to be done in this respect. In the system of planting, as above described, seeds rather than cuttings are employed. The bean is taken for planting fresh from the pod, with the whole saccharine pulp adhering. On some farms cuttings have been planted, but the result is not so satisfactory. The districts of Balao and Machala, where there is constant moisture throughout the year, yield better crops than the plantations at Arriba. These districts are traversed by the Rivers Balao and Jubones respectively, which fall into the Jambeli Channel to the south of Guayaquil. This greater produce is due rather to the climate than to the soil, as the seeds from those districts, when planted at Arriba, do not appear to produce better than the customary seeds of that district.

It has been stated [1] that an area of 100 square yards, which may easily contain 1,325 trees, will yield, according to location and other circumstances, from 500 to 2,000 pounds of cacao. A fairly well attended plantation, even when the crop is ordinary, will give 12 per cent. per annum on the capital invested. Cacao is the safest and easiest crop to be raised in Ecuador. Foreign enterprise of late years has seen the advantages offered by the cultivation of cacao in Ecuador. There are two German companies working the Clementina, the Puga and the Seminario cocoa estates, and in 1910 an important company was formed in London to carry on the administration and extend the plantation of the largest cocoa estate in the Republic, that of the Tenguel, on the borders of the Machala district. In addition to the cocoa, the estate has rubber plantations. It also produces coffee, and has an immense extent of ground suitable for plantations of all the usual tropical products. The estate is in one of the best-watered districts of the country, with a regular and constant rainfall, not falling off, as is the case in

[1] In Colonel Church's work on *Ecuador*.

BANANA PLANTATION.

[To face p. 330.

some of the other districts of the Arriba and Santa Rosa zones.[1]

Rice, although it grows well in many places, is cultivated on but a small scale. The plantations are situated in the damp plains or on the low-lying lands along the rivers. The supply does not nearly satisfy the demand. In the Guayas valley, especially on the flooded lands of the Boliche, the possibilities of rice-growing are considered to be very wide, and Guayaquil might become a large rice-exporting centre.

The same condition of supply and demand obtain with regard to maize in the coast region, where cultivation is somewhat similar. Each dweller plants what is required for his own family use, and as an article of commerce the maize grown in the uplands is more important.

Tobacco is cultivated with preference in the low-lying river lands or the fertile plains adjacent thereto. The Ecuadorian tobacco is of very good quality, but little known abroad, as the country does not produce more than enough for home consumption. The better classes of tobacco are from the plantations of Daule, Esmeraldas, and Santa Rosa, the Daule tobacco being distinguished by its strength, and that from Esmeraldas by its agreeable aroma. The first-named, it is stated, might, if properly treated, rival the tobacco of Havana, from which it is descended in a direct line, as the cultivators import fresh seed from time to time from Cuba.

The *plátanales*, or banana plantations of Ecuador, are of some considerable extent, and provide not only their own districts with the fruit but also the Sierra districts, and even the towns on the Peruvian and Chilean coasts, to which regions quantities are exported. The *plátano* forms practically the daily bread of the poorer classes on the Ecuadorian littoral.

[1] Foreign Office Report for 1910, issued January, 1912.

It is eaten either green and boiled, or baked in that state, or half ripe, and baked, or ripe, whether raw or fried. In the first state it tastes like bread. For eating raw the aromatic kind, the *plátano de seda*, is preferred, or the various species of *guineo*, equally aromatic. The cultivation of these plants is exceedingly simple. Once sown no further care is necessary, except that of gathering the bunches, which yield all the year round. New shoots constantly replace the old ones. It might be said that the banana and its kindred belong to that series of " providential " plants with which the tropical zones have been dowered, and which yield foods for even the idlest inhabitant, almost without effort.

Coffee in Ecuador is cultivated up to an elevation of about 5,000 feet above sea-level, but only in the lower zones are large plantations found and coffee grown for export. The Ecuadorian coffee is of excellent quality, better, it is stated, than that of Brazil, and it might be more extensively cultivated. The good price obtained for the product, and the demand in the markets of Chile and of Europe, has led to an increase of planting.

Rubber has been planted to a very limited extent on the Ecuadorian littoral, but the soil and climate are favourable to its production. The *tagua*, or ivory nut, has also been planted to a small extent. This possesses the advantage, in its wild state, that it is not necessary to fell the tree, as has so frequently been the case with the rubber and the cascarilla, in order to gather its harvest.

Tagua is a forestal rather than a cultivated product, and is one of the most valued of Ecuadorian exports. The nut is used abroad in the manufacture of buttons largely.

Agriculture in the inter-Andine region has a European aspect, to some extent, except as regards the small plantations of coffee, sugar, and bananas

in the very low valleys of the zone.   In addition
to the natural pastures or *potreros*, the common
forage in the Sierras is alfalfa, cultivated everywhere
for horses and mules.   This valuable exotic from
Europe has a very wide range of cultivation vertically,
from the low, hot valleys up to the cold uplands.
The traveller in the Andes, throughout their vast
extension of thousands of miles, from Ecuador to
Peru and Chile, has good reason to be grateful
for the presence of this forage plant, as without it
the horse and the mule, often the only motive power
and means of transport in those regions, could not
exist.   The traveller may at times be obliged to do
without bread in his journeys there, but without alfalfa
for his beasts he would be reduced to inaction.   The
leaf of the maize plant may be used as a substitute
for forage in some cases.

Of European cereals only wheat and barley are
cultivated in Ecuador, oats being almost unknown.
Wheat produces well up to an elevation of 10,000
feet, and barley up to rather less than 11,500 feet.
The product is scarcely sufficient to meet the demand
in the interior provinces, and the coastal centres
are supplied by import.   The cultivation of maize
is general, but it yields well only in fertile, sheltered
places : in the arid *altiplanicies* it is poorer and later.
Maize forms at the present time, as it did in the most
remote periods of the country's history, one of the
principal articles of diet of the people, as in Peru,
Mexico, and other American lands.   On the table
of the well-to-do class, the boiled maize-ear, the
mazorka or *choclo*, when green and tender, is eaten.
Among the poor, toasted maize, known as *mote*, or
in Peru as *cancha*, is the ordinary bread, and the
traveller in the Andes will at times have to content
himself with this—to him—unsatisfactory bread diet.
A vast quantity of maize is used in the Andine countries in the making of *chicha*, or native beer, a

drink preferred by the Indians to all else, and in itself
nourishing, although to the foreigner its taste is at
first peculiar.　It has various qualities analogous
with beer.　Almost equally important, in earlier times,
in the Andine countries, was the quinua (*Chenopodium
quinua*), which was, after maize, the principal grain
food of the Indian.　At the present time it is relatively little cultivated, and only in the higher regions.
Several edible tubers are cultivated by the Indians,
among them the oca (*Oxalis crenata*), but these are
not nearly of the importance of the potato, known
in the Andes as the *papa* (*Solanum tuberosum*).　In
the uplands the potato is, for the Indian, what the
banana is in the lowlands.　It grows from the elevation near the *páramos* as far down as the valleys
with a middle temperature, but not on the hot plains.
Whether Chile was the real home of the potato, as
has been asserted by some writers, cannot be
decided, but its cultivation dates from the most
remote times, probably beyond the Inca period, and
was one of the gifts of the Andes to the world.
It was brought to the early notice of the Spaniards
near Quito.

The usual small vegetables, peas, beans, gar-
banzas, etc., are largely cultivated in this zone, and
the vine has done well in sheltered situations.

The Ecuadorian pastoral industries are in the same
backward state as characterises agriculture in the
country.　Any good results obtained are due to
favourable natural conditions rather than to improved
methods.　To the breeding of saddle horses some
attention has been given, but cattle-breeding is backward.　The wool of the *páramo* sheep is of inferior
quality, but there is little doubt that with the intro-
duction of better stock it would be capable of
improvement.　The pasture is good, and the milk
yielded by the cows of the uplands of excellent
quality.　It has been asserted that the interior of

UPLAND FARMING AND LLAMAS

[To face p. 405

Ecuador is capable of producing cattle to an amount ten times greater than that required for home consumption, and that an export business could be established. At present only hides are exported, to the annual value of about £52,000. The best grazing lands are on the lower elevations of the Pacific slope of the Cordilleras, and in some of the plateau districts of the higher Andes, such as those near Antisana and Chimborazo. A small export trade in horses and mules is done, but the wool-clip is all employed in home manufacture. Sheep-farming is undoubtedly capable of extension. On the coastal lands the natural pastures are also used, and at times improved for cattle. In forming artificial *potreros* or meadows the gamalote, a native grass, is encouraged to flourish, and the *Janeiro*, introduced from Brazil, grows exceedingly well. As before described, alfalfa is also largely employed.

The llama is much less used in Ecuador than in Peru, Bolivia, and northern Chile, as before remarked. This useful beast of burden feeds itself on the wayside pasture in its journeys, and so costs nothing for its upkeep. It was the only beast of burden existing in America in pre-Hispanic times, and has many valuable attributes. The characteristic, graceful form of the American sheep-camel is an invariable adjunct of the Andine landscape.

From the economic standpoint the *páramo* region is of great value to Ecuador (as elsewhere in the Andine countries) for pastoral purposes. The wealth of many *haciendas* consists solely in the many square miles of *páramo* which they control, supporting cattle, sheep, and horses. The poor Indian of these bleak yet invigorating and valuable regions may not possess a rood of land of his own, but he is enabled to maintain his own beasts on the communal *páramo*, and thus the existence of great bands of domestic animals, with hundreds of proprietors, is a feature which the character of these regions has so far preserved.

Ecuador has been described by some writers as one of the most fertile countries in the world, and whilst this may be true of certain districts, it is not so of the inter-Andine region. Under more intensive and intelligent cultivation this zone, like all other zones and countries, could produce far more abundant food supplies, but it cannot be looked upon as naturally fruitful, in comparison with other agricultural regions of the earth's surface. The cereal-producing belt is of limited extent, and half of it uncultivable, due to its broken character, sterility, and frigid temperature. This latter characteristic, however, in view of the cultivation of wheat in Canada, which has been pushed much farther towards the cold north than was ever supposed possible, may be overcome. But the flat lands in the cereal belt are small, and in comparison with the whole appear almost like oases. The uplands of Riobamba, Ambato (with the exception of its valley), Latacunga, and Quito, although in the country itself often described as fertile, are scarcely so in comparison with truly fertile lands. There are, of course, many beautiful and productive valleys in the zone, with an ideal climate, as before described, as, for example, part of the province of Imbabura, the valleys of Tumbaco, Chillo, and Machachi, in the provinces of Cuenca and Loja, where the rainfall and fertile soil produce abundant harvests, and where the *haciendas,* surrounded by myrtles and fruit trees, form delightful spots. But this is not the case with the whole territory, and the long description of fruits and vegetables produced in such districts tends somewhat to give an exaggerated idea of the fruitfulness of the country as a whole. The same remark, indeed, applies to the Andine countries generally. The fertile spots are accentuated by the sterility of the deserts, as ever. " Inexhaustible natural resources " is a favourite term of Spanish American writers, who, in many cases being unacquainted with the broad, fertile lands of Europe or North America, are led away in their descriptions unintentionally to exaggeration. It is, of course, natural that in countries where, in the European or North American sense, there is no winter there is found a large variety of species and products, but not for this reason can such lands be described as necessarily more fertile. The great need of agriculture in Ecuador and its sister republics is more scientific methods, the employment of artificial irrigation, manures, and a better system of tilling the soil. Whilst higher Ecuador could support a much larger population than at present, it could not carry so many people as the thickly settled lands of Europe, nor could it expect to export food products. Its exports must continue to come from its tropical lowlands. Furthermore, the economic life of the labouring classes must be uplifted and the feudal conditions of land-holding altered if a peasant class is to flourish. The burden of peonage must be lifted.

As before remarked, wasteful and negligent methods of farming in Ecuador have caused the land to deteriorate in parts. This destruction by man is part of the same history that has laid waste many other portions of the earth's surface, and if mankind is to maintain itself and multiply it will have to be the subject of that science of conservation to whose necessity even the most advanced nations have only just begun to awaken.[1] In Ecuador, however, Nature has been harsh in places, and the great areas of pumice, which proceeded from the destructive Cotopaxi, are largely responsible for the sterility

[1] The Author, in his lecture on " Human Geography and Industry Planning " before the British Association in 1913, dwelt strongly on this point.

of the region around it.   These pumice deposits
absorb the water and cause rapid evaporation,
without yielding dew-producing conditions.   Nothing
but a future system of tree-planting and other atten-
tions can cause these particular areas of Ecuador
to produce freely for their populations.

CHAPTER XXI

MINERAL RESOURCES AND MINING

In the occurrence of metalliferous minerals Ecuador is much poorer than its neighbours Colombia and Peru, or than the more southern Andine republics of Bolivia and Chile. The great lodes and deposits of gold, silver, copper, lead, coal, and other minerals which the Andine countries generally contain have not been shown to exist in the portion of the Andes which traverses Ecuador, although exception must be made in the case of the important goldmines of the Zaruma district. Copper exists in small quantities, and with gold was mined and used by the ancients, and quicksilver has given its name—Azogue —to one district ; but these minerals are not found in commercial quantities. Iron, lead, and platinum all exist geologically. Petroleum has begun to furnish a source of industry. Further expert knowledge of Ecuador may reveal hitherto unsuspected sources of minerals.

The Andes throughout almost the whole of their great course are auriferous, certain portions being extremely rich in gold. In Colombia both lode-mining and placer-mining are extensively undertaken. In Peru there are enormous deposits of alluvial gold-bearing material on the summit or water-parting of the Cordilleras, especially in the southern part of that country, and in Bolivia the same formation occurs. Gold-bearing quartz-lodes are exceedingly numerous and often rich and extensive,[1] and southern Ecuador contains the important Zaruma mines, of much historical and commercial interest.

The Zaruma mines were first visited by the Spaniards in 1549, when Captain Mercadillo ascended the Tumbez River. The town of Zaruma and the *Real de Minas* of that name was then founded. The same year the Spaniards penetrated to the eastern forests of Loja, and founded the famous town of Zamora, described as " one of the most beautiful and populous of the old kingdom of Quito," and the royal mines of Cangasa and Yacuambi were established. Eight years afterwards, in 1541, other gold-mines were discovered, and the foundations of the towns of Valladolid and of Loyola, on the banks of the Chinchipe, were laid, and the *Real de Minas* of San José established. The same adventurous spirits, in 1552, entering the regions to the east of Cuenca and Riobamba, founded Logroño del Oro and Sevilla del Oro, on the banks of the Paute and Upano Rivers respectively. So great was the reputation of these districts that a veritable " gold rush " followed, many Spaniards abandoning their mines in Peru for the new field of Ecuador. The newly established towns reached a high grade of prosperity in a short time. The greed of the Spanish authorities, however, principally that of the Governor of Macas, residing in Sevilla del Oro, caused the sudden downfall of these flourishing places. In the year 1599 the Jibaros Indians, headed by Quiruba, rebelled, destroyed to their foundations the towns of Logroño and Sevilla, and murdered the inhabitants and the odious Governor. The insurrection extended to Zamora and Valladolid, whose inhabitants fled in fear at the Indian approach. Thus, after forty-seven years of life, those flourishing centres were lost to the Crown of Spain.

[1] Described in the Author's *Peru.*

After the fall of these places mining in Ecuador was limited to the *placers* of Esmeraldas and the quartz lodes of Zaruma, under the *Alcalde Mayor de las Minas de Zaruma*. But exploitation was not very active. Lack of appliances for the extraction and treatment of the auriferous quartz prevented extensive operations. The miners had not sufficient metallurgical knowledge for mines of that character ; they threw away the pyritous mineral, thinking it contained no gold, or were unable to extract such, and (as was invariably the case among the numerous early Andine quartzmines) they worked only the surface or oxidized ores. The workings were carried out at haphazard, and drainage was impossible with their limited resources. The only method of treating the ore was in the primitive mills of that time, crushing a few *quintals* daily and extracting what gold was possible. Even thus the town of Zaruma had a population of 5,000 or 6,000 inhabitants, dependent upon the mining ; but in 1891 this had fallen to 700 or 800. Zaruma was visited by La Condamine in 1743, but the mines were almost abandoned at that time.

At the beginning of the nineteenth century (1815) the Zaruma mines were examined by Loayza, and this expert rendered a very favourable report to the Spanish Government, advising the establishment of a bank for facilitating the mining industry. The mine which according to tradition had been most actively worked was the celebrated " Sesmo," close to the town, and of this mine fabulous stories were told. Other largely worked mines were the " Leonor " and the " Amoquillados," probably on the same lode, with at that time some 1,600 feet of workings. From Zaruma towards the River Amarillo run the Castillo hills, and these contained various mines, the ruins of whose primitive mills abound, one below the other along the stream which served as water-power. The same remains were to be seen in the Vizcaya ravine, an hour's distance from Zaruma. A considerable number of mines in the surrounding district, among them the " Portovelo," worked by an English company, attested the importance of the region. The " Zancudo " vein was also reopened at that time. After the War of Independence the mining industry of Zaruma was prostrated, and at length became only an historic recollection. In 1876 the Government of Ecuador charged Dr. Wolf, the State geologist, to examine the mines, and he reported that Zaruma would fill one day an important place in the mining industry. Later, various foreign engineers and miners visited the place, all rendering favourable reports and confirming the statements of Dr. Wolf, and some companies were formed.[1]

The lodes or veins of the Zaruma mines are described as in a porphyritic rock, but there was no outcrop, and the surface appeared to have been naturally levelled by the action of water. A capping of earth covered the lodes, overgrown with thick vegetation. Under this the surface of the lode was oxidized to a depth of twenty or twenty-five metres, as commonly occurs with quartz lodes, and it was in this " toscon," as it was locally termed, the disintegrated part of the lode-filling, that the earlier mining was carried out, in a fashion familiar to the engineer who is acquainted with the mines of Peru and Mexico.[2] The lodes of Zaruma were described as strong and well formed, true fissure veins, several kilometres long, varying from fifty centimetres to three or four metres in width, with one metre as the average, a strike of north and south, and a dip varying from the vertical to forty-five

[1] *El distrito aurifero de Zaruma*, Señor Saenz de Tejada, published in Guayaquil, 1886.
[2] The Author has examined many of these.

degrees to the east. The fracture-zone is extensive, some six leagues in length, with a large number of lodes. The vein-filling is quartz, compact and with iron pyrites, the gold occasionally visible, the upper portion being oxidized, as described, and carrying copper pyrites, galena, and blende, the gold both free and in combination, with some silver. Ores were described as extraordinarily rich, some of the workings yielding to assay as follows : " La Quebrada," up to 39 oz. gold and 47 oz. silver per ton of ore ; " Pacay Urcu," 36 gold, 21 silver ; " Zancudo," 19 gold, 40 silver ; " Favorita," 4 gold, 6 silver ; " Immaculada," $3\frac{1}{2}$ gold, 7 silver. The " Zancudo " at 100 feet depth gave also 5 to 6 per cent. of copper. These were naturally not average values, the average being placed at four ounces of gold per ton from extensive ore-bodies. In the " Portovelo " mine of the English Zaruma Gold Mining Company the ore as treated in a twenty-stamp mill gave an average of one ounce per ton of free gold, the " sulphurets " or tailings being neglected, although rich in gold. The " Telefono " mine, or " Pacay-Urcu," was rediscovered by accident in 1881, a heap of quartz overgrown with vegetation giving indications of its richness. Some excitement was aroused, and the English company entered into negotiations with the owner, and $7\frac{1}{2}$ tons of ore were sent to London, yielding thirty-six ounces of gold per ton. But the vein was not at first discoverable, and the old ore deposit became exhausted. In 1889 the vein was again sought and found, and assays gave $2\frac{1}{2}$ oz. of gold and $\frac{1}{2}$ oz. silver per ton as the average, excluding the richest portions. A company was formed in France in 1890 to work the mine. Other mines of somewhat similar character at Zaruma of the *Compañía Minera Nacional Felix* were the " Cristina," " Mercedes," " Francesa," " Zancudo," " Caridad," " Fenix," " Leonor," and " California." The altitude of this district is 1,400 metres above sea-level, and the climate agreeable. At 100 feet depth the values in some of the workings gave two to four ounces of gold per ton and five to ten of silver ; others an average of $1\frac{1}{2}$ gold and five silver, with 4 to 5 per cent. of copper and 7 to 8 per cent. of lead. The total cost of obtaining the gold was given as equal to half an ounce per ton. The mines of the Compañia Explotadora were equally important, covering a considerable area. Those of the English Zaruma Gold Mining Company were the only ones in active exploitation, however. The company was formed in London in 1880, with a capital of £250,000, to work the " Sesmo," " Portovelo," " Jorupe," " Bomba de Vizcaya," " Bomba de Pacchapampa," " Toscon Blanco," and " Curi-pampa " mines. All these were reputed as fabulously rich, and as having, in remote times, yielded great quantities of gold ; but when the English company acquired them no careful examina-tion had been made to prove their richness ; and what is more remarkable, the sale was carried out in London without the examination of the mines by any expert or anything to prove the truth of the traditions. Further, instead of beginning a syste-matic exploration of the lodes, the company began the survey of a railway and entered on the con-struction of a wagon-road, brought in from the United States expensive machinery, which remained abandoned at the port of Santa Rosa because the pieces were too heavy for mule transport, and estab-lished a large body of employees, all at enormous cost. The capital of the company was in conse-quence " shamefully wasted." [1] At this period a revolution arose in Ecuador against the dictator

---

[1] Tejada, *op. cit.* This proceeding is an old story in various English mines in Spanish America.

Veintemilla, and the manager of the mines raised a column of soldiers among the employees, and himself was killed in action. A fresh manager was sent out, who, after examining the position, advised liquidation. But work was continued, and good ore was struck in the " Portovelo " mine. Funds running short, the company raised a loan of £30,000, and brought in machinery. But other difficulties arose, and a fresh company was formed with the name of the Zaruma Gold Mining Company, Limited. Various experts took charge in succession, and considerable success was attained. The average value was found to be one ounce of gold per ton, and the average costs equal to half an ounce ; a forty-stamp mill was erected, to which additions were later made, and regular shipments of gold were made to Europe.

The production of gold from the Zaruma mines in 1910 was approximately £25,000 in gold and £26,000 in cyanide slimes.

Apparently the whole extension of the eastern Cordillera of the Andes, where composed of the ancient schists, is auriferous, although much richer in certain districts. In Ecuador the richest *placers*, and those exploited in antiquity, are found in the province of Azuay, from Allcuquiru to Yana-Urcu, in the province of Loja. At the present time the *lavaderos* are found on the western versant of the Cordillera Real, although it may be that such exist on the eastern slope at the heads of the tributaries of the Paute River. The *lavaderos* are found not only on the streams but as " dead " river deposits, remote from existing streams, and high up on the slopes, as at Collay and Ayon, the ancient level of the water-courses. The thickness of the gravel banks or deposits varies ; some, as at Collay, are several metres thick, but generally they are from one to two metres, in more or less level deposits. Although all the rivers of the eastern Cordillera are auriferous where they traverse the schistose formation, they are not necessarily worth working for their gold. Many are very poor in gold and small in volume. Collay appears to have been the goldmine most famed in its province by the ancient Indians, as is shown by old workings of large extent, in which have been found implements of copper and wood, such as they used. Immense quantities of material exist, which have been brought down by three torrents which join at the foot of the two hills of Cari-Collay and Guarmi-Collay. The altitude above sea-level is 9,000 feet, and the climate not inhospitable. The ancient Indians ran galleries into the deposits, but later great earthslides took place. It is stated that material in great quantities remains to be worked. The thickness of the alluvial varies from six to twelve metres. Gold in grain and dust is encountered, and also gold as amalgam with native mercury. The quicksilver is also found pure, disseminated through the mass in almost microscopic globules, and oxidized. The presence of the quicksilver is a curious phenomenon,[1] and was also noted in a *lavadero* at Los Rios. In spite of the relative poorness of the material at Collay, it was considered that work on a large scale might yield commercial results, although the surrounding topographical conditions are difficult to overcome. The *lavadero* of Samanamarca, in the province of Loja, also belongs to the eastern Cordillera.

The *lavaderos* in the porphyritic formation generally carry very little gold, and only that brought down from metallic lodes, as that of Zaruma. The gold in the Zaruma basin, carried down by its rivers, is concentrated in the alluvials of the Tumbez River, from the confluence of the Calera with the Amarillo, as far as Puyango, where the river leaves the mountainous region and enters upon the

[1] Wolf, *op. cit.*, who quotes Isschot.

quaternary formation. From the earliest times of
the Conquest up to the present, gold has been recovered in this district, at first with very small
irregular workings. Only since 1885 have the great
deposits been scientifically studied and their importance been grasped. In 1891 " denouncements "
or claims were taken up, sixteen kilometres long, and
calculations were made, upon a basis of a thickness
of pay earth of two metres and a value of three
sucres per cubic metre of material.

In the province of Esmeraldas the gold-washings
of the fluvial system of the Santiago, which discharges into the Pacific in the north of the republic,
generally contain platinum in addition, although often
in insignificant quantities. This metal is more freely
found in Colombia, to the north. It does not appear
that the *placers* of Esmeraldas are of value as large
commercial enterprises, although the Indians work
them. The ancient Indians doubtless obtained gold
from the beds of the streams, a common operation
in South America, especially east of the Andes in
Peru.

It is a matter for speculation where the Indians
of Ecuador obtained their gold, and in view of the
poorness of the *placers*, the answer has seemed difficult. But it is to be recollected that gold was not
obtained in " commercial " quantities at that epoch.
In Azuay (and in Peru) the Incas could dispose of
large bodies of labourers, who obtained gold under
State orders. The gold was not used as money
necessarily, nor taken away from its particular districts, but was used for purposes of adornment. The
gold taken by the Spaniards was therefore the result
of accumulations from long periods of native work
before their advent. The condition that it did not
" pay " to extract the gold did not enter into consideration among the early Peruvians. Furthermore,
the gold had been concentrated by Nature in the

beds of the streams, and many of the richest *placers* had doubtless been exhausted before Pizarro arrived. Probably the smaller gold-bearing streams and *placers* of the Andine territory will never yield returns to ordinary company-promoting methods, and if the gold is recovered at all it will be by the laborious Indian, the true son of the soil, for whom Nature has intended it. The quartz goldmines are in a different category, however, and lend themselves to commercial methods, and indeed can only be exploited by machinery and scientific appliances.

Quicksilver is not now found in Ecuador in commercial quantities. Old mines, where apparently mercury was extracted in some form, either in a native state or as cinnabar ore, exist in the quartzite and sandstone formation of Azogues, near San Marcos, in the Huaizhun hill, in the province of Cañar. There are extensive galleries, well worked, and it would appear that the mines were good, or such considerable workings would not have been made otherwise. A remarkable condition (according to Reiss and Wolf) was that no vestiges of quicksilver were discoverable when the mines were examined with the utmost care by them and samples analysed. Neither sulphide of mercury nor globules of the liquid native metal were found. Other writers thought the supposed mines were in reality only " ancient quarries."

The petroleum deposits of Ecuador are of some importance, as far as it is possible to judge from present conditions. The district which has received most attention so far is that of Santa Elena, on the littoral. The peninsula of Santa Elena forms almost the most westerly point of South America, and it is reputed to be petroleum-bearing throughout the greater part of its area. At the western end of the peninsula, close to the sea, oil prospectors have dug a number of hand-pits, in depth from four to fifteen metres, and from many of these a considerable quantity of surface oil is collected, amounting in the aggregate to some 4,000 barrels of petroleum per month from this source at the close of 1913. This surface oil is of good quality, although it has naturally lost some of its lighter constituents. A more serious attempt to exploit the petroleum deposits of the district is being made by a London company,[1] which is drilling a well for the purpose of proving the existence of oil deposits at depth. In a well drilled by this company petroleum of a very high quality, containing a large percentage of motor-spirit, has been found. If the fields are found to be as important as is anticipated, the high quality of the oil found on the Santa Elena peninsula, combined with the favourable position of the district on the seaboard and its relative proximity to the Panama Canal, might be expected to bring this field into considerable prominence. The course of the steamers [2] plying between Panama and Guayaquil and the Peruvian and Chilean ports lies a few miles off Cape Santa Elena.

From the small port of Ballenitas, near Santa Elena, a railway is to be built to Guayaquil, a sum of money amounting to 400,000 *sucres* having been raised by the municipality of that town for the purpose.

In 1913 a large concession was applied for by a powerful British company [3] to cover mining rights throughout a great part of the area of the republic, and was provisionally agreed to by the Government. The clauses of the concession called for the expenditure of a sum of £100,000, within a term of ten

---

[1] The Ancon Oil Company of Ecuador, Limited.

[2] Royal Mail and Pacific Steam Navigation Company of London.

[3] S. Pearson and Sons, the well-known contractors and oil-field owners, of London and Mexico. The negotiations were carried out in Ecuador by Lord Murray of Elibank, on behalf of the firm.

years, upon exploration and development work, with the object of discovering deposits of petroleum or allied mineral substances. The concessionaire was to have the right of free access to all national lands, and " the right to expropriate, on terms to be stipulated by an engineer to be chosen by the Government, on the one part, and the concessionaire, on the other, any lands, estates, or properties in private ownership in any part of the republic, and should further be entitled to take over and develop any other petroleum wells, land, or mines which might be the property of the Government." This proposed concession was characterized by the London Press as a triumph for Great Britain. It was, however, bitterly denounced by a portion of the Guayaquil Press as a sacrifice of national rights on too easy terms, and was at first thrown out by the Ecuadorian Congress. Later the concession was modified. There is always a party in the Latin American Press ready to oppose such concessions. The matter admits of discussion. On the one hand, there has been a tendency among Latin American Governments to hand over vast concessions to foreign capital without adequately considering the future rights and necessities of the nation ; on the other, such resources cannot be developed without foreign capital and enterprise, and it is undeniably of advantage to such a country as Ecuador that a strong foreign country should develop its mineral resources.

CHAPTER XXII

COMMERCE, FINANCE, INDUSTRIES

THE industrial and commercial life of the republic of Ecuador is but little developed in comparison with that of the larger Latin American communities. Those manufacturing industries which have been developed are mainly of a primitive character and supply local wants, the exception being the interesting native industry of " Panama " hat making. The export of *cacao* or chocolate beans is that which renders Ecuador most noteworthy as far as foreign markets are concerned. The poverty of the bulk of the inhabitants, and the native lack of initiative, together with the conditions of landholding and the frequent political disturbances, operate against the natural development of the country's resources. Foreign capitalistic holdings in the republic have in the past suffered considerable reverses, and the name of Ecuador has been unfavourably known to financial centres abroad. This condition is not peculiar to Ecuador, but has been shared by its neighbours of Peru, Colombia, and other Latin American States. Ecuador, moreover, has of late showed a much greater attention to the needs of meeting its foreign obligations, and so is redeeming its credit.

The agricultural and pastoral industries have been dealt with in their special chapters, and in the descriptions of the flora and fauna of the country, and the mining industry is also specially described elsewhere. The industries that depend directly upon agri-

351

culture, especially in the littoral provinces, tend to increase. The industry of straw hat or " Panama " hat
manufacture merits some descriptions. Its origin was
in very remote times, and the industry is an instance of
the patient labour characteristic of the aboriginal race
of Latin America. The fine texture of the Panama hat
is well known in foreign markets, and in Britain and
the United States and elsewhere the demand for this
form of head-covering has greatly increased of late
years. The hats are known in the country of their
origin as *sombreros de paja toquilla* and *macora*.
The finest qualities come from the towns of Jipijapa
and Monte Cristi, near Santa Elena, in the province
of Manabi. It is only by reason of their export via
Panama that these articles have earned their popular
nomenclature of " Panama " hats. The material of
which they are made is from two kinds of plants,
commonly known as *paja toquilla* and *macora*. The
first named is that from which the finest hats are
woven, as also the straw cigar-holders ; the second
being used for second quality hats and for the beautiful woven hammocks which are made in the district.
Both plants are wild, with the difference that, in the
case of the *toquilla,* its propagation is tended, the wild
plants being pulled up and transplanted at distances
of a yard and a half apart and kept free of weeds.
The *toquilla* plant looks like a small trunkless palm
whose fan-shaped leaves rise directly from the ground.
At Manglar Alto, in Manabi, the conditions of climate
are exceptionally favourable for the growth of the
plant, but there are other places along that coast
which are suitable. The portion of the plant used for
weaving the hats is separated therefrom before it
begins to open, as, if left longer, the fibre becomes
hard, green, and brittle. It is then subjected to
certain processes in preparation for weaving. Only
at certain states of the weather, when a certain temperature prevails, is the fibre collected. The *macora*

SHOE FACTORY AT GUAYAQUIL

[To face p. 352

grass grows wild in abundance on the hills and needs no attention beyond gathering.

The value of the export of Panama hats from Ecuador has increased considerably of late years. In 1900 the value was £32,700 ; in 1902, £67,700 ; in 1909, £232,000 ; in 1910, £258,500. The rapid growth of this trade is noteworthy. The principal market for the hats is in the United Kingdom, the United States, and Germany, the first-named country taking about half the product. The declared value, as in the figures given above, is generally under the actual price. As the material costs very little the value is mainly that of the manufacture. A protectionist duty on export was established by the Ecuadorian Government in 1899 of one *sucre* per kilogram on the export of the straw. This was partly aimed at the similar industry carried on at Payta in Peru, from which port also large quantities of " Panama " hats are exported, the manufacture of which depends largely upon the fibre imported from Ecuador. The Ecuadorian makers have learned recently how to adapt the shapes of the hats manufactured to modern European requirement, and to this is due, in large part, the sustained demand. Fine qualities of the hats were at one time worth from £20 to £30 each,[1] which amount is an indication of the vast labour and time expended in weaving, involving also great care in the selection of the straw. Hats of this character are now manufactured at Dresden and elsewhere, and can be purchased for 30s. or 40s., and there are also much cheaper varieties.

The main article of export from Ecuador is cocoa, which furnishes about one-third of the world's demand. This export has long been of much importance, although it has fluctuated from time to time.

[1] The Author has been offered hats at even higher prices at Guayaquil.

The following list shows the amounts of cocoa brought into Guayaquil or exported during a long series of years. The amounts are in quintals, equal to 106·61 lb. avoirdupois :—

Year.						Quintals.
1840	...	...	...	...	...	142,670
1850	...	...	...	...	...	110,660
1860	...	...	...	...	...	168,000
1870	...	...	...	...	...	233,140
1880	...	...	...	...	...	338,800
1890	...	...	...	...	...	365,000
1900	...	...	...	...	...	292,200
1910	...	...	...	...	(doubtful)	790,000

The nature of Ecuadorian exported articles is shown by the following list, together with their values [1] :—

				Kilos.	Sucres (2s.).
Cocoa	...	...	...	36,305,192	21,057,011
Coffee	...	...	...	3,938,224	1,535,917
Tagua, unshelled	...	...	...	9,213,431	2,211,223
Tagua, shelled	...	...	...	7,520,167	2,556,845
Rubber	...	...	...	552,596	2,065,904
Hides	...	...	...	931,238	528,240
Straw hats	...	...	...	—	2,584,342
Straw	...	...	...	95,415	88,398
Gold and gold amalgam and specie				—	1,239,600
Fresh fruits ...	...	...	...	—	126,862
Various	...	...	...	—	276,746
Total	...	...	...	...	34,271,088

For the previous year the total value was 30,006,211 *sucres*.

Of the above exports, France took a value of £984,000 ; the United States, £840,000 ; Germany, £462,000 ; and Great Britain, £234,000.

The character of the imports will be gathered by the following,[2] with their Custom House values. It

[1] For 1910 ; the latest figures available at the close of 1913, no Foreign Office Report having been issued of a later year.

[2] 1910.

is probable that these are considerably under the actual cost, as there is no check upon declaration beyond the Consular invoice from ports of origin :—

		Sucres.
Food products	... ...	2,641,793
Ironware	... ...	1,125,893
Lumber	... ...	131,743
Machinery	... ...	719,924
Paper, etc.	... ...	314,722
Paints, oils, etc.	... ...	243,979
Clothing	... ...	698,352
Jewellery	... ...	9,386
Textiles	... ...	3,532,846
Silk fabrics ...	... ...	133,132
Wines, etc. ...	... ...	719,716
Candles	... ...	256,060
Firearms	... ...	222,853
Boats, etc. ...	... ...	38,752
Cement	... ...	112,028
Leather goods	... ...	432,591
Rope ...	... ...	303,606
Crockery and glassware	... ...	234,623
Gold and silver	... ...	2,056,000
Coal ...	... ...	480,079
Drugs, medicines, chemicals, etc.	... ...	476,830
Sundries	... ...	1,600,694
Total	... ...	16,476,603

Of these imports the value of £512,000 was from Great Britain ; £463,000 from the United States ; and £323,000 from Germany.

The table on p. 356 is useful as enumerating the Ecuadorian seaports and the amount of business done thereby.[1] The names marked * thus are minor ports, for export only.

The history of Ecuador's foreign debt is a chequered one. Under the Convention of 1834, Ecuador was made responsible for 21½ per cent. of the original Colombian debt, or £1,424,579, upon which

[1] 1910.

the arrears of interest amounted to £683,798. From that year to 1854, however, Ecuador paid no interest at all upon this sum. In 1855 an arrangement was made under which (1) the total debt was fixed at £1,824,000, of which £400,000 was given in exchange for £1,000,000 of the arrears of interest ; (2) the balance of the arrears amounted to £1,482,120 ; of this £400,000 was cancelled and land warrants (subsequently taken over by the Ecuador Land Company, Limited, now holding about

PORT.	IMPORTS.		EXPORTS.	
	Kilos.	Sucres.	Kilos.	Sucres.
Guayaquil ...	61,078,512	14,356,521	45,200,896	21,993,470
Puerto Bolivar ...	140,011	57,709	305,221	76,524
Ballenita * ...	—	—	104,035	57,030
Manglar Alto* ...	—	—	614,035	112,512
Machalilla * ...	—	—	1,022,335	292,452
Cayo *	—	—	1,784,400	788,356
Manta	3,569,779	913,362	5,374,585	2,127,890
Bahia de Caraquez	4,103,245	799,344	5,065,280	1,784,220
Esmeraldas ...	1,186,934	313,861	4,592,503	810,528
Macara	54,376	33,158	26,103	11,530
Tulcan	14,065	2,648	14,550	7,852
Total	70,147,822	16,476,603	64,103,943	28,062,364

200,000 *cuadras* in the Pailon and at Atacamos) were issued against £566,120, whilst $860,000 in Peruvian 4½ per Cent. Bonds were given in satisfaction of the remaining £516,000. These latter bonds were paid by Peru to Ecuador in liquidation of a debt contracted prior to 1834 with the old republic of Colombia, of which Ecuador then formed part ; (3) interest on the new debt was to be paid at the rate of 1 per cent. as long as the Customs receipts at Guayaquil should not exceed $400,000 per annum. Of any excess over

CIGAR AND CIGARETTE FACTORY AT GUAYAQUIL

[To face p. 430

this sum the bondholders were to receive one-fourth until the maximum rate of 6 per cent. was attained.

In 1868, however, the loan went into default. In 1888-9 various unsatisfactory proposals were made for the settlement of the debt, still in default, but without result. In 1890 an arrangement was drawn up for the conversion of the 1855 bonds, with progressive rates of interest and a sinking fund, the proceeds of an additional import duty being assigned by Congress as security for the service of the debt. This arrangement was accepted by the bondholders subject to the old bonds being deposited in the hands of trustees and cancelled only in the same proportion as the corresponding new bonds were received. But the Government refused this condition, and in 1891 the Ecuador National Railway Company, holding the concession for the completion of an important line with a Government guarantee, offered to give £15 in fully paid-up railway shares in respect of each £100 new bonds. The bondholders accepted. After this came laws suspending payments, followed by various arrangements, acceptances, refusals, etc. In 1897-8 a contract for the construction of the Guayaquil-Quito Railway was entered into between the Government and the representative of an American Syndicate, Mr. Archer Harman. The capital of the company was to consist in gold bonds—$12,282,000, at 6 per cent. interest, 1 per cent. sinking fund, the principal and interest being guaranteed by the Government by a lien on its Customs duties, with other Government subsidies and guarantees. The Ecuadorian foreign debt in 1878 was assured by the railway company, the Government guaranteeing interest on the sum of £2,525,000 railway mortgage bonds for thirty-three years, also recognizing the external debt at 35 per cent. of its face value. In Ecuador the feeling had grown that the part of the old debt taken by the republic in 1830, was a much greater share than should have been borne, and some allowance has been, made for this feeling in taking into account the financial career of Ecuador.

Further agreements and modifications in regard to the bonds took place after 1898, which it would be tedious to enumerate. In some cases they were protested against by the English bondholders. There was also failure to remit funds when such fell due. In 1908 a settlement of the debt was effected under a contract signed at Quito on the 30th September between the Government of Ecuador, the railway company, and the representative [1] of the Council of Foreign Bondholders. This contract was approved by Congress on 1st November, with certain modifications. The main provisions of the arrangement were as follows :—

The principal of the railway bonds of 1897 to be reduced from $12,282,000 to $10,808,000, by the cancellation of the $1,474,000 bonds redeemed by the sinking fund to date. The interest to be also reduced from 6 to 5 per cent., and the sinking fund to be 1 per cent. on the reduced principal. In compensation for the reduction of interest, non-interest-bearing certificates to be issued at the rate of $100 per $1,000 railway bonds. The July, 1907, coupon to be surrendered to the Government, and the three coupons of January, 1908, to January, 1909, inclusive, to be exchanged for Ecuador Government Four per Cent. " Salt " Bonds at par. Part of the issue of " Salt " Bonds to be appropriated to provide for the payment in cash of the interest in arrear on the Special Series Bond, and for expenses. Prior Lien Bonds of the railway company to be created, the proceeds to be applied to (a) the retirement of the Special Series Bonds outstanding ; (b) the repair and equipment of the railway ; (c) the provision of working capital for the railway company ; (d) the settlement of the company's debts, and (e) the payment of the expenses connected with the arrangement.

The Board of Directors of the railway to be reconstituted, and to consist of eleven members, three of such members to be nominated by the bondholders. The agreement to be regarded as a final

---

[1] Mr. James Cooper, whose work in this connection was highly commended in London financial circles.

settlement of all disputes and controversies which had arisen in the past between the Government, the railway company and the bondholders.   The arbitrators appointed to decide the questions in dispute between the Government and the railway company to be requested to notify their respective Governments that they accepted the agreement as a definite settlement of all points referred to their decision.   The Government to bind itself unconditionally to remit the sum of $859,740 per annum (being the full-service of 6 per cent. interest and 1 per cent. sinking fund on the original principal of $12,282,000) until the Prior Lien Bonds are redeemed, and thereafter 5 per cent. interest and 1 per cent. sinking fund on the reduced principal of $10,808,000.   The service of the bonds to be a first charge on the entire Customs revenue.   The quota of the debt service to be placed daily without intermission, by the bank charged with the collection of the Customs, to the account of the Council, and remitted fortnightly to London.   The Government not to constitute in the future any charge on the Customs revenues to the prejudice of the bondholders' rights.

The following are the particulars of the new securities issued under the above arrangement :—

(1) $2,486,000 Guayaquil and Quito Railway Six per Cent. Prior Lien Mortgage Gold Bonds, issued at 90 per cent. in February, 1909, in London.   Redeemable by an accumulative sinking fund at 2¼ per cent. per annum, by tender or by drawings at par.   Secured by a preferential mortgage on all the property, etc., of the company. and on the Customs revenues.   The bonds can be paid off on six months' notice at the rate of $1,050 for each $1,000 of bonds. (2) $1,075,050 Four per Cent. Ecuador Government Salt Bonds, redeemable by a 4 per cent. accumulative sinking fund by tender or by drawings at par.   Secured on the Government salt monopoly ; the Government to deposit monthly in one of the Guayaquil banks the due proportion of the proceeds of the sales of salt, and six days after the receipt thereof the bank to remit to the Council one-twelfth part of the full service for the year.   (3) $1,080,800 Guayaquil and Quito Railway non-interest-bearing compensation certificates of $100 each, redeemable out of 25 per cent. of the net earnings of the railway, after payment of the company's fixed charges.

In June, 1909, an issue of 7,000,000 fr. of bonds of the Compagnie Française de Chemins de Fer de l'Equateur (Bahia de Caraquez to Quito) was offered for subscription in Paris by the Banque Commerciale et Industrielle at the price of 84½. The bonds bear 5 per cent. interest, and are redeemable by a sinking fund of ½ per cent. by purchase or by drawings at par, commencing in 1913. They are secured on the Customs receipts of the province of Manabi, subject to the portion already allocated for other services. According to the prospectus of the loan, the total authorized issue of the company is 23,000,000 fr., and the Government guarantees to the company for thirty years 6 per cent. interest on the capital employed in the construction of the railway up to 25,000,000 fr., in so far as the net receipts of the line are not sufficient to cover the same, in proportion as each section costing at least 200,000 fr. is opened to public service.

The Government of Ecuador defaulted on its obligations under the contract of 30th September, 1908. The necessary funds for the first application of the sinking fund on the First Mortgage Bonds of the railway company due July, 1909, were not provided. After meeting the two coupons due July, 1909, and January, 1910, on the First Mortgage and Prior Lien Bonds and the sinking fund on the latter, due on the same dates, further payments were discontinued. Owing to the remittances for the service of the Salt Bonds being short of the proper amount, the sinking fund on these bonds, due July, 1910, also fell into arrear.

In December, 1910, the Government contracted with Messrs. Speyer & Co. for a loan of £300,000 (3,000,000 *sucres*), secured by Six per Cent. Treasury Certificates of the same amount, issued to Messrs. Speyer & Co. at 85 per cent., and repayable within twelve months of their issue, such certificates to be used exclusively for the payment of the export duties. Fifty per cent. of these duties were assigned to the service of the loan, as well as 500,000 *sucres* of the Treasury's portion, in 1911, of the alcohol tax, and, subject to the existing liens, the whole of the Customs revenues. [Under the contract of 30th September, 1908, the entire Customs revenues, which necessarily include the export duties, were preferentially pledged to the holders of Guayaquil and Quito Railway Bonds.]

An issue of £200,000 Six per Cent. Gold Bonds of the Central Railway of Ecuador (Manta to Santa Ana), guaranteed by the State of Ecuador, and secured by a special assignment of one-third of the duty on the export of vegetable ivory from the province of Manabi, was offered for subscription in Paris at about 97 per cent., redeemable in thirty-three years by a sinking fund of 1 per cent. [The remarks made above with regard to the loan of 1910 apply also to this loan.]

In November, 1911, the Government of Ecuador resumed the remittances for the service of the railway bonds. A revolution then broke out, and the re-mittances were suspended until March, 1912, when they were again resumed. During 1912 the service, both interest and sinking fund, on the Prior Lien Bonds was brought up to date, and in January, 1913, the July, 1910, coupon on the Five per Cent. First Mortgage Bonds was paid. With the exception of the sinking fund being in arrear for two years, the service of the Salt Bonds has been maintained.

The President of Ecuador, General Plaza, has striven to maintain the financial obligations of the republic, and informed the Council of Foreign Bond-holders in London that " he did not consider that any circumstances, even civil war, could justify a suspension of the remittances." Thus confidence in Ecuador financially, long rudely shaken, is being built up.

As regards the service of the Guayaquil and Quito Railway Bonds, the report of the Council of Foreign Bondholders says :—

" On the 20th of February, 1912, the Provisional Government issued a resolution setting aside the product of certain taxes for the service of the railway bonds. This resolution, which was to remain in force for the year 1912, was in all respects similar to the Order issued by the Government on October 30, 1911. With reference to the above resolution, the Council understand that since the resumption of payments in March, 1912, the entire product of the taxes mentioned therein has been remitted to London. The total so remitted has certainly been considerably in excess of the amount fixed by the contract of September 30, 1908, and this result is not only creditable to the Government, but beneficial to the bondholders. At the same time the Council must again point out that the bondholders have a preferential mortgage on the whole of the Customs revenues, so that these resolutions of the Government, setting aside certain percentages, not only of the Customs but also of other revenues which have not been assigned to the bondholders, must only be regarded as measures taken by the Government for its own convenience, and which cannot in any way override the stipulations of the above-named contract."

The currency of Ecuador consists in the *sucre,* equal to practically two shillings, and its multiples and parts. Gold is the monetary standard, legal tender of silver being limited to ten *sucres.* The British pound sterling is legal tender throughout the republic (as in Peru), at the value of ten *sucres,* or one *condor.* The paper money in circulation consists in the issues of two Guayaquil banks—the *Banco del Ecuador* and *Banco Comercial y Agricola.* Other banks are those of Quito and Pichincha.

The French metric system was adopted in 1856, but the old Spanish *quintals, libras, varas,* and *fanegas* are still used.

The Budget estimate for the republic for 1913 was as follows :—

ESTIMATED REVENUE, 1913.

	Sucres.
Cash in hand	268,156
Import duties...	9,958,290
Export duties	4,158,426
Aguardiente	833,493
Octroi	274,911
Rent of mines, etc.	70,808
Contribucion general	321,372
Consular dues	697,696
Salt	553,075
Registers, etc.	42,557
Stamps...	397,883
Patriotic tax	1,700,000
Tobacco	70,335
Gambling Tax	71,264
10 per cent. on municipal revenues	51,632
Telephones	13,172
2 per cent. on profits of banks	18,350
Extraordinary receipts	56,507
Contributions in arrear on 31st December, 1912	400,000
Loan from Banco del Ecuador for various purposes	138,000
Sundries	290,656
Total	20,386,583

ESTIMATED EXPENDITURE, 1913.

	Sucres.
Legislative power	168,930
Executive power	51,260
Ministry of Interior	32,980
„ of Foreign Affairs	278,820
„ of Finance	113,340
Railway services	3,092,234
Printing Office	49,360
Police and penitentiaries	1,358,250
Public works	324,958
Governments...	121,560
Beneficence...	2,129,270
Justice	437,532
Carried forward	8,158,494

Sucres.

ESTIMATED EXPENDITURE, 1913—(*continued*).

	Sucres.
Brought forward	8,158,494
Public instruction	2,117,833
Posts	290,000
Telegraphs and telephones...	340,000
Statistical Department	235,224
War and Marine	4,702,596
Treasuries	113,300
Collectors	199,486
Customs	988,062
Salt	150,000
Public debt	2,260,470
Municipality of Guayaquil	180,000
Unforeseen public works	172,838
Extraordinary expenditure	315,248
Sundries	163,032
Total	20,386,583

For the year 1911 the figures were : Actual revenue, 17,722,824 *sucres;* and actual expenditure, 13,356,854 *sucres.*

As regards the political relations of the republic of Ecuador with its neighbours on the continent, the most friendly and enduring are those with the republic of Chile. There is considerable sympathy between the two republics. This is due to some extent to the fact that (being separated from each other) there is no boundary question, which question has been a serious cause of enmity in general among Latin American nations. With Peru, as shown elsewhere, the question of boundary has been a rankling source of contention. Peru is a stronger and more numerous community than Ecuador, and the latter has had to accept conditions as regards its position with that republic by reason of its comparative poverty and weakness. On the other hand, Peru and Chile have been mortal enemies, and are still divided by rankling questions of boundary, in Tacna and Arica. The Chileans for their part are well aware that an unwritten alliance or association with Ecuador is of strategic value to them, as concerns their relations with Peru, whilst for Ecuador the friendship of Chile partakes to some extent in the influence of an elder brother.

As showing the possibilities of industrial development in Ecuador the following from a recent (1910) Foreign Office Report (British) under the heading of " Progress in Ecuador " is instructive :—

" Notwithstanding the very remarkable progress which has been made in this republic in the development of its agricultural resources during the past eleven years (from a value of £1,567,140 in 1900 to £3,000,062 in 1910), there are still vast tracts of land on the lower west coast region suitable for development of the cocoa, coffee, and rubber growths. There is likewise a considerable field for the establishment of other industries, such as the cultivation of hat and hammock straws, henequen or maguey, the *tagua* or ivory-nut, annato, valuable timber, and many other articles, some already known to science and others only awaiting discovery and the mode of working them profitably. The development of the actual branches of cultivation, however, affords full employment for all available labour, and the absolute requirement for the further progress of the country is the encouragement of immigration. Unfortunately, the conditions of the law, the character of the natives (who are all jealous of, and inimical to, foreign competition), and the insanitary conditions of Guayaquil and some of the agricultural districts prohibit this immigration, and thereby retard the rapid and profitable development of the country. Whilst the western coast districts could and would provide ample products for export of possibly five to ten times of the present value, the interior districts offer vast fields for the growth of cereals, vegetables, potatoes and fruits, and fodder for the support of cattle of all kinds. There is

undoubtedly in the country means for the easy subsistence of more than 50,000,000 inhabitants instead
of the present 2,000,000 or less, and for the profitable employment of their labour, either for export
produce or home consumption. It is to be hoped
that with the proposed sanitation of the port of
Guayaquil an impetus may be given to immigration
and the development of agricultural wealth." [1]

The above, being an official statement, is doubtless
well considered. Possibly the estimate of 50,000,000
inhabitants as the capacity of the country is open
to question, or at least under the industrial methods
of civilization in general at present. Possibly also
the jealousy of foreign competition will not be an
obstacle to development.

Turning finally to matters of general social evolution, the most urgent requirement for Ecuador, like
that for most Latin American countries, is the up-
lifting of the masses of its people, who are in bulk
poor and ignorant. The sociologist, in his study
of the Latin American communities,[2] observes the
enormous undeveloped resources and potentialities
and the great amount of land still remaining as the
property of the State ; yet, notwithstanding these
possibilities for prosperity and progress, the bulk of
the people live in poverty. The labouring classes
of South America in general own no land, carry on
no occupation profitable to themselves, live in mud
or wattle houses, are insufficiently clothed, their food
is of the most primitive and scanty, their education
neglected, and they are subject by the lack of sanitation to epidemics of disease. The wealth and education of the republics is in the hands of a small

[1] A contract has recently been let to a British Company for this
work.

[2] In his work, *The Republics of Central and South Americas*
(Dent and Son : London, 1913), the Author has fully dealt with the
sociology of Latin America.

oligarchical, plutocratic class, and this, having the
control of government, moulds circumstance to its
will. Roads, schools, and civic improvements are
insufficient. As regards the development of public
works, the cry is for the foreign concessionaire and
his ready gold. But this alone will not prove a
substitute for self-development and homely energy.

The high cost of living, and evils resulting therefrom, are becoming increasingly marked in Ecuador
(as in the whole of South America). This is due
in part to high Custom-house dues on imported
articles, followed by the monopolistic methods as
regards foods and markets of the middlemen, as
also the high cost of transport by the railways and
other methods of carriage. The lack of houses for
the working classes presses heavily upon the populations of the towns. Dwellings are of the most
miserable and insanitary character. Rents are very
high, and the cost of building almost prohibitive,
due in the main to the cost of material and to duties
and taxes. The cost of living has risen 50 per
cent.[1] of very recent years. Due to the poor
conditions of life, the lack of proper food, clothing,
and shelter, tuberculosis develops among the working
classes with great rapidity, and the mortality among
children is very high. These evil conditions exist
in spite of the fact that timber, food, material of
all kinds exist in plenitude within the republic. There
is another class which suffers in Ecuador, as in
other lands : that section of the people which, to
dress itself with elegance, stints its own food, its
income being insufficient for both. This is a marked
feature of middle-class life in Spanish American
society.

There are some efforts at co-operation in the
matter of food supply, and labour tends towards
trade organization. In all Latin American countries

[1] According to the Guayaquil Press.

there is to be noted a growth towards socialistic thought and action, and strikes are not infrequent. These matters are inevitable, and might take rapid strides in these communities. No permanent political and sociological improvement can be expected in the smaller South American republics until a better spirit takes hold of the governing classes, with a resolve to awaken and to prosper, to exploit the land for the benefit of the great bulk of its humble citizens.

On the other hand, Ecuador contains many valuable elements, and its people many excellent qualities. It is not a country yielding vast exports, such as the coffee or rubber, the wheat, cattle, or nitrate that some of its neighbours possess ; but an impartial view will not see in this necessarily a matter for regret. Great exports and imports do not of themselves alone bring prosperity to the bulk of the citizens : a fact certainly marked strongly enough in South America ; for even in Argentina, Brazil, or Chile—countries which export valuable products and do a large trade—the same miserable conditions among the working class exist. To develop their own resources for the national benefit, to invite foreign capital under conditions equitable to national rights, and of future as well as momentary advantage ; above all, to spread education and knowledge of agricultural and homely arts by example and kindliness — these will best carry forward the Spanish-American civilization of South America, which contains many pleasing traits and elements of enduring value.

Ecuador possesses its own individuality and powers, which, duly exercised, could ensure its prosperity and progress. With its physical beauties and advantages the country has much to be proud of, and if the spirit of true patriotism and generous social development will but expand, the republic could set an example to its neighbours in the settled arts of life and the solution of Latin American problems in the coming years upon that fruitful continent. Like its neighbours, Peru, Colombia, and others, Ecuador should be open to a fuller sympathy on the part of European nations and the United States, and susceptible to greater industrial co-operation therewith, and should share in that tide of world-development which is to be expected of this century. Amid all the present vicissitudes of industrial and international circumstance the student of world-affairs and human geography discerns promise and progress, and the lands of the South American Pacific coast have an important part to play in this development.

INDEX

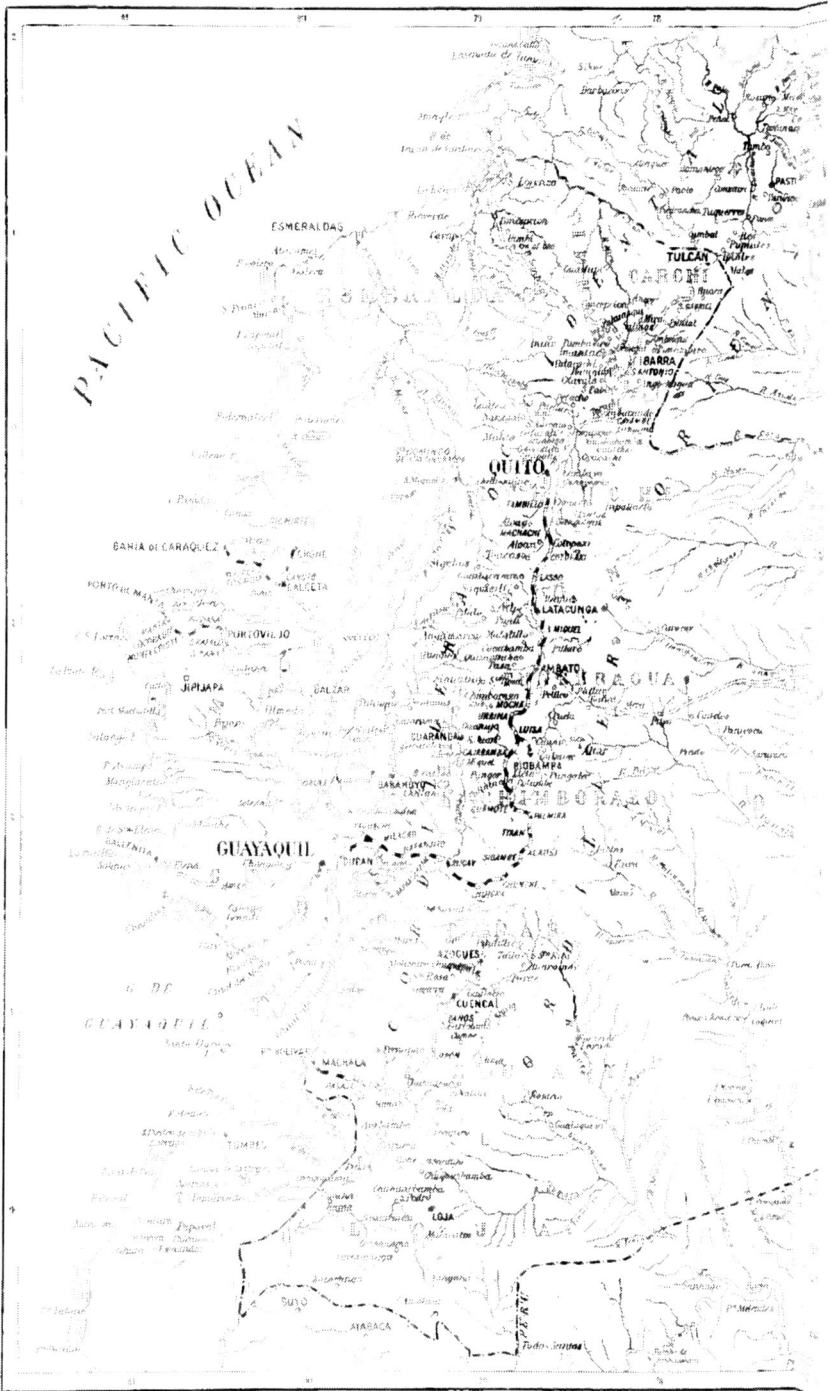

RICHARD MAYER LONDON E.C. 42 OLD BROAD STR. COPYRIGHT

MAP OF ECUADOR

TO ACCOMPANY ECUADOR BY C.R.ENOCK F.R.G.S

RAILWAYS in operation ━━━ in construction ▬▬▬ proposed ▬▬▬

SCALE 1:4 500 000

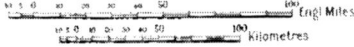

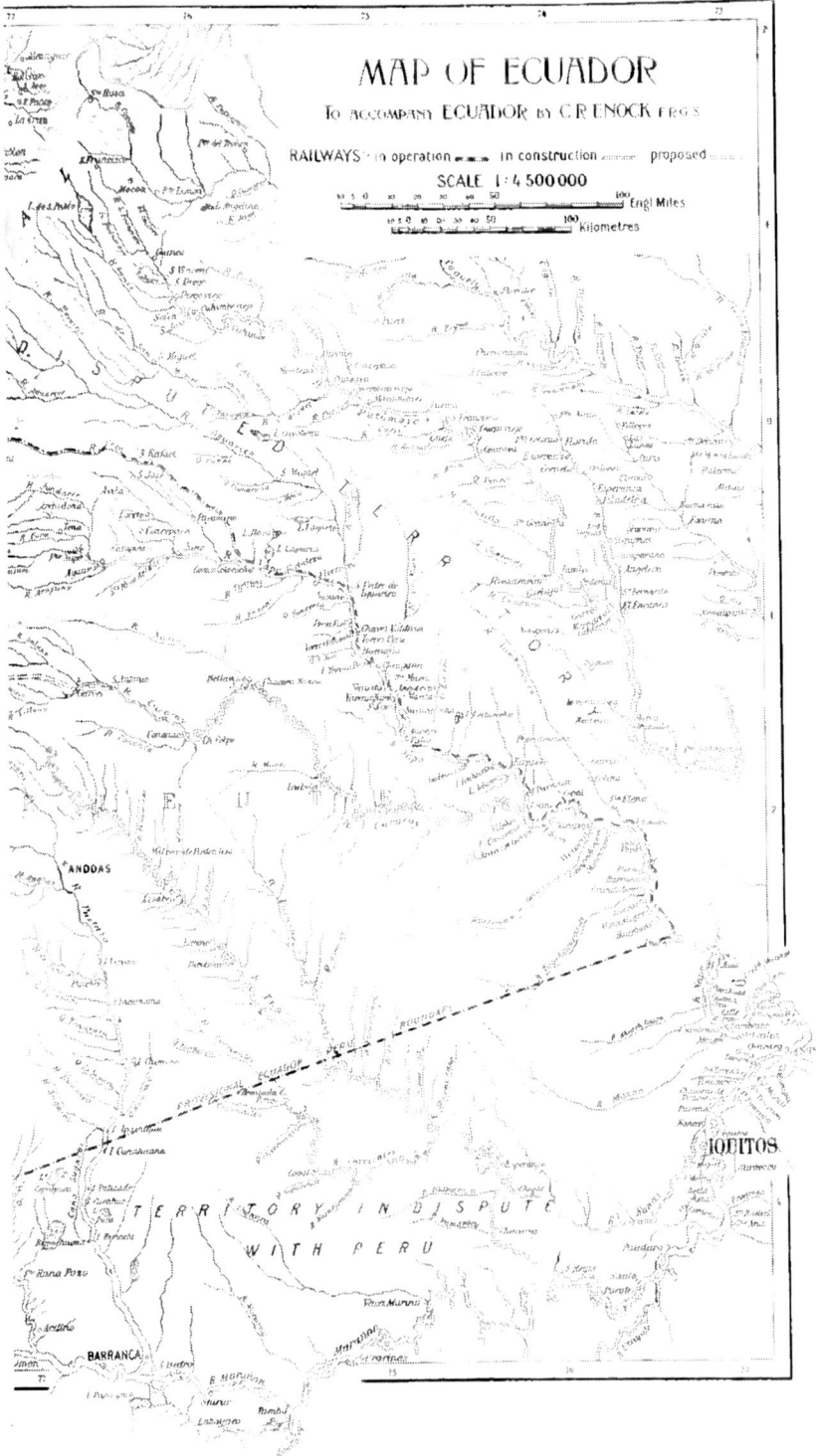

Engl Miles

Kilometres

DISPUTED TERRITORY

TERRITORY IN DISPUTE WITH PERU

ANDOAS

IQUITOS

BARRANCA

ImTheStory.com

Personalized Classic Books in many genre's

Unique gift for kids, partners, friends, colleagues

Customize:

- Character Names

- Upload your own front/back cover images (optional)

- Inscribe a personal message/dedication on the
  inside page (optional)

Customize many titles Including
- Alice in Wonderland
- Romeo and Juliet
- The Wizard of Oz
- A Christmas Carol
- Dracula
- Dr. Jekyll & Mr. Hyde
- And more...

CPSIA information can be obtained at www.ICGtesting.com
Printed in the USA
LVOW07s2120080414

380850LV00022B/463/P

9 781313 161114